WHAT PEOPLE ARE SAYING ABOUT

MEETING S

This is an extraordinary　　　　　　　　_y woman.
Meeting Shiva is about the a　　　　　.ross the Himalayas,
an adventurous search for lo　　　.herself. The search took her
into the arms and bed of a sworn ascetic monk and beyond, into
the dark spaces of her soul. What she discovered is incredibly
revealing for anyone on a similar quest. She ripped the covers off
of romantic love, and looked at the can of worms underneath it.
Highly recommended.
Tony Crisp, author of *Dream Dictionary* and *Liberating the Body*

This book is able to touch the heart of the reader. Simply wonderfull!
Katja Sundermeier, author of *Simply Love* and *Relationship License*

Immediately engaging, fast-paced, exquisitely written: Tiziana
takes us into the essence of love which surprises the ego with
much more than it knows. The result is a story that can only
come from life – and grace… makes *Fifty Shades of Grey* look like
Madame Tussaud's by comparison…
Jay Ramsay, author of *Crucible of Love: The Alchemy of Passionate Relationships*

What happens when a 21st-century woman goes out into the
world looking for her soul mate? Seeking and finding a spiritual
man to seduce and fall in love with, only to find he has mighty
feet of clay, as does she, and that she has inadvertently plunged
herself into the web of her own shadow projections. This is
Tiziana's true story. It's a great read and eventually after much

emotional delving, leads to the healing of childhood and karmic wounds.

Kathy Jones, author of *Priestess of Avalon, Priestess of the Goddess* and *The Ancient British Goddess*

Meeting Shiva is the true story of a romantic collision between a Himalayan monk under a vow of celibacy and a Western woman seeking her own spiritual truth. Elegant in its simplicity, deceptive in its depth, the book is an expedition into the realms of romantic entanglement, exploring the differences between love and lovers, sensuality and sex, reason and illusion, desire and glory.

Set against a backdrop of Gods and ashrams, deities and icons, temples and altars – the wild religiosities that shape India – *Meeting Shiva* is an encounter with raw honesty and rare openness, an insider's story of self-reflection, identity and longing told by a Western voice interlaced with the wonder of the initiate.

A journey of embarkation, return, release and, finally, resolution, author Tiziana Stupia's exploration of the truth of her existence is a seductive invitation to other women to uncover the truth of their own.

Stephanie Dale, author of *My Pilgrim's Heart*

Tiziana invites us to join her on her outer and inner journeys of discovery. The sounds, smells, sights and characters of India rise vibrantly out of the pages. More significantly she shows us the healing power and potential of relationship when the erotic and spiritual come together. I was captivated and curious from the first paragraph.

Sophie Slade, Imago relationship therapist, workshop presenter and clinical instructor

Meeting Shiva

Falling and Rising in Love
in the Indian Himalayas

Meeting Shiva

Falling and Rising in Love
in the Indian Himalayas

Tiziana Stupia

CHANGE
MAKERS
BOOKS

Winchester, UK
Washington, USA

First published by Changemakers Books, 2013
Changemakers Books is an imprint of John Hunt Publishing Ltd., Laurel House, Station Approach,
Alresford, Hants, SO24 9JH, UK
office1@jhpbooks.net
www.johnhuntpublishing.com
www.changemakers-books.com

For distributor details and how to order please visit the 'Ordering' section on our website.

Text copyright: Tiziana Stupia 2012

ISBN: 978 1 78099 916 6

A CIP catalogue record for this book is available from the British Library.

Design: Stuart Davies

Printed and bound by CPI Group (UK) Ltd, Croydon, CR0 4YY

We operate a distinctive and ethical publishing philosophy in all
areas of our business, from our global network of authors to
production and worldwide distribution.

For Rudra, who tore open the doors of my heart
so that love could enter

'How long have you known me?' he asked playfully, eyes sparkling, head propped on one hand, as we lay on the bed in his secret room.

'Oh, I don't know... years? A lifetime? Millennia? It seems like a very long time,' I replied with a smile. In truth, I felt there was never a time I did not know him.

'Yes.' He suddenly grew serious, and a dark shadow fluttered across his dreamy brown eyes, like a ripple on a still summer lake. 'We're connected by birth.'

Shiva's Song

The young *sannyasi* entered the temple quietly and sat cross-legged on the floor. He wore the flowing saffron-colored robes of his religious order, with the top half draped elegantly around his upper body. His face was round, beautiful in an almost child-like way, with full, sensuous lips and smooth skin the color of almonds. Fleetingly, he looked across the candlelit temple, which was filled with Indian worshippers ready for the evening's *aarti* ceremony. From my place near the right side of the altar, where I sat sandwiched between two Bengali women in saris, I caught his glance briefly. Was it my imagination, or was there a hint of melancholy in his dark brown eyes?

The *sannyasi* directed his gaze towards the altar, took a deep breath and began to play the small harmonium that stood in front of him. As the accordion-like sounds started to weave their way around the temple, it seemed to transform from a dreary, cold concrete structure into an enchanting sanctuary. Suddenly, over the evocative, almost mournful chords of the instrument rose a strong, clear voice that sang a song so haunting, filled with such passion and devotion, that my body began to tingle all over.

Fascinated, I listened to the chant of '*Om Namah Shivaya*', an ancient Sanskrit mantra in praise of the Hindu God Shiva, and felt as though I had somehow, magically, been transported into a different, faraway age. The melody reverberated around the temple and drifted out of the barred windows into the snow-covered mountains that surrounded us.

I was transfixed and could not stop looking, no, *staring*, at the *sannyasi*, who, with his eyes closed and head tilted back, appeared completely lost in his act of worship, until another, elderly monk sat down in front of me and blocked my view. I looked across the sea of faces towards my friend MJ, who sat kneeling near the rear of the room, and noticed tears running down her face from beneath closed eyes. I turned back towards the altar. My heart filled with the sweetest ache. I had never heard anything so beautiful in my entire life.

In the weeks and months that followed, I would often think back to this moment. I would remember the clear, melodious voice of the *sannyasi*, the cold stone wall against my back, the dense smoke of incense in my nostrils, and wonder how different my life would have turned out if I had left the temple that day and never returned; if I had made the choice to go and therefore escaped what was to become an encounter that would turn my world upside down and shatter everything I knew about love.

Prologue

This is a story of love. It is not a conventional love story, but the tale of an unusual meeting that had the power to change my life completely.

In the spring of 2008, I was at the end of an epic overland trip through the Himalayas. I had left my hometown of Leamington Spa in England eight months previously for a train journey that had taken me through many different countries, including Russia, Mongolia, Tibet and Nepal. After reading a newspaper article about a tribe called the Kalash who lived in the Hindu Kush Mountains, I had set out to Pakistan to celebrate the Winter Solstice festival with them. With a great passion for travel and spirituality, I'd been fascinated to learn about this colorful tribe who lived a life filled with ancient Gods, temples, fire rituals and feasts. I wanted to meet them and at the same time fulfill my life's dream: to travel the world.

This was my first big trip. I'd always wanted to travel, ever since I was a little girl. I dreamt about adventures in strange lands, treasures that were to be uncovered and destinies that had to be fulfilled. But, apart from short trips, my job as a manager in the music business had not allowed me to leave everything behind and follow the wind. It took a severe burn-out at the age of twenty-seven and a breakdown for me to trade workaholism and revelry in for a degree in psychology and a calmer way of life. I started to practice yoga and meditate and slowly discarded layers of an old personality that did not fit me any longer.

When I turned thirty-five, I decided that the time to live my dream of traveling had finally come. I sold my house, surrendered my remaining work responsibilities and gave away most of my possessions to follow the call of my soul. And not prone to doing things in halves, I chose to travel overland to fully experience the countries I was about to cross. I wanted to appreciate the journey as well as the destination, and I knew that this trip would become the adventure of a lifetime.

Before I left, I set several intentions for my trip. One of my quests was to get fully aligned with my soul's purpose. I wasn't entirely sure what exactly my soul purpose, my mission in life, was, but I wanted it to reveal itself to me. I trusted that the journey would lead me to where I needed to be and show me what I came to this planet to do – something I had inklings about but had yet to discover fully.

My other major intention had to do with love and the ancient spiritual path of Tantra that I had recently become interested in. Tantra is a passionate path. It is a route to enlightenment and bliss that does not require abstinence from worldly pleasures: its practices work with the human passions, instead of against them. And in stark contrast to most religions, in Tantra sexual union is not seen as impure but believed to have the potential to be a prayer and a meditation.

These ideas resonated strongly with me, the niece of a Catholic priest; tired of dogma, I'd given up religion two decades earlier to concentrate on a more life-affirming, female-friendly spirituality. That sex could and was indeed revered as sacred confirmed something I'd felt deeply in my bones for a long time. Although I had never experienced lovemaking in this conscious way, I'd had glimpses, and knew it to be true. I just didn't know how to find it.

I'd explored some Western Tantra courses in the past, but found them to completely miss the point by focusing primarily on erotic techniques between strangers – something that didn't seem to have much to do with spirituality or love. So I hoped that I might find a spiritual teacher on my travels through the Himalayas, where Tantra originated. Somebody who could lead me more deeply onto 'the path' and show me what Tantra, this union of opposites, actually meant in real terms.

Deep down, I was of course hoping to meet a man; somebody

who lived and breathed Tantra and would share his knowledge with me. I wanted to meet the person who could teach me about love, about opening my heart, and about the transcendental lovemaking that could connect us with the Divine. I was craving this connection more than anything else, and more than that, I was craving transformation.

Ultimately, I was on a quest to meet my soul mate. With a string of failed relationships behind me, I felt that I hadn't yet met my match. For one reason or another, I'd walked out of every single relationship in my life, but still believed in meeting 'The One' – and for me that meant a spiritual man who would see and love me as I was, without wanting to change me or curb my freedom.

And so I wandered through the Himalayas in Tibet, Nepal and Pakistan, but my tantric soul mate didn't materialize. Apart from a brief fling with a Pakistani mountaineer in the Hindu Kush and an even briefer encounter with a Mongolian horseman, nothing amorous occurred. And except for some Tibetan Buddhist nuns who did not speak English and a Nepalese shaman who chain-smoked Marlboro, I didn't even come close to meeting anyone who knew much about Tantra.

Not wanting to go home empty-handed, I decided to cross the border to India and go to Rishikesh, a small town in the Himalayan foothills. Rishikesh, one of the most sacred pilgrimage sites for Hindus, has the reputation of being the world's yoga capital. Maybe I could find my tantric soul mate here, I thought. And so, on the banks of the Ganga, I spent my time studying yoga and immersing myself in Hindu spirituality, meditation and rituals. I even moved into a yoga ashram. But, although I met some amazing people and had a wonderful time, the man of my dreams didn't appear. I had been so sure that I would meet him before I started my journey, but now started to wonder whether he existed at all.

After four months in India, I decided that enough was

enough. The soul mate had had ample time to show up. I was tired and wanted to go home. I'd had enough amazing experiences to last me for a lifetime, and maybe my intuition about the tantric man had all been an illusion. So, without much further ado, I booked my ticket back to Europe.

To leave India on a high, I set out on one last adventure. Together with my French-Canadian friend MJ, short for Marie-Josée, I left for a camping trip to the Himalayas. We wanted to immerse ourselves in glorious mountain landscapes, visit ancient temples, meet mystical *sadhus* and have a magical time before going home with a treasure chest full of great experiences.

This book is the story of 'what happened then', in those final weeks after I had resolved to go home. Strangely, on the first evening after my departure from Rishikesh and under unlikely circumstances, I met the man I had been waiting for all my life. He was the man I had dreamt of and who in many ways exceeded my wildest expectations. My match. What I hadn't bargained for was that he was a *sannyasi*, a celibate Hindu monk who lived in an austere ashram in the remote Himalayas. This is the story of our meeting.

PART 1

SOMEWHERE IN
THE HIMALAYAS

But now the destined spot and hour were close;
Unknowing she had neared her nameless goal.
For though a dress of blind and devious chance
Is laid upon the work of all-wise Fate,
Our acts interpret an omniscient Force
That dwells in the compelling stuff of things,
And nothing happens in the cosmic play
But at its time and in its foreseen place.

From 'Savitri', Sri Aurobindo

1.1: The Flip of the Coin

On a stifling hot morning in May, I stood on the dusty balcony of a yoga ashram in Rishikesh and shielded my eyes against the intense sun. My friend MJ leaned against the railing next to me with a glass of sweet, milky *chai* in her hand. We had spent the last four months in this small Himalayan town by the Ganga, studying yoga under the guidance of a young bearded yogi who, with his long black hair and white robes, looked like an Indian version of Jesus.

'Do you think they will come?' I asked and craned my neck. We were about to leave the ashram for the wilderness of the Himalayas and were waiting for a driver to collect us. Before MJ could answer me, a weathered VW crawled down the dirt path that connected the main road with the ashram, leaving a cloud of dust in its wake. When the car had come to a halt, a wiry young man with a goatee beard, an Italian flat-cap and trendy sunglasses jumped out of the car and waved at us vigorously. We grabbed our backpacks and ran out to meet him.

'Sanjay!' he beamed. 'Welcome! I am your guide.' He heaved our backpacks onto the roof of the car and strapped them onto a luggage rack that was already packed with tents and sleeping bags.

'*Chalo!*' he hollered, 'Let's go!', and ushered us into the back of the car. With a final wave of goodbyes and '*Namaste*'s to Mata-ji, the yogi's imposing mother, who had come to see us off with the ashram's cooks, we set off on our trip: towards the Himalayas, and into the Unknown. I watched with quiet excitement as we edged out of Rishikesh, past the little *chai* stalls, German bakeries and internet cafés, the stoned and dreadlocked *sadhu*s in the Shiva temple, the Western tourists clad in hippy clothes with red *tilaks* on their foreheads, obese cows, beggars and street children. With all of its contradictions, I had grown fond of Rishikesh – a lively mix of East and West, with more yoga schools, ashrams, temples and spiritual bookshops than you could care to imagine.

Guide Sanjay, whose ear was glued to his constantly ringing mobile phone, had a look and demeanor so Sicilian that we named him Al Pacino before we reached our first stop. In contrast, the driver, Ram, was of stocky build. Clad in a blue-grey driver's uniform, he sported a thick bush of shiny black hair, a black stubbly beard and even blacker circles beneath his eyes. Eyebrows furrowed and knuckles white, his speedy driving style consisted of leaning over the stirring wheel while laughing hysterically from time to time. Consequently, his nickname could be no other than Maniac.

I turned to look at MJ, who shook her head and smirked as we flew through a precarious bend with screeching wheels. I laughed. MJ was a tall woman with piercing sky-blue eyes and shoulder-length blonde hair. We had met at the ashram, and I liked her for her complex nature. Generally lively and emotional, she had a wry sense of humor and was prone to frequent outbursts of 'Tabernac!' and other religiously inspired swear-words when things didn't go as planned. There was also a deep, thoughtful and vulnerable side to her. We were on a similar wavelength and often enjoyed long, intense conversations about things that mattered to us. I was looking forward to going on this adventure with her. What a fantastic way to end my epic journey to the East.

Accompanied by an abundant diet of high-pitched Hindi disco music, we drove for hours through lush wooded, mountainous landscapes, and occasionally sighted the sparkling Ganga in the desolate valleys beneath us. Absorbed in the scenery, we didn't speak much. It was strange, I mused as we passed a small shrine dedicated to the Hindu elephant god Ganesh, that I ended up in India. And even stranger that I liked it so much. When I was younger, I'd never wanted to go to India. *Ever.* Since I could remember, I had harbored a strong, irrational aversion to this vast, bewildering country of holy cows, moustachioed men and haloed Gurus. There was a time when even the smell of Indian food would make me feel sick.

My hippie friend Kassandra, on the other hand, loved India. While I spent my early twenties running a record label in England, she repeatedly pilgrimaged to the Holy Land, as she called it, in search of spiritual enlightenment. I would receive a flood of letters and postcards bearing vivid descriptions of life in India from her, bursting with tales of crazy *tuk-tuk* rides, gawking crowds, silent mountain monasteries and ominous Gurus with names like Sai Baba and Osho. These Gurus, she said, could magically produce sacred ash and wristwatches out of thin air and sometimes appeared in your dreams to grant you boons, if you recited the right mantras.

Kassandra's quest was unfathomable to me. 'Why are you going to this crazy Third World country?' I would question her dismissively. '*Why?*'

I don't know where my aversion to India came from. I had never been there and knew preciously little about the country. I just knew I hated it. And now, through an odd series of circumstances, I was here and had completely, irrevocably fallen in love with the country. How interesting and contradictory life could be sometimes.

We stopped in a small town to buy supplies for the week ahead. The place bustled with market stalls, cows and donkeys. As so often in India, I was mesmerized by the colorful mix of human beings, deities and animals, the traders and their strange wares on offer. A young girl, sitting in the back of her parents' four-wheel drive, threw up through the open window all over the road with a woeful expression on her face in near proximity to our car. I watched her with a mixture of sympathy and curiosity, while MJ groaned in disgust. The girl shot me a 'What?!' look, and I pondered the 'sick women on Asian buses' phenomenon.

It was a sight that I'd grown accustomed to all over Asia:

women with green faces and suffering expressions leaning out of buses, long black hair fluttering in the wind, throwing up while sympathetic relatives patted their hands. Invariably, the victims were women, while cheerfully chattering men leant back in their seats and smoked. One time, when I was returning from a temple in Tibet, the bus stopped en route and we were treated to the sight of a long line of women who all leant against a wall and purged their stomachs in unison. Why was it only women who got sick? I wondered.

Maniac inhaled some lunch at one of the roadside stalls; MJ and I followed Al Pacino through the afternoon heat down cobbled alleyways to the vegetable market, where he bartered with different traders. Meanwhile, MJ and I were befriended by a group of young Muslim vegetable sellers in blue *shalwar kameez* outfits who enthusiastically fed us cucumber slices and involved us in a fervent discussion about Allah. I was in a good mood, excited to be on the road again.

Al Pacino signaled that he had finished his purchases, and we headed back to the car to continue our drive. That night, we were supposed to stay in a 'beautiful and remote wooden cabin in nature overlooking a river'. At least that's what it said on the itinerary.

However, as we soon found out, our trip was very loosely organized. When we arrived at said location, the cabins were being renovated by an army of moustachioed workers. Admittedly, the location was glorious, quiet and wild, but with their smell of fresh paint and damp, the huts didn't promise to be an inviting place to spend the night. After a short debate, we decided to move on and climbed back into the car. We stopped at various places in search of a room, but without much luck. The promising ones were fully booked and what was left were places we weren't keen to stay in.

Dusk set in, and MJ was losing her sense of humor when we were shown to a tiny cramped shed by the roadside that had a man's moldy Y-fronts draped gracefully over the wardrobe. At this point, I was tired and just wanted to stop somewhere, but she flatly refused.

'Forget it,' she spat and stomped back to the car. 'I'm not staying in that hole! And have you seen those… underpants?! *Putain!* They are crayzeee to charge money for zis!'

Glumly, we carried on driving for another hour. It was getting dark. After eight hours of having to endure Maniac's driving to the backdrop of Al Pacino's hysterical Hindi disco music, I'd had enough.

'Right,' I said, 'we're stopping at the next place. I don't care where or what it is. I'm tired.' Al Pacino and Maniac nodded grimly in the front seats, clearly as irritated about the situation as I was.

The road snaked up a mountain, and in the fading light of dusk, I could make out some habitation: little houses by the hillside, trees and fields. It looked idyllic, and I spotted a sign informing us of a nearby guesthouse. This looked promising. A few yards onwards, a large yellow building caught my eye. 'ASHRAM,' big letters exclaimed on the sign that accompanied it.

'Oh!' I cried out. My mood perked up dramatically and I jabbed Al Pacino on the shoulder. 'An *ashram*! Look! That's where I want to stay!' He gave me a bemused look. MJ turned towards me and raised an eyebrow.

'No, no, guesthouse!' Al Pacino shook his head and pointed towards the left, where foretold guesthouse was located.

'No, no, ashram!' I insisted, leaning forward.

Maniac stopped the car. While Al Pacino set off to check out the guesthouse, I ran over the road to the ashram and skipped up its stairs with a bedazzled Maniac in tow. The ashram was a big multi-storey building with a seemingly endless number of steps that were framed by steel banisters and balconies with wire mesh around them. With its yellow walls and contrasting green window shutters, it looked like a prison made from Lego. The ashram stood at the edge of a steep hill that overlooked a gorge, at the bottom of which ran a torrential river. On one of the landings, a black Alsatian raised its head and eyed us curiously. In the ashram's office, located at the end of the first flight of stairs, I caught sight of a young Indian man dressed in saffron-colored robes – probably the *sannyasi* in charge. He had a beautiful, round, almost child-like face, with short black hair and a small tuft of longer hair at the back of his head. Our eyes met briefly. Then the weirdest thing happened. Suddenly, as I was standing in the doorway of this ascetic ashram office, space and time transcended. I felt myself flinching with surprise – it was almost a feeling of physical pain that started in my belly and rapidly shot through every inch of my body. Perplexed, I dived into the *sannyasi's* deep brown eyes as if to search for the answer to a question my mind hadn't even formed yet. The astonishment I found in them mirrored mine, and in this moment, I knew that, whatever it was, he felt it, too.

The moment only lasted for about two seconds. Not knowing what to make of it, I shook my head slightly and diverted my attention to Maniac, who asked the *sannyasi* whether rooms were available for the night.

'*Haa,*' the *sannyasi* affirmed in Hindi, and instructed a skinny young man in jeans who was hovering nearby to show us the room.

We followed him down two flights of stairs, and watched him unlock a heavy, dark green steel door. He switched on a neon light. Curiously, we inspected the concrete-floored room. It had pale dirty yellow walls and housed five single beds plus a small table covered in dust. The en-suite bathroom consisted of a squat toilet, two grimy buckets and a copper tap on one of the walls from which cold water emerged sporadically. The window was obstructed with green iron bars and heavy shutters that rattled synchronous with the sharp mountain winds. On the upside, the sturdy beds were adorned with beautiful pillow cases depicting red roses. I was smitten.

I ran back up the stairs and waved MJ, who still languidly reclined in the car, over animatedly. She climbed out of the car in slow motion and followed me down the ashram stairs. She glanced at me doubtfully when I, proud as a mother hen, showed her the room. 'Let's look at the guesthouse, too,' was all she could muster. 'I'm sure it's more comfortable.'

'Okay, if you want to...' I mumbled, and we made our way back to the ashram office to inform the *sannyasi* that we would have a look at the guesthouse, too, 'for comparison'.

'Sure,' he replied curtly from behind his desk.

Across the road, things were indeed more luxurious, though smaller. The guestrooms had showers, comfortable beds, a sink, and even carpets. MJ's eyes lit up, but I wasn't convinced. I had my heart set on the ashram. It was more austere, sure, but as I told MJ, it was also more interesting. 'There's love in the place, a friendly dog, the *sannyasi*...'

'Think about how much you're paying for this tour,' MJ interrupted my thought processes sharply. 'Do you really want to stay in that cold ashram? What for?'

I didn't reply. Suddenly, comprehension entered her clear blue eyes and she sighed with exasperation. 'It's just because he's cute!'

I grinned. She knew me too well already. Yes, I admitted, he was, but that wasn't the main reason. There was something else that drew me to the place. I wanted to stay in an authentic Indian ashram and see how it compared to the relative comforts of the Westernized yoga ashram we'd lived in for the past months. We were in the Himalayas, after all, and what could be more appropriate than to live among the religious and righteous of rural India for a while?

Unable to find a consensus on the matter, we flipped a coin, and, impartially, the decision was made. We moved into the ashram. I beamed, whereas my three companions shrugged their shoulders and followed me with an air of resignation. And thus, my fate was sealed.

1.2: In Lord Shiva's Abode: Chubby Gurus, Barred Windows and Rose-Covered Pillows

After we'd moved our bags into our new home, I curiously walked through the ashram to find out what spiritual activities I could get involved in. I discovered a handwritten note on the ashram's office door. *Aarti 7.30 pm*, it read. I glanced at my watch. It was seven pm now. This promised to be exciting. I loved *aarti*, a Hindu ceremony in which oil lamps are offered and songs are sung in praise of a deity. I wondered what it would be like in this remote mountain ashram.

A few people were sitting on a bench nearby. As I looked towards them to greet them with the traditional Indian *'Namaste'*, I saw that the young *sannyasi* was among them. He sat on the edge of the bench with a *mala*, a chain of prayer beads, in his hands and recited mantras quietly. I wondered how old he was. Late twenties, early thirties maybe? He raised his head and nodded in acknowledgement when he saw me. I smiled and edged towards him.

'Swami-ji,' I addressed him formally, 'did I read this correctly? Your *aarti* is at seven thirty pm?'

He cleared his throat. 'Yes,' he answered. 'But try to come earlier. I start the hime at seven fifteen in the temple, just over there.' He pointed towards the end of the corridor.

'The hime?' I asked, confused.

'Yes, you know, a… a song. We chant it together every evening before the *aarti*,' he said, still counting the prayer beads with his right hand. 'At seven fifteen.'

'Oh', I said, 'the *hymn*! Yes, great. I'll be there.'

When he turned his attention back to his *mala*, I walked to our room to tell MJ about the *aarti*. She was unpacking and said she'd meet me in the temple. On my way back, I ran into Al Pacino and Maniac and tried to inspire them to accompany me to the *aarti*.

My attempts were unsuccessful, as they had already made plans to spend the evening in the car to consume liquor and listen to disco music. Undeterred by their blatant lack of piety, I made my way to the temple alone.

The temple's heavy steel door was ajar, and with a tingling feeling of anticipation in my belly, I entered the room cautiously. It was brimming with Indian pilgrims who sat with crossed legs and bent backs on the concrete floor, which was partially covered with patterned rugs. Perused by the curious eyes of the congregation, I tiptoed towards the altar at the far end of the room. There was a space by the wall between two large Indian ladies in saris. I made my way across to them and slid to the floor. One of the ladies turned towards me and smiled kindly. Relieved, I returned her smile. I was never quite sure how welcome I was in Hindu temples, as some of them were closed to Westerners.

It was cold, and I was glad that I had brought my Tibetan blanket. My eyes wandered curiously over their new surroundings. The temple itself was sparse, with pale yellow walls, a black ceiling and barred windows. The altar sat on a raised platform, and its centerpiece, a gigantic oil painting of the ashram's Guru, dominated the room. It portrayed a chubby man with round cheeks and long wavy hair. Dressed in orange robes, he stared wistfully into the distance with an expression that seemed... wise on one hand, but there was something else, too. It was almost a look of mischief, an '*I know something you don't know*', mixed with mockery and a hint of cynicism. He also seemed focused and tough. I was not at all sure that I liked him.

The altar was dressed elaborately with flower garlands, colorful fabrics, and ritual objects such as knives, swords, brass bowls, candles, incense holders, and seashells. I looked for pictures or statues of Hindu deities such as Krishna or Durga, but there were none, apart from a tiny image of Lord Shiva, the austere God of yogis, on the altar. Thick incense wafted through the room and mingled in my nostrils with the buttery smell of flickering oil lamps.

As I pondered my surroundings, the young *sannyasi* entered the temple quietly and sat cross-legged on the floor. Fleetingly, he looked across the candlelit room. From my place near the right side of the altar, I caught his glance briefly. Was it my imagination, or was there a hint of melancholy in his dark brown eyes? I wasn't sure.

After ruffling his short hair and taking a deep breath, the *sannyasi* began to play the small harmonium that stood in front of him. As the accordion-like sounds started to weave their way around the temple, it seemed to transform from a dreary, cold concrete structure into an enchanting sanctuary. Suddenly, over the evocative, almost mournful chords of the instrument rose a strong, clear voice that sang a song so haunting, filled with such passion and devotion, that my body tingled all over.

Fascinated, I listened as the *sannyasi* chanted the words 'Om Namah Shivaya' over and over again – an ancient Sanskrit mantra that praised Lord Shiva. I felt as though I had somehow, magically, been transported into a different, faraway age. The melody reverberated around the temple and drifted out of the barred windows into the snow-covered mountains that surrounded us.

I was transfixed and could not stop looking, no, *staring*, at the *sannyasi*, who, with his eyes closed and head tilted back, appeared completely lost in his act of worship. Everything faded into insignificance – my body, the other worshippers around me, the cold – and only the *sannyasi* and his voice remained. I stared at him in a state of near-trance for almost the entire song, until an elderly monk sat down in front of me and blocked my view.

Irritated, I shifted around and looked across the sea of faces. I spotted MJ, who sat kneeling near the rear of the room, and noticed that tears were streaming down her face from beneath closed eyes. I turned back towards the altar. My heart filled with the sweetest ache. I had never heard anything so beautiful in my entire life.

Then the song was over. The *sannyasi* bowed and touched the ground with his forehead. I had a lump in my throat by then and tried hard not to break down in tears, although I wasn't sure why exactly. After a few moments of silence, the *sannyasi* got up to kneel down in front of the altar. This marked the beginning of the evening *aarti*.

The assembled congregation began to chant a litany of Vedic mantras, while the *sannyasi* conducted ritualistic acts to honor Guru-ji, the man in the painting. He blessed him with the elements of air, fire, water, earth and spirit through the raising and circling of various objects, including incense, candles, and water.

Two Indian ladies, wearing elegant saris and expressions of stern purposefulness on their faces, stood to the left and right of the altar. One of them swung an object that resembled a large hairy duster (or 'Santa Claus beard', as MJ called it) through the air, whereas the other woman wafted a big colorful shield in rhythm with the chants. A golden tray on the altar held a pair of wooden sandals, presumably the Guru's. The *sannyasi* washed and dried them carefully before anointing them elaborately with ghee and flowers. With great reverence, he formed pretty patterns and symbols on the shoes while the congregation continued to chant. I recognized some of the Sanskrit mantras from my stay at the yoga ashram, and joined in with the singing whenever I could.

At some point, the *sannyasi* stood up and picked up a large ritual knife. He contemplated it for a few seconds, then held it to his heart and looked at Guru-ji. Then, seemingly out of nowhere, the demure chanting was interrupted by a loud noise. I flinched and turned around. A band of young Indian men had appeared at the back of the temple and together, they rang bells, crashed cymbals and banged drums with great vigor. It sounded like they were playing a rock song, full of energy and purpose. The worshippers around me pulled themselves up from the floor and now stood facing the altar. I copied them.

As if on cue, the *sannyasi* began to perform an extraordinary martial dance. He swung the knife from left to right, held it up towards the picture of Guru-ji, stabbed the air, jumped, and uttered what seemed to be shamanistic cries. All eyes were on the *sannyasi* now, and an elderly man to my right recoiled in horror when the ritual knife came dangerously close to his face. It was a spectacular sight and drew me in completely with its potent energy, reminding me of ancient ritual dramas. The *sannyasi* was a great performer. I had a flashback to the times when I worked in the music industry, and leather-clad, face-painted Metal bands were very fond of doing a similar ritualistic display of weapons on stage. Who *was* this guy, I wondered?

The music quietened down again, and a young boy started to make his way through the temple with a wicker basket in his hands. From the basket, he handed each of us flower petals and then smeared some *tilak* paste on the point between our eyebrows to bless us. The *sannyasi* took his seat again at the harmonium and began another chant, seemingly in honor of Guru-ji. One by one, the Indian devotees filed to the altar, knelt down in front of Guru-ji's portrait, and placed the flowers – and their foreheads – on his wooden sandals.

I faced a conflict. I wanted to be respectful, but something in me resisted bowing down to an unknown human deity. Especially this one. I came up with a compromise: I would make my way to the altar and put the flower petals in front of the tiny picture of Lord Shiva, and bow down to him instead. Yes, I could live with that. When I returned from the altar, I saw that MJ was doing the same.

The *aarti* finished with another chant and the distribution of *prasad*, blessed food. The same boy who had given us the flower petals came around and now distributed pieces of fruit and sugary sweets with a shy smile in his eyes. I thanked him by holding a piece of apple to my third eye and then eating the sweet fruit. The pilgrims around me started to chatter and move out of the temple slowly. I looked around for the *sannyasi*, but couldn't see him anywhere.

MJ and I met in the corridor. I grabbed her arm.

'Did you hear that? Wasn't that just amazing?' I asked her.

'My God!' she exclaimed and shook her head. 'That was so beautiful. I couldn't stop crying. What *was* this song?'

'I don't know, but I've never heard anything like it. It was incredible.'

Together, we walked down the landing towards our room. We passed the ashram office. The *sannyasi* was inside it amid a crowd of Indian people who all seemed to talk to him at once. In his robes, he reminded me of a shorn Jesus with a band of excited disciples around him. As I walked past the office, he caught my eye and flashed me a big smile. My heart jumped. Had he really just smiled at me? I smiled back quickly and then elbowed MJ in the ribs.

'Did you see that?' I whispered. 'The *sannyasi* just smiled at me.'

'Yeah,' she said nonchalantly, 'he smiled at me, too.'

We unlocked the clunky steel door and entered our musty, dark room. It was cold and damp, but I didn't feel it. I still had fragments of the song swirling around in my mind, mixed with images of the *sannyasi's* radiant smile. MJ dropped onto one of the beds with a sigh and wrapped a duvet around her. I couldn't sit still.

'I'll just go and find Al Pacino to see what we're doing tomorrow, okay? I'll be back in a few minutes,' I said and opened the door.

'Okay,' MJ said and yawned. 'It's so damn cold in this place. Could you bring me some tea please if you can find some?'

'Yes, sure, there might be some in the canteen,' I replied and left the room to find Al Pacino. Maybe he was still in the car with

Maniac.

The corridor was full of Indian pilgrims who smiled and nodded at me. Smiling back, I navigated my way around them and climbed up the stairs towards the ashram's entrance. There, a group of inquisitive middle-aged Indian ladies in saris zoomed in on me and began to bombard me with questions in Hindi. *What is your name? Where are you from? What are you doing here?* they seemed to say. Not knowing how to respond, I shrugged my shoulders and laughed. *'Hindi tora-tora,'* I said, 'little Hindi.' They laughed, too.

Suddenly Al Pacino, who must have heard the commotion, came to my rescue. He addressed the ladies in Hindi to seemingly tell them all they wanted to know. Once their curiosity had been satisfied, they dispersed.

'Thanks,' I said with a laugh. 'Al Pacino...'

'Yes!' he beamed. He obviously liked the nickname we'd given him.

'Al Pacino, I want to know if there is meditation or yoga in this ashram in the mornings. Can we ask somebody?' I said.

He nodded vigorously. 'We ask Swami-ji!' he suggested. *'Bhai!'* he called to a moustachioed man who stood leaning against the ashram wall with a cigarette in his hand. The man tilted his head. I heard the words 'Swami-ji' and the man pointed towards the ashram stairs.

'He says that we find Swami-ji in kitchen,' Al Pacino told me. *'Chalo.* We go find him.'

Together, we skipped down several flights of stairs. The ashram seemed to be full by now, and the landings were populated with women washing their saris in buckets, wide-eyed children, and men in white undershirts who sat on wooden benches.

The kitchen was in the basement of the building. As predicted, we found the *sannyasi* in the adjacent canteen, standing again in the midst of a group of merry pilgrims. I was surprised to see men smoking and shouting into their mobile phones. The ashrams I had visited before had a no-smoking policy, and many forbade the use of mobile telephones also. Ashrams were generally secluded Hindu hermitages in which a Guru lived and gave spiritual advice to others. People came there to meditate, practice yoga and follow a *sattvic* lifestyle by eating a light, vegetarian diet and abstaining from toxins like cigarettes and alcohol, as well as external distractions such as TV. Detachment from luxurious living was believed to aid spiritual development, and strict routines as well as *karma yoga*, selfless service for others, were a big part of ashram life. *What kind of ashram is this?* I thought indignantly as I saw a small bottle of liquor peek out of another pilgrim's pocket.

Meekly, we edged our way towards the *sannyasi*. 'Swami-ji,' Al Pacino said and pointed at me. The *sannyasi* looked at me and smiled. *Wow*, I thought as I stood in front of him. *He is beautiful.* His skin was smooth and almond-colored, and he had full, sensuous lips. His dark eyes looked thoughtful and kind.

Quickly, as if to shut up the voice in my head, I started to chatter.

'Thank you for the beautiful *aarti*,' I gushed. 'It was the best *aarti* I've seen in the whole of India.'

Yeah, the little voice in my head popped up again, *as if you've seen so many. Don't be so stupid. You've only been to Rishikesh!*

The *sannyasi*'s face lit up. 'Oh… thank you,' he replied. 'You enjoyed it? This is nice to hear.'

'Do you have yoga or meditation sessions here, too?' I asked timidly. For some reason, I was feeling self-conscious talking to the *sannyasi*. Something about him put me on edge.

He nodded. 'We do *pranayama* in the mornings,' he said.

'*Pranayama?! Great!*' I enthused, as though he had just offered me instant enlightenment. 'Can I join?'

'Yes, of course,' he replied with what I thought was an inter-ested look in his eyes. 'You can come at five am for an hour's practice.' He had a nice accent, very colonial, stilted almost. I liked the way he rolled his r's. *Morrrrning. Prrranayama*, I repeated reverently in my mind. I loved accents, and could amuse myself with mere words and peculiar pronunciations for endless, happy hours.

'And what about the *aarti*?' I asked, eager like a puppy about to be taken for a walk.

'That is at four thirty.' *Fourrr thirrrty*, I repeated devoutly.

'Can I come to that, too?' I asked aloud.

The *sannyasi* regarded me with a sardonic smile and raised his eyebrows slightly. 'Sure – if you can get up that early,' he shrugged, 'then you are most welcome.' With that, he turned to speak to a pilgrim. I was thrilled: it was a challenge set.

'What!?' wailed MJ in her French-Canadian accent when I returned to our room with two steaming cups of *chai* in my hands. 'You're going to get up at four o'clock? You're crayzeeee!'

'What's the big deal?' I smiled as I set my alarm clock with grand ceremonial gestures.

I felt very virtuous indeed when I turned off the light half an hour later, and heard MJ mutter and shake her head on the pillow beside me.

1.3: A Private Education

I slept fitfully. In the ashram, doors banged and phones rang. People shouted and coughed and spat all through the night. As we later found out, our abode was more of a spiritual hotel than an ashram. Indian tourists stopped here on their way to famous pilgrimage places. It explained a lot.

I dreamt that I was in a car with the others. I had to get to the *aarti*, yet they wanted to buy petrol at a faraway petrol station. I realized that I would not make it to the *aarti* if I stayed in the car, so I jumped out and ran, without knowing where I was going. I asked people in a panic and eventually spotted the ashram, just in time.

I woke up with a start. It was four am. All was quiet now. I had a quick wash, brushed my teeth and wrapped a large blanket around me before I left the room. The heavy metal door creaked, and I hoped it wouldn't wake MJ up. Outside, it was still dark, and armed with a torch, I silently glided towards the temple.

Expecting to find a similar congregation and spectacle as on the night before, I was surprised to see only the *sannyasi* and an elderly monk in the brightly neon-lit room, chanting with subdued voices towards the Guru's sandals. I quietly sat down at the back of the room, pulled my shawl around my head and observed the monks as they performed the *aarti*, which was a bit of a let-down after yesterday's imposing event.

After that, I was excited to note, I had a private *pranayama* class with the *sannyasi*. *Pranayama* is a form of breath control used in yogic practice. It's a method whereby *prana*, the life force, can be activated and regulated so that practitioners can attain a higher state of vibratory energy. Again, I had expected a large class of practitioners, so having this one-on-one encounter with the *sannyasi* unsettled me somewhat. I hoped that I would be able to keep up with him.

Sitting cross-legged on the floor to my left, the *sannyasi* instructed me earnestly in various types of breathing exercises, including *kapalbhati* (frontal brain cleansing breath, performed through short, rapid abdominal out-breaths through the nose), *nadi shodhana* (alternate nostril breathing, a calming breath performed to balance the left and right hemispheres), and *bhramari* (the 'humming bee breath', used to improve concentration). I knew most of these practices, but found the ten-minute long continuous *kapalbhati* hard-going.

'Is it… *paining*?' the *sannyasi* asked me with concern when I took a breather after several rounds.

Suppressing a laugh, I quickly replied, 'No, no, not at all. It's not paining.' Full of zeal, I started again. It helped to have an attractive teacher.

The *sannyasi* also taught me some exercises to better my eyesight. He was appalled that, at my young age, I already wore glasses.

'Do you work much at the computer?' he asked me with furrowed eyebrows.

'Yes,' I responded, 'I write a lot.'

'That is why your eyesight is bad then,' he diagnosed.

'No,' I shook my head, 'I wore glasses long before I used a computer. Short-sightedness runs in my family.'

'Anyway,' he continued brusquely, seemingly irritated by my response. 'Thinking is also important. You have to think: *Every day, my eye problems are becoming less.*'

I nodded obediently and continued to follow his instructions. Together, we rolled our eyes to the left on our in-breaths, then to our rights on the out-breath, while we silently repeated the mantra 'All my eye problems are going away.' We also performed a peculiar vocal exercise in which we imitated the high-pitched sound of a helium balloon (this was a very good exercise for singers, apparently) and another form of *pranayama* in which we blew up our cheeks and then exhaled the air in short rapid bursts.

I tried to keep a straight face. It was hard.

Overall, I enjoyed the class. Some of the breathing exercises demanded stamina, but I was pleased to note that my two months at the yoga ashram as well as the yoga training I'd done back in England were falling into place. Without them, I would have been lost here.

After class, the *sannyasi* excused himself politely, then turned and asked, 'What are you doing today?'

My ears pricked up. He wanted to see me again?

'I think we're going to a temple this morning,' I said while I pulled my blanket tightly around my shoulders. It was only six am, and it was freezing.

'Temple? Oh yes, the temple in the village. That's only a kilometer away. Are you free at four o'clock?' The *sannyasi* tilted his head and looked at me questioningly.

'Hmm, maybe,' I replied, playing hard to get. 'Why?'

'We can meet here for another *pranayama* session. If you are free, of course.' He pulled his saffron-colored robes into shape and draped the upper part elegantly over his torso. It looked almost like a Roman toga.

Flattered, I enthusiastically nodded my agreement and watched the *sannyasi* leave the temple to perform his ashram duties.

The evocative hymn to Lord Shiva haunted me all day and I couldn't wait for the evening's *aarti* to hear it once again.

1.4: Fire Ceremonies and Sword Dances

The day was clear and bright, and after breakfast, MJ and I idly strolled down the mountain road to visit the village temple. Al Pacino trundled along several steps behind us and busily shouted into his mobile phone. We passed isolated cottages with red roofs and stopped every few yards to take in the view. Many of the surrounding hills had finely layered agricultural terraces hewn into them, giving them a rugged look that reminded me of Machu Picchu in Peru. The trees were blooming with fragrant purple flowers.

The clouds had lifted from behind green-brown hills, and we were treated to a majestic view of the Himalayas that had been hidden from us the night before. A range of snow-covered peaks, obscured partially by white clouds, spread out before us, peak after peak, like mono-colored patchwork. We greeted the local women who worked on the fields with hands folded in front of our hearts and a cheerful 'Namaste!' which they returned with radiant smiles and warm eyes. I stopped and breathed in the clean air, feeling blissfully happy to be here. This village was unbelievably quiet. All we could hear was birdsong and the occasional passing car.

The temple was located at the end of a narrow little lane. I bought the traditional offerings of flowers, coconut, incense and puffed rice from a little roadside stall. Before entering the temple compound, we took off our shoes, as is custom in India. By the wall, an old lady in rags, cowering on a stick, stretched out a rough, wrinkly hand towards us.

The ancient complex was vast and contained bright, colorful woodwork and hidden alcoves in little convoluted alleys. Shiva *lingams*, stone pillars representing Lord Shiva's divine phallus, representative of the fountain of life, stood interspersed with black statues of Mother Goddesses, intricate stone carvings of deities and sculptures of Ganesh, whose elephant head had been marked with yellow and red *tilak* powder. The pagoda-like rooftops looked almost Chinese in style, and were held in place by electric-blue pillars.

The main sanctuary's entrance was guarded by a seated stone Nandi, Lord Shiva's bull. We rang the heavy brass bell that hung over the entry's threshold, and entered the temple's inner sanctum respectfully. Inside, a striking, intellectual-looking *pujari* with short, black oiled hair, thin-rimmed spectacles and a white *kurta* sat cross-legged in front of the elevated stone altar, which was set back in the walls of the building. He explained the layout and significance of the temple to us while preparing his ritual tools to bless us with a small *puja*.

I smiled when I remembered my surprise after I had set foot into India for the first time. Bizarrely, though I had resisted anything Indian for so long, I felt like I had come home. It was the spirituality that spoke to me most. Somehow, I understood it instantly, as though I was merely remembering something long forgotten. Everything made perfect sense: India's many multi-faceted deities, the rich mythology, the Sanskrit language, the rituals, the temples, the sanctity of rivers and mountains and other places in nature. I was fascinated by the colorful images of the Hindu deities Shiva – an incredibly attractive, muscular God with blue skin, long flowing hair, three eyes and snakes coiled around his half-naked body – and his beautiful consort Shakti, who were often pictured sitting side by side in the Himalayas.

The Hindus lived a life filled with vibrant rituals, prayers and fire ceremonies, fueled by a fervent devotion to hundreds of Goddesses and Gods, each of which fulfilled a different function. The fact that there *was* a Goddess, many Goddesses that were revered sincerely, touched my heart deeply. In India, God was male *and* female, as well as androgynous, and I loved the celebration of fertility, of life, of Mother Earth. This was exactly what had interested me about Tantra: the balance between male and female energies, and the recognition that the sacred is reflected in everything – the male, the female, animals, the elements, nature, in every object and in every being.

On our way back to the ashram, we took a stroll through the village. It possessed a bustling market with an array of small shops, selling everything from bright material for saris to fruit, vegetables, medicines, mobile phones and cosmetics. For a tiny mountain village consisting merely of a handful of streets, it seemed thriving. Smiling men, women and children stared at us curiously.

'*Woh log kaun hai?*' they asked Al Pacino. 'Who are they?' 'Where are they from?'

Overall, life seemed laid-back here. In a little tea store, we enjoyed a deliciously sweet *chai*, prepared by a burly man with the most luscious, twirly moustache I had ever set eyes upon.

Back at the ashram, we hungrily devoured a simple yet tasty lunch of lentil *dhal*, okra and potato *sabji* with hand-rolled chapattis. Thick, heavy clouds began to darken the sky in the early afternoon, which caused MJ and me to snuggle up in bed in our equally dark room to rest and read. The wind howled through our barred windows and a violent thunderstorm ensued. Fatigued from my early-morning start, I drifted in and out of sleep.

At four pm, I reluctantly crawled out from beneath my cozy duvet and made my way towards the temple to meet the *sannyasi* for my next *pranayama* session. He was already waiting for me at the top of the staircase and checked his wristwatch.

'Oh good, you're on time,' he mumbled, surprised, as he watched me climb the stairs towards him.

'Sure,' I smiled, and together, we ambled along the concrete corridor towards the temple in silence. We cast off our sandals at the entrance, entered, and sat cross-legged on the floor. The *sannyasi* prostrated before Guru-ji's portrait, whereas I nodded curtly in his direction.

We began to practice some *pranayama* exercises, but our session ended prematurely as the *sannyasi's* mobile phone rang near-constantly. 'Excuse me,' he said apologetically between calls, 'but the pilgrim's season has just started. I am the only one in charge here. You just continue.'

As he was speaking, I took a closer look at the *sannyasi*. Under his dark eyes, I noticed deep, black circles. Beneath his outwardly authoritative, energetic demeanor, he looked exhausted. I decided to ask him a few questions between telephone calls. I was intrigued as to why a young, attractive man like him had renounced the world to become a *sannyasi*. Did religion run in his family? Was it a calling?

His answer was astounding. He did not come from a religious background, he said, and contrary to what I had imagined, had spent his early adulthood in the Indian army, leading a relatively normal life in his native Varanasi. His life changed completely after he met Swami-ji, a senior disciple of Guru-ji. He decided to give up his career, leave his parents, and followed Swami-ji across India to become a *sannyasi*.

'How did this happen?' I asked, amazed.

'I did not believe in anything at the time. I was a complete atheist. In fact, I was making fun of Swami-ji for being so religious. *Why are you doing this puja all the time?* I was asking him. He simply said to me: *Just try this meditation for one month. It does not matter if you believe in it or not; just try it for one month and afterwards, we will speak again.* And so I did. It was a challenge, and I was curious.'

He smiled reflectively as he recalled the events of his past.

'And well, after that, I decided to give up my job, and leave everything – my job, my family, my friends – to come here. This meditation changed my life forever. Now I have been here for seven years. But I have no regrets. The life is fantastic here, really.' He straightened his back and nodded. 'Fantastic.'

After some preliminary study with Swami-ji, the *sannyasi* was posted to the Himalayas and now managed Guru-ji's ashram single-handedly. The ashram focused primarily on education – it ran a school for local children, taught through the medium of English, and aimed to elevate poor areas. This mission was financed through money from the pilgrims that passed through the ashram and left donations. In addition, the *sannyasi* was an Ayurvedic doctor and treated both villagers and pilgrims with his medicines.

I felt inspired. Not only did he possess outstanding physical beauty ('What a waste of a beautiful man,' MJ had sighed), but he seemed to be inwardly beautiful, too. Lost in thoughts, I left the temple to reconvene with MJ.

At precisely seven pm, we made our way to the temple again. To our dismay, the *sannyasi* was not there for the evening *aarti*. Instead, we were treated to a performance by the elderly monk, who crooned the beautiful hymn to Lord Shiva painfully out of tune to the woeful sounds of the harmonium. I was gravely disappointed. This was our last night at the ashram, and I'd been craving to hear the haunting song one more time.

Later in the evening, however, the *sannyasi* entered the temple for the weekly *havan* fire ceremony. This excited me, especially since I had just spent the past two months studying Vedic fire ceremonies and was curious to see how they compared. *Havan*, also called *yajna*, is an ancient ritual in which offerings such as ghee and sacred herbs are placed in a ceremonial fire to the chants of Sanskrit mantras.

In Hinduism, fire ceremonies are a form of communication with the Divine. Everything offered into *Agni*, the sacred fire, is believed to reach the Gods. In return, it is hoped that the Gods will shower some blessings on the devotees who so fervently place precious offerings into the flames. Symbolically, by placing offerings into the fire, practitioners let go of negative emotions and surrender to the fire of transformation.

This *havan* was enormously intense, and unlike anything I'd ever experienced before. It was like switching a TV from black-and-white to color. In the yoga ashram, the fire ceremonies had been rather tame affairs, with quiet monotonous chanting around the fire pit and a meek uttering of the '*Svaha!*' that accompanied the offerings. Here, in this small Himalayan temple, the walls were shaking with the collective chants of the gathered congregation. I could literally feel the blazing presence of Agni, the Fire God, in the room, scorching the minds and hearts of those present.

A charged excitement pervaded the temple as the small fire burnt brightly in its tray. Four people, including the *sannyasi*, sat around the fire and vigorously offered ghee and herbs into the flames after each mantra. The rest of us gathered around them in a circle and chanted the Vedic mantras. '*Sva-ha!*' we thundered in unison, bodies reverberating with spiritual fervor. 'We offer!'

Gradually, the smoke in the room became thicker and I could see now why the temple ceiling was black. People began to cough and disappeared into clouds of smoke, until two of the ashram boys quickly opened the doors and windows.

The *sannyasi* was focused and raised the energy ever higher with his emphatic chants and movements. From time to time, he placed small pieces of wood into the fire with dramatic gestures. Once again, I was mesmerized. I felt as though I had entered a different world – a magical kingdom of ancient rituals, fires, deities and mountain temples. This was what I had been looking for all along, and suddenly, when I least expected it, I found it. Near-ecstatic, I continued to chant the mantras with the Indian worshippers. Towards the end of the *havan*, we all filed towards the fire to place offerings of fruit and flowers into it as our offering to the Gods.

The *aarti* that followed the evening's *havan* was more

elaborate. Instead of the knife dance, we were treated to a special sword dance, in which the elderly monk swung a hefty sword slowly around his head. I half-expected the *sannyasi* to join him for a sword fight.

That night, still carrying the glow of the *havan* in me, I told MJ that I would like to spend more time at the ashram. I was enthralled by what seemed to be a higher level of esoteric rituals and yogic practices. I was keen to learn more about them, and here was a fantastic chance to further my knowledge. In addition, I wanted to help the *sannyasi* out. He seemed so busy and couldn't even do his *pranayama* in peace without being interrupted by the telephone or pilgrims. If he had more help, maybe in the form of a PA, I thought, he could focus on his spiritual practice. After all, this was imperative for a *sannyasi*, no?

MJ looked doubtful. 'Look,' she said sharply, 'this man is old enough. You don't need to rescue him.'

'I don't want to rescue him, I just want to offer him some help. And why not? I have some time left, and it would be great to work with the children. I really admire the work they do here.' I shrugged my shoulders.

'I guess… If that's all it is…' Evidently, MJ was not convinced.

I had to admit that it was mainly my curiosity about the *sannyasi* that inspired me to offer my help in the ashram. I was keen to find out more about him, his way of life and his spiritual practices. I wanted to learn the fire ceremonies he led and the beautiful hymn to Lord Shiva. I thought that maybe I could write an article about him and the ashram's work. And I was keen to practice more *pranayama* with him. It seemed ideal: I could have a Guru all to myself, and a good-looking one at that.

MJ suddenly smiled: 'Just imagine him in his army uniform,' she giggled. 'He is really well-built!'

We laughed and turned off the light.

The next morning, I attended a final pre-dawn *pranayama* session with the *sannyasi*. After a night's sleep, I wasn't sure whether I still wanted to offer him my volunteering services. Somehow, it felt inappropriate, presumptuous even. Maybe I should just forget about the whole thing, cherish what I had experienced here and move on.

Confused, I decided to ask Guru-ji for advice. He was the deity here after all, I reasoned, so maybe he could help me out. With all the respect I could muster, I looked at his face in the gigantic painting and addressed him in my thoughts.

'Look, Guru-ji,' I said, 'I am thinking of doing some *seva* in your ashram. I'm not sure if this is right. But if this guy needs help with anything, if this is meant to happen, and if you want me to return, then give me a sign.'

Nothing happened. Unmoved, Guru-ji continued to stare wistfully into the distance. The *sannyasi* and I continued our *pranayama* session earnestly. *Okay*, I thought, strangely relieved, *maybe I am not supposed to come back here after all*. I remembered my original travel plans to visit the marriage place of Shiva and Parvati for a few days. Yes, that would probably be better anyway. Who knew what kind of trouble I might get myself into in this ashram otherwise.

After *pranayama*, the *sannyasi* turned to leave the temple. With a sideward glance in my direction, he straightened his *dhoti* and addressed me cheerfully: 'So it is time to depart!'

'Yes,' I responded, 'we're leaving later on today.' I sat on the floor in a yoga stretch, while he towered above me with a playful smile on his round face.

'When are you coming back?' he asked, half in jest.

This was my cue. *Okay, Guru-ji*, I thought, *you're on.*

'Soon,' I said. 'I was actually wondering whether you needed some help here at the ashram. You seem really busy, and I have a few days left after my Himalayan tour. I could come back and help you out.'

The *sannyasi* looked at me intensely for a moment. He seemed confused. Then my offer sank in and he grew animated.

'So you *are* coming back?' he asked.

'Well, if you have anything to do for me here, then yes.' I smiled up at him.

He grinned. 'There is not just any thing you can do here – there are *many* things you can do.' He sat down on a table. 'You can teach a few English classes in the ashram school, and you can tell the children stories. Yes! And, of course, you can do yoga here. This place, the Himalayas,' he pointed towards the window, 'is much better than where you were before. The *prana* is so good here.' The words tumbled from his mouth.

'Yes. I am also very interested in the fire ceremonies.' His enthusiasm was infectious. This was going better than I'd dared to hope.

'I will teach you everything!'

'And the hymn to Lord Shiva?'

'Everything.'

'Okay, it's a deal.'

We smiled at each other warmly for a moment. I was pleasantly surprised. It seemed that he had enjoyed practicing *pranayama* with me – something I hadn't been able to deduce from his serious and professional manner towards me.

Still smiling, he left the temple, only to return a minute later to ask me, 'Do you like Indian sweets?'

'Yes,' I lied. He handed me some sugary balls wrapped in newspaper with the words 'This is for you', before he left the room again.

Proudly clutching my Indian sweets, I ran back to our room. MJ was still in bed and slowly opened her eyes as I charged into the room.

'I have a new job!' I proclaimed. MJ peered up at me from beneath her duvet and yawned.

'Really?! Wow! So you are going to volunteer here?' Curiously, she was excited for me. 'This is your thing! That's great! So now you will leave India on a good note, as you wanted!' she enthused while munching the sweets I handed her.

Suddenly, as if on cue, the fragments of a triumphant martial anthem drifted through our barred bathroom window. *'I love my country! I love my parents! Thank you, God!'* the jubilant phrases resounded, accentuated by vigorous, repetitive drumming. Curious, MJ and I darted to the window to find out where the cries were coming from. We peered out over the fields to the ashram's school. A flock of beaming, uniformed children was gathered on the school's rooftop and belted out the chant fervently in unison with a smiling saffron-robed *sannyasi* and a couple of school teachers. We cracked up laughing and shook our heads.

We had some breakfast at the canteen across the road and prepared to leave. While Al Pacino and Maniac loaded our trusty car, we ambled down towards the ashram school. The school children were still assembled on the flat roof and performed exercises to the sound of drums. A middle-aged teacher with thick spectacles wagged his index finger vehemently at one child and smacked another across the head.

Exuberantly, the children ran towards us, smiled and waved. 'Good morning, Ma'am!' 'How are you, Ma'am?' they shouted laughingly at the top of their voices. Gathering his robes around him, the *sannyasi* descended gracefully from the rooftop to bid us farewell.

'See you next week,' I said, and climbed into the car. With a dazzling smile, he tilted his head Indian-style in acknowledgement and strolled leisurely towards the ashram.

1.5: Where Earth Meets Sky: The Sacred Mountains

I was so excited as we drove up the curvaceous mountain road that not even Al Pacino's disco music managed to bother me. I still couldn't believe that I'd be returning to this ashram in a few days to work with the *sannyasi*.

But for now, the Himalayas and new adventures were waiting for us. I looked out of the window down the steep, wooded valleys and thought back to when I had my first real glimpse of the Himalayas in Tibet. It was November then, and I'd been on my way to Nepal. Together with two Frenchwomen, I was traveling on the Friendship Highway for a week in a jeep, stopping every night in a different, frozen village.

Visually, it was mind-blowing. *Kamba-la*, the final mountain pass at almost five thousand meters altitude before the road drops down towards the Nepalese border, almost took us by surprise. It appeared after we'd climbed the precipitous road for a long time. We knew that we'd arrived at a pass because Pupu, our eccentric Tibetan driver, had uttered the hissing shamanic blessing we heard every time we approached one.

We got out of the jeep and into the icy wind that numbed our skin and blew furiously through our hair. I took a few steps and then stopped abruptly. My mouth dropped open. Ahead of me was a universe made from countless, rugged white peaks, so beautiful that they appeared almost surreal. It looked like a kingdom made from thousands of unique crystals.

A brown, desert-like landscape separated us from the mountains. It was vast and uninhabited, accentuated only by little stone pyramids the Tibetan people left as a mark of respect, and a few discarded yak skulls. Next to me, thousands of bright prayer flags fluttered dauntlessly in the fierce wind on wooden poles to carry blessings to all living beings.

I stood completely still and immersed myself in these giant mountains. I almost didn't dare to breathe in case they'd disappear. Feeling like a small child, I looked and looked until my face and fingers became numb. With every second, my awe grew bigger. Enveloped in stillness, I experienced a moment of pure perfection. Natalie, one of my companions, came to stand beside me. She saw the expression on my face and began to cry.

'This is God to me,' she said quietly and pointed at the scene in front of us. 'These mountains are God.'

Jampa, our guide, joined us. 'These mountains are sacred in Tibet,' he nodded, wrapping his windbreaker tightly around him. 'They also have different names. For us, Mount Everest is called *Quomolangma*. It means "Mother of the Universe" or "Goddess Mother of the Snows". Together with the two mountains next to her, she symbolizes the triple Goddess of Maiden, Mother and Crone.'

He paused and looked at Natalie. 'So you are not wrong when you call them God. All expeditions here start with a devotional ceremony. Team members leave offerings for the Gods of the mountain, for protection.'

It was this sanctity that drew many yogis and *sadhus* to the Himalayas, either to travel between sacred sites, or to meditate in the solitude and peace of mountain caves, far from the Western tourists that flocked to the East in search of enlightenment. I'd heard that some of these yogis possessed extraordinary powers, and that mythical beings, the so-called 'Masters of the Himalayas', were said to live here eternally, existing on nothing but *prana*, the life force. I wondered if I could meet one of them, and how. If they really existed, they had to possess so much wisdom.

Now I was on the other side of the Himalayas. Our first stop was a tranquil lake on top of a mountain. It had taken us about an hour to climb up on a small trail, laden with backpacks, food and sleeping bags. We were to camp here for a few nights. The lake was surrounded by woodland, and apart from a small canteen nearby, there was little else around. After the chaos of the pilgrims' ashram, this suited us just fine.

I sat down on a wooden picnic bench and watched while Al Pacino and Maniac erected our tent. MJ stretched out on the bench next to me and took a nap in the morning sun. A few people were sitting near the lake on plastic chairs, sharing picnics. It was idyllic and quiet, apart from the occasional Indian hikers who'd make a point of standing at one side of the lake and shouting across it to their companions who had placed themselves strategically on the other side.

'Namaaaaṡteeeeeeeeee!' their voices echoed across the still waters. 'Hellllllllllllooooooooooooooooooooo!'

We didn't do much over the next few days. We slept, ate and read books. MJ and I spent much of our time sitting outside our tent and contemplated the dramatic landscape ahead of us – big skies, snow-capped mountains, green hills, and the clear lake. From time to time, beautiful mountain women in bright saris came to visit us in the company of their energetic buffaloes to share a cup of milky *chai*. And every evening, our faithful Al Pacino cooked us delicious vegetarian meals accompanied by fresh *rotis*. They were simple and rustic, yet, in this evocative location, everything tasted as divine as the Food of the Gods.

I loved the straightforwardness of our existence in the Himalayas. It was mainly the silent beauty of the mountains and the pure, clean air that gave me a heightened perception of everything. Just being here made my heart sing. I had everything I needed: food, good company, nature, alone time and a warm place to sleep. Wasn't this all that mattered?

I'd noticed that I was happiest when I traveled, when I lived from day to day and was open to whatever and whoever came my way. And more than anything, I relished the detachment from things that didn't contribute to my peace of mind – telephone, internet, and all the other trappings of modern life.

In this meditative setting, MJ and I had many deep conversations about our pasts. Our family backgrounds were remarkably similar in their dysfunction. We'd both grown up with an alcoholic parent, and knew the misery this brought even in adulthood. I was amazed to find that, like me, she'd experienced a frustrating pattern with unavailable men in her life. She'd been involved with alcoholics and dope smokers in the past, too, and none of her relationships had lasted very long.

Because of our similar childhoods, we were able to relate to each other with sensitivity and compassion. We felt that it was no coincidence that we, two single women in their mid-thirties from different parts of the world, had randomly met in India and embarked on this adventure together. There were just too many synchronicities.

India was working on me in the stillness of the mountains. Triggered by my conversations with MJ, I was thinking about my relationships with men, and where things were going. Or not going.

'No wonder you're celibate, Tiziana,' MJ laughed one night after I complained that I hadn't had sex for almost six months. 'You keep surrounding yourself with unavailable men! You live in ashrams, hang out with monks and yogis who think that sex is bad… I mean, come on!'

She had a point. And now I had somehow met another unavailable man – the *sannyasi* – and would spend yet more time in a religious institution where sex and relationships certainly weren't a priority.

So, one afternoon, I climbed up a hill to sit underneath a tree that overlooked the lake. Perhaps I could get a glimpse of enlightenment about what was going on in my life right now. The area was deserted. The canteen boys were taking a siesta and MJ was reading in front of our tent. I absorbed the stillness that was only occasionally interrupted by birdsong, the raspy croaking of tree frogs and the monotonous humming of bees. The sky was hazy, and the mountains ahead of me looked like frozen blue ghosts against their milky background.

I leaned my back against the rough bark of the tree and watched the turquoise light that shimmered on the water below me. So much had already happened on this little mountain trip. My time in the pilgrims' ashram had certainly been interesting. All the practices I'd studied in Rishikesh – the fire ceremonies, the Sanskrit mantras, the *pranayama* – made sense and fell into place at the *sannyasi's* place. It felt as if I had moved up a level. Considering that I'd only had a rudimentary knowledge about yoga before I left England, this was an impressive development.

And really, I was amazed at how much I had changed through the course of my journey. I almost didn't recognize myself anymore: I voluntarily got up before dawn, practiced rigorous yoga routines, lived on a diet of Indian food and sang devotional songs. I wore saris and prayed to Indian Gods. *Me.* And now I was about to become an English teacher in a Himalayan mountain village.

I raised my eyes when I noticed two brown eagles that slowly circled over my head. They flew towards each other and away from each other, again and again. It looked as though they were dancing. Maybe they were *dakinis*, I thought as I watched them, the Tibetan tantric deities believed to be a female embodiment of enlightened energy. *Dakinis*, the mythical sky dancers who transmitted sacred teachings to their disciples.

I'd often wondered why it was so hard for me to stay in an intimate relationship with a man. I'd been involved with many men in my life, some of them very nice and caring. Without fail,

I left all of them – sometimes out of boredom or restlessness, sometimes because the relationship became too painful or complicated. In the latter situations, I left as a last, desperate measure to gain control over an otherwise uncontrollable situation. Leaving had become a blueprint for me, ever since I left my parental home aged sixteen because I couldn't cope with the violence that took place between my parents any longer.

Though my five serious boyfriends had been lovely men, I'd also always held a fascination for lonely, introverted *Steppenwolf*-type men. I had harbored crushes and become involved with just about anyone who displayed signs of vast unsuitability and unavailability, including prisoners, drug addicts and skinheads. These men interested me because they were 'different' and had a certain depth, a way of looking at the world I could relate to, just as I could relate to the feelings of despair and loneliness they seemed to radiate. It was always the loner and the nerd I felt sorry for and befriended, the 'bad boys' I defended. I adopted the dog nobody wanted and loved the men no woman in their right mind would even look at. The dark side of human behavior fascinated me, and I always wanted to find out 'why' first-hand.

Sometimes, my inquisitiveness backfired. The last man I'd been involved with before I set out on my big trip had been a huge wake-up call in that respect. For some strange reason, I had fallen in love with Steven, an existentially despairing artist. Mentally tortured and on the brink of suicide, he lived a lonely existence in a squalid tower block bursting with lost hopes and broken dreams. Steven fascinated and scared me in equal measures. I'd never met anybody like him before. Against my better judgment, and with great persistence from his side, I started to go out with him.

Steven challenged all of the carefully constructed concepts I held about myself and the world. Intellectual and manipulative, he played my mind like a toy, and I became more and more drawn into his derelict world, until I was not sure of anything anymore, least of all my own sanity. I became hopelessly addicted to the oscillating cycle of abandonment and enmeshment our ill-fated affair consisted of, because in the midst of all the emotional mayhem, we shared moments of true beauty and soulful connection. I thought if only I'd hang in there long enough, *la bête* would turn into the beautiful prince he was meant to be, transformed by my all-encompassing love. But just when I thought I'd grasped him, he challenged my beliefs again. Somehow, I had lost myself in the pages of the book I had been reading for so long.

Things spiraled out of control, and by the time I managed to leave him, I was a shadow of my former self. I had stopped working, eating and, like Steven, was hardly leaving my house. In a last attempt at self-preservation, I drove all the way to London in my pajamas to my friend Suzanne's flat. There, I collapsed into a nervous breakdown and a crippling depression, from which I didn't emerge for months. I was a tough cookie, but Steven had managed to crack me open. My heart broke from its protective shell, and anguish surrounded me like an impenetrable fog for a long time to come. I think I cried almost non-stop for several months in those days, overwhelmed with feelings of grief and a loss I couldn't fully understand. Most unbearably, the belief that I could handle and control everything was swiftly taken from me and crushed.

It took me two years and many sessions of psychotherapy to fully recover after Steven. I came face to face with my demons. Years of buried hurt slowly emerged from my psyche and I finally started to feel the impact my volatile childhood had had on me, and for which I had tried to overcompensate by becoming extra tough. I stopped pretending that I was fine and began to show my vulnerability. In the process, thick layers of an old, false identity were chipped away, and a softer, yet subtly stronger new Self came to the surface. I emerged into a richer, more authentic and creative life.

In retrospect, I choose to call my breakdown a breakthrough. It needed to happen. Some people call this the 'Dark Night of the Soul', a place at which one's spiritual journey really begins. This was certainly the case for me. I began to read spiritual books and immersed myself in yoga, something which balanced and soothed me greatly. And, after I picked myself up again, I vowed that troubled men had lost their appeal for good. I wanted to meet a different type of man now. Spiritual, self-aware and sane.

Somebody like the *sannyasi*, for example. I smiled when I remembered his serious demeanor and clipped tones during *pranayama*. What an inspirational man. I loved that he had a strong spiritual practice and dedicated his life to teaching and healing others. And, most amazingly, he worshipped Lord Shiva, the God of Tantra. Was he a tantric, I wondered? What were the teachings of Guru-ji like?

By now, I'd managed to bore MJ to tears with my musings about the *sannyasi*. I constantly speculated about him, his life and what it'd be like when I returned to the ashram. I felt a tingling of excitement in my solar plexus whenever I thought about him. I wasn't sure what to think about this attraction – most of the time I tried to deny it and talk myself out of it. But at the same time, I also knew that it was there.

Yet, of course, as I reminded myself with an invisibly raised index finger from time to time, he was a celibate renunciate, a spiritual man who certainly didn't have women on his mind. I cautioned myself to be careful. Things might be different if the *sannyasi* wasn't a *sannyasi*. But he was.

I shook my head and got up to go for a walk. It was time I stopped thinking along those lines before I seriously convinced myself that my meeting with the *sannyasi* carried more meaning than it actually did. I was going to work and practice *pranayama* there, and that was it. Therefore, it was important that I remained centered and didn't lose myself in romantic projections before I embarked on this new venture.

1.6: How Shiva Killed the God of Love

'You cried at the Shiva temple?' the *sadhu* asked, eyes warm with compassion. The fire in front of him crackled softly. Orange and yellow, it cast a golden glow over his face.

I didn't answer and stared into the dancing flames instead. Yes, I had cried there, at this isolated mountain temple dedicated to Shiva and Parvati. Set deep in the woods, it had taken us a few hours to hike here, along a steep, narrow and rocky trail. The small stone structure was hidden behind shrubs and rocks, but I knew we had arrived when I saw Shiva's trident placed in an elegantly shaped stone *yoni* on the ground ahead of me. Yellow wildflowers peeked at me through crags in the irregular stone slabs that surrounded it. I crouched down to offer some incense.

It was the last day of our week-long Himalayan camping adventure, and we were near Kedarnath, one of the most sacred pilgrimage sites for Hindus. I'd been feeling strange all day. Restless. Distracted. And once I arrived at the temple, I literally fell apart. It was the stone plaque of the Mother Goddess in the main sanctuary that had done it. An ancient plaque radiating such power that I started to cry as soon as I set eyes on it. It showed a carving of a small, round figure of a woman with voluptuous breasts and wide hips. Snake-like hair framed her face, and her hands were clasped prayer-like in front of her chest. An imposing Shiva *lingam* stood next to her.

The image and the temple felt so familiar to me, like something I knew with all my heart but had forgotten a long time ago. It was as though I knew every stone and every crevice and every image in this temple intimately. It was filled with a strong, pulsating Goddess energy that shocked my body and ripped my heart wide open. I'd stood in the ancient building for a long time, with sobs coming from a deep place beyond my heart. Outside, black ravens circled low.

Now it was raining. When we came down from the temple to seek shelter, a dark-skinned *sadhu* with long matted dreadlocks reaching down to his buttocks invited us into his little hut. Dressed in the orange robes of renunciation, he sat cross-legged on the dirt floor in his little mud home and stirred a pot on his fire hearth with a stick. The familiar scent of wood fire filled my nostrils and I felt instantly comforted.

'This place,' he made a sweeping hand gesture, 'this place has very much power. This is the place of Shiva and Parvati. You feel it, yes?'

I nodded and continued to watch the flames. It was powerful indeed, like some of the other sacred sites I knew. Glastonbury was like that, Callanish stone circle on the Isle of Lewis, and some of the ancient Goddess temples in Sicily I'd visited. The energy in these places seemed to weave patterns of its own, often stirring strong emotional reactions in those who were sensitive to it.

'Yes. I can feel it,' I said finally. The tears were still burning behind my eyes and my heart was filled with a heaviness I didn't understand.

The rain was coming down strongly now and the wind howled around the hut. Shivering, MJ and I huddled together on a narrow mattress near the fire. With a kind look in his eyes, the *sadhu* stood up, fetched a woolen blanket and gently placed it over us. Al Pacino, who obviously knew him well, took out supplies from his backpack to cook us a meal.

I took a closer look at the *sadhu*. The saffron robes hung loosely around his sturdy body. He was young, thirty maybe, although it may have been his thick, curly beard that made him look older. Around his neck and arms he wore the traditional *Rudraksha* beads, sacred to Lord Shiva, and various amulets made from crystal and silver.

'You know the story of Shiva and Parvati?' the *sadhu* asked. He slowly poured milky *chai* from a little pot into narrow steel cups. He handed me and MJ one, then poured some for himself and Al Pacino.

'A little bit,' I said and gratefully took a sip of the hot tea. It was thick and sweet, and I could taste and smell the aromatic *masala* spices in it.

'*Om Namah Shivaya*,' the *sadhu* chanted softly. 'I will tell you. It is a very, very famous story in India.'

'Great!' I suddenly perked up. He'd tell us about Shiva? How auspicious! I propped up on my elbow and looked at him expectantly. With his matted locks and *Rudraksha* beads, this *sadhu* even looked a bit like my favorite God. His voice was dark and soft, and in slow, lilting tones, he began to tell us a magical tale. The sounds of the rain and wind mixed with the crackling of the fire and gave his words an atmospheric backdrop.

'Lord Shiva, yes,' he began. A slight smile was playing on his full lips. 'Lord Shiva lives on Mount Kailash, in the Himalayas, in Tibet. He is God of yoga, only interested in meditation. He is only sitting and meditating, all day and all night long. He only cares about the *atman*, the soul. He has no time for women. Marriage is like prison for Lord Shiva.'

The *sadhu* laughed and tossed more kindling on the fire. Little sparks flew. 'A little bit like me. We *sadhus* do not like marriage.' With a mischievous grin, he winked at MJ, who stared at him with fascination. I glanced at her and smirked.

'But Brahma, our God of creation, he wants to see this yogi fall in love, you know? Lord Shiva was always laughing at him. Always laughing at the poor other Gods who did so many stupid things because of the women. Fighting, killing, all these things, because of the women. Brahma is angry. *Let Shiva feel it, too*, he says, *and see if he will still laugh*. So Brahma makes a plan. He performs *tapasya* for Maha Devi, the Divine Mother. You know what is *tapasya*?'

I shook my head.

'It's... how you say... penance? You treat your body very

harshly. You do not eat, you go in cold water, you stand on one leg. Such kinds of things.'

'Oh, like the *sadhus* we sometimes see in Rishikesh? Those guys who hold their arms up in the air for three years at a time?' MJ asked.

'Yes, yes,' the sadhu nodded, 'is like that. It is a *sadhana*, and if you practice seriously, it brings *moksha*, liberation. It is also done as sacrifice, to please the Gods and pray for something. Brahma performs this *tapasya* for praying to Maha Devi so she will take birth and be Shiva's wife. Because only Maha Devi can be a wife to a God so powerful like Shiva.'

'So what happened? Did she become his wife?' I asked and edged a little closer to the fire.

'Yes. She finally took a birth as a girl called Sati. Sati, since she was a small girl, she was painting pictures of Lord Shiva and she was always singing songs about the God. Always singing. *Om Namah Shivaya. Om Namah Shivaya.* Parents think she's crazy, yeah?'

He tapped his head. Al Pacino, who listened just as intently as us, smiled at me from across the fire where he was cutting up potatoes.

The *sadhu* continued. 'So when Sati grows up, she tells to her parents that she will go to forest to do *tapasya*, yes? Because she knows that she will marry Lord Shiva, and only way to get Shiva is to do *tapasya*. Shiva, he is *Lord* of tapasya. He likes *tapasya* very, very much. This is why Sati goes to the forest and does the *tapasya* for one year, two years. Not eating, not drinking, just *tapasya*. At same time, Brahma and another God, Vishnu, they go to Mount Kailash. They go there together and they pray to Lord Shiva to take a wife. *Please, Lord Shiva*, they say, *please, you marry!* But the Lord Shiva, he sits in meditation, like this.' The *sadhu* crossed his legs into lotus pose, closed his eyes and put his hands in *gyan mudra*, his index finger joining his thumb.

'Like this, yes? And then he begin to laugh very, very much.

He open his eyes and he laugh at Brahma and Vishnu like crazy. *Why you say such stupid things? Why you ask me to marry? You know marriage is not good for me. I am yogi! I am always practicing* tapasya *and meditation. I go to the* smashan *where they burn the dead people, and my friends are the ghosts and monsters. How can I marry? Please, you go away.* And Lord Shiva close his eyes again.'

The *sadhu* closed his eyes again, too, for a moment.

'But Brahma and Vishnu,' he continued, 'they do not go away. They pray to him again. *Please, Lord Shiva, please, you marry. Please,* they pray. *Om Namah Shivaya.* Then finally, Lord Shiva, so tired to listen to this, he says, *Good. If you can find a woman who is perfect for me, then I will do the marriage. You look for a wife who is yogini, and a good wife also. And most important: you find woman who leave me alone when I meditate. If you can find this woman, then you come back.*

'Of course, Lord Shiva knows there is not such a woman. But Brahma, he is excited! He says, *Oh! But I show you this woman!* And he tells Lord Shiva about Sati, how wonderful is she, and they go to see her. And when Lord Shiva sees Sati in the forest... something strange happens to him. Sati is sitting and doing *panchagni* – she sits in the middle of five very, very hot fires – and she is chanting *Om Namah Shivaya* all the time. Not even sweating. Lord Shiva is confused. He has never seen such a woman. He thinks, Who is she? Who is this yogini who can perform such strong *tapasya*? And he likes her. He agrees to do the marriage.'

'Wow,' I said. 'And then, what happened? Did Lord Shiva like being married?'

'Oh, he liked it,' the dreadlocked *sadhu* laughed. 'Lord Shiva liked it very, very much. Sati was perfect for him. She was so beautiful, with black skin like the night. She was like him, a yogini. She meditated. But then something terrible happens. Not so long after the marriage, Sati... she dies.'

'Oh! Really? How?' I asked.

The *sadhu* looked into the fire for a moment, then turned around to face us again. 'You know what is *sati*? Not Ma Sati, but the practice of *sati*? You know it?'

I looked at MJ. 'Isn't this the practice in which a wife throws herself onto the funeral pyre when her husband dies?' I had heard about *sati*. Though very controversial, it was apparently still practiced in some rural areas of India.

The *sadhu* nodded. 'Yes, it is this. It comes from Sati, the wife of Lord Shiva. She kills herself in the fire because her father Daksha... he did not invite Shiva to a *havan* ceremony. Daksha hated Lord Shiva. So Sati got very, very angry. She throws herself in the fire with anger and she dies.' He threw another log of wood onto the fire.

'When Lord Shiva find out about this, oh... he was so sad. He screamed and he cried because he was so sad. *Now* he feel what this love, this desire was. And it pains him very, very much, here.' The *sadhu* pounded his fist against his heart.

'The Lord Shiva, he walked through the world looking for Sati, thousands of years. The Earth became dry. Everything broken. Everybody so sad. Lord Shiva finally, he begins to meditate again and he says, *Never again a woman. The only bliss is in meditation, in the atman.* And so he sits again on Mount Kailash and meditates for thousands of years.'

Lost in thoughts, the *sadhu* played with the *Rudraksha* beads around his neck.

'But then a demon came and he made a lot of trouble for the Gods. He was powerful, this demon, and only a son of Shiva could kill him. But Shiva would never marry again. So the demon went on to create trouble. He burnt and killed and did many bad things. So Brahma and Vishnu once again asked Maha Devi to take birth, so that Shiva can have a son. Maha Devi agreed and was born as Parvati.'

'Ah,' I piped up. 'So Parvati was a reincarnation of Sati?'

'Yes, yes. Oh, Parvati, she was very, very beautiful. Like Sati, she was dreaming about Lord Shiva and singing *Om Namah Shivaya* all the time. She also goes to the forest to do *tapasya* to make marriage with Lord Shiva. And again Brahma and Vishnu went to Mount Kailash. But this time,' the *sadhu* shook his head and laughed, 'this time, Lord Shiva did not say yes. *Leave me alone,* he says to the Gods. *I will never marry again. Remember what happen the last time I listen to you? Forget it.* He will not even listen anymore. So the Gods make a plan. They send Kama to Lord Shiva. Kama, he is God of Love. He has bow and he shoots the heart of people.'

'Oh, like Cupid!' MJ said.

'Yes. So Kama comes and shoots at Lord Shiva with the arrow. Lord Shiva is in meditation and he is feeling this thing hurting him. He opens his eyes and he sees Kama behind a bush shooting arrows. You know what does Shiva? He open his *ajna*,' the *sadhu* pointed at his third eye, the area between his eyebrows, 'and *whoosh!* He kills Kama with fire coming out of there. Dead. Nothing left. Kama is like this.' He pointed at the ash from the fire. 'Finish.'

I laughed and sat up. 'What, Shiva actually *killed* the God of Love? No way!'

'Yes,' the *sadhu* said and took a swig from his *chai*. 'He kills Kama. Shiva will never love again. Never.'

'And so will nobody else, by the sound of it,' MJ commented wryly.

The *sadhu* nodded. 'But Parvati, she continues with her *tapasya*. She *knows* she will marry Lord Shiva one day. In hot summer, she practice *panchagni*, the five fires. In Monsoon time, she sit in cold, cold water and ice for many days. She stop eating and she stand on one leg for three thousand years. Oh, the world became so hot! It nearly burns like Kama.'

As if to underline his words, the *sadhu* poured the rest of his *chai* into the flames, which evaporated with a hiss.

'So Gods go to Mount Kailash again. *Please, Lord Shiva, you marry Parvati, before whole world burns down!* Lord Shiva still says no. But now he also knows that Parvati is Sati. But he still... afraid, yes? What if Parvati die like Sati? So he sends a *sadhu* to Parvati. *Give up,* the *sadhu* says. *Lord Shiva is no good. He is beggar. Why you want to marry this God? He will never make marriage with you.* But Parvati will not give up. And Lord Shiva, he cannot say no anymore. He goes to Parvati and... yes, they marry. Parvati is very, very happy. And Lord Shiva is happy. And then...'

The *sadhu* smiled at MJ. It was almost dark now, and his eyes glowed like coals in the light of the fire.

'They make love for two thousand years. Shiva and Parvati, in a cave, alone, making love.' He laughed and held MJ's gaze for a just a moment too long before turning back to the fire.

'Wow, what a story,' I said. 'And two thousand years of lovemaking? So her *tapasya* was worth it!'

The *sadhu* laughed again. The rain had stopped by now. We shared a small meal of potatoes and *dhal* and then got up to leave. The *sadhu* took MJ's hand and pressed a *Rudraksha* bead into her hand.

'This will bring you luck,' he said and folded his hand over hers. She smiled her thanks and we left the hut.

Outside, the sky was still overcast and the fresh smell of rain clung in the air. Al Pacino and MJ, eager to get back to our camping spot, marched swiftly down the muddy path. I fell behind and walked back down the mountain slowly, glad for the solitude. Fragments of the *sadhu*'s story were still resounding in my head. Finally I had found out more about this transcendental love story.

I was familiar with the myth of Shiva and Kali, who was the ferocious version of Parvati. But I'd known nothing about Shiva and Parvati's courtship so far. Yet their images had drawn me in so much when I saw them for the first time. It had all been intuitive, and now that I knew more, I felt even closer to them.

I liked what the *sadhu* had said. I loved how Parvati had

managed to win the aloof ascetic's heart through her fierce love and single-mindedness. Because of her desire, Parvati, also known as the Goddess of Love, became an ascetic; and the austere Shiva surrendered to the power of love. They were such opposites, asceticism and eroticism, and yet, seemingly anything was possible when they met and mingled.

1.7: A Flirtatious *Sannyasi*

Our Himalayan excursion was drawing to a close, and it was time to return to the *sannyasi*'s ashram. By now even MJ, who didn't enjoy the cold and rain that had been with us almost daily, was excited about it. Admittedly, a week's camping without a toilet or washing facilities made the prospect of visiting the austere hermitage seem enticing. We were looking forward to snuggling up in a real bed beneath warm duvets, barred windows or not.

To arrive not completely unkempt at my new employer's abode, MJ helped me to wash my straggled hair with the aid of a grimy bucket, filled with cold water. It was an ambitious undertaking, keenly observed and photographed by a group of passing pilgrims, who relished the sight of the foreigner crouching on her knees with her head bent towards the wet ground below a *chai* stall.

Through the pouring rain, we slowly drove down the wooded mountain road towards the ashram. I stared out of the window and contemplated my next steps. I was nervous. Now that the time had come, I had mixed feelings about staying at the ashram by myself. Maybe it wasn't such a good idea after all. MJ read my mind.

'Don't do this unless your intentions are right,' she said. 'If you really want to help out and work with the children, then do it. But don't do it because of *him*.'

She had a point. I was wondering whether I would be so eager to spend my last days in India working at the ashram if it was run by an old bearded monk instead of the luscious *sannyasi*.

'Well, I'll see how I feel when I get there. I'll ask him a few questions and if it doesn't feel right, I can still leave,' I replied as I watched the raindrops slide down the car windows.

In retrospect, I don't think that I had much of a choice. It was as though what came to pass was already written.

It was still raining when we arrived at the ashram. Al Pacino unloaded the car while Maniac, MJ and I climbed the steps towards the ashram's office. The *sannyasi* sat enthroned behind his desk, immersed in paperwork. When he saw us approaching, he smiled warmly and got up to greet us.

'*Namaste*, Swami-ji,' Maniac cried in his usual exuberant, slightly deranged manner.

'*Namaskar*,' the *sannyasi* replied politely and tilted his head. I felt a twinge of disappointment. With crumpled robes and a dark stubble that framed his handsome face, he looked even more tired than I remembered him. What did I expect? That he'd dress up and shave for my return?

'Hello again,' I said. 'We're back.'

'Welcome,' he said and smiled. 'Please sit and I will check you in.'

I took a seat in front of his desk and suddenly felt very small. Bemused, I craned my neck to look up at the *sannyasi* and realized that the chairs surrounding his desk were lower than the one he sat on. I was reminded of the Buddhist temples in Tibet, in many of which a gigantic, wide-eyed figure of Guru Rimpoche loomed ominously over unsuspecting devotees as they entered, often scaring them witless.

'So,' the *sannyasi* regarded me earnestly, 'what have you decided? Are you still going to stay with us?'

I shifted uncomfortably in my seat. Suddenly, I wasn't so sure whether I wanted to stay here any longer than I had to. All the questions I had carefully prepared in my head – *How could I leave from here? What would my working hours be? Where would I stay?* – came to an abrupt halt in my throat before I could ask them. For some strange reason, I felt shy and tongue-tied.

'Hmm, yes, I think so,' I replied vaguely.

'Good!' He appeared satisfied and glanced at his desk calendar. 'We will discuss the classes later. You can come to school with me right away tomorrow morning.'

'Okay,' I said.

'How long are you staying?' he asked. 'One year?' He leaned towards me and looked straight into my eyes. His smile was almost overwhelming.

'I'm not sure, Swami-ji,' I said meekly. 'I have a flight booked in about ten days. Let's just see how it goes, okay? And... could you tell me how I can leave this village once I am done here? Is there a bus or taxi service?'

The *sannyasi* furrowed his brow.

'It's important to always have a sporting mind about every-thing,' he advised me sternly.

A sporting mind?! What did he mean by that? Confused, I glanced at MJ, who observed our interaction from a chair by the office window. She shrugged her shoulders.

'There is a bus service once a day,' the *sannyasi* continued. 'It leaves at seven am. And remember, your friends are only a telephone call away.'

Duly chastised, I gave a brief nod and decided to override my doubts. It was decided then. I was going to stay here for the next few days.

'You will come and practice *pranayama* with me this afternoon?' the *sannyasi* asked before I left his office. In his clipped Indian tones, it sounded more like a command than a question. I agreed to meet him in the temple at the usual time.

MJ and I checked into our room, a different one this time, but like the previous one, it contained a similar array of wobbly beds, grimy buckets, musty smells, and the all-important rose-covered pillows. We collapsed onto our beds for a short nap.

At five pm, I made my way to the temple for my *pranayama* date. *Namaste*, I greeted the imposing portrait of Guru-ji silently and jovially, as though I was saying hello to a *chai wallah*.

So you're back? his ironic smile appeared to say. *Good for you.*

Wrapping a woolly blanket around my shivering body, I knelt on the carpeted floor and waited for instructions from the *sannyasi*, who sat in lotus pose diagonally across from me. However, instead of practicing *pranayama*, he wanted to chat to me. Shifting around in his robes, he ruffled the tiny tuft of hair at the back of his cranium and smiled awkwardly.

'I am very happy and pleased that you are back,' he said after a pause.

'Good,' I responded quickly, feeling slightly embarrassed. 'I am very happy and pleased to be back, too.'

He turned his head towards the left to look at me fully. *Damn,* I thought, *here's that smile again.* 'You know, this is the first time I am coming in such close contact with a woman. I have never met a Western woman like you before, with such deep thinking.'

Perplexed, I blinked. What did *he* know about my thinking? We had hardly spoken to each other.

He continued. 'You know, India is all about chastity. We are brought up with this concept. Purity. Chastity. This is what our society thrives on.' He frowned and looked towards the altar.

Chastity?! Why was he talking like this? Despite my curiosity and admiration for the saffron-robed *sannyasi*, this felt a bit too familiar for comfort.

'Why are you talking about chastity? I mean, you can't have contact with women anyway as a *sannyasi*,' I tried to deflect.

He shrugged and turned towards me again. 'Eighty percent, no, maybe ninety percent of humanity is corrupted. There are no morals anymore in the modern world.'

'Is that so?' I murmured.

He changed the subject. 'What is your name?'

'My name? Tiziana.'

'Ti-zi-aa-na,' he repeated slowly, as if tasting every syllable with his mouth. 'Oh, that's sweet.' He smiled gently. '*You're* very sweet.'

I was thoroughly confused now. What was this? Was the *sannyasi* trying to flirt with me? Surely this couldn't be.

'Not always,' I said defensively and shook my head. 'Definitely not.'

My answer seemed to please him.

'Oh, that's good. That's definitely good for me.' He nodded approvingly.

I began to feel like I was riding on a fast, uncontrollable horse. Had the *sannyasi* been a normal Indian man, I would have interpreted the increasingly familiar tone of our conversation as flirtatious. As it was, my mind disputed my feelings. The *sannyasi* was a spiritual man who had surrendered his life to Guru-ji and the upliftment of the poor sections of society. Certainly women were the last thing on his mind. I was sure that I was somehow misinterpreting our exchange, perhaps through language barriers, even though my gut tried to tell me a different story. To change the subject, I asked for his name.

'My name is Rudra,' he said and shifted out of lotus pose. He stretched his legs towards the side of the temple, then folded them again to sit in a simple cross-legged pose.

'Rudra,' I repeated. 'Nice.'

Given that the ashram worshipped Lord Shiva, the name suited him. Rudra was an early form of Shiva, in his guise of God of storm and wind. In some traditions, Rudra is also known as the Lord of Tears. It is said that after performing austerities for thousands of years, Rudra's mind began to tremble with compassion for the human condition. It was then that Rudra's eyes opened and tears began to fall from them, tears that are believed to have sprouted into the *rudraksha*, the blue marble tree. Thus, the seeds of the *rudraksha* tree, believed to destroy the most dreadful karma, are worn around the neck by followers of Shiva. I saw that Rudra wore one of them, too.

'I will move you up to a different room tomorrow,' Rudra

interrupted my train of thought, 'near to my room.'

The strange feeling in my solar plexus didn't shift. Near to his room?

'Where is your room?' I asked cautiously.

'I will show you tomorrow.' That smile again. He stood up.

'I have to go back to the office now, but I will see you at the *aarti* tonight, yes?' He tilted his head and left the temple.

I stayed for a few minutes longer and pondered what had just been said. Rudra seemed excited at the prospect of my company over the next ten days. I was flattered, but somewhere in my head, little alarm bells started to ring ever so quietly. I shut them up quickly.

'MJ,' I said when I returned to our room, 'if I didn't know better, I'd say that this *sannyasi* is hitting on me.'

MJ looked up from her book with a skeptical expression on her face. I told her about the conversation I'd had with the *sannyasi* in the temple, but she was not convinced. Instead, she reprimanded me.

'Sometimes,' she said and sat up in her bed, 'we can imagine things that are not really there. He may simply not be used to being around women. Perhaps he is just curious to spend some time with you. It's probably a novelty for him to practice yoga with a foreign woman. I don't think he's hitting on you.'

Maybe she was right. Perhaps I had simply projected my own desire onto him and thoroughly misinterpreted his words. Embarrassed, I banned the thoughts from my head.

1.8: Pondering Ashram Life and the Philosophy of *Karma Yoga*

The next morning, the hour of departure had arrived. I walked MJ, Al Pacino and Maniac, my trusty companions, to the car and hugged them goodbye with mixed feelings. With his demented smile, Maniac grabbed the steering wheel and started the ignition while simultaneously hitting the accelerator. With a screech, the battered VW rolled down the mountain, back towards civilization. Standing next to a tree, I followed it with my eyes until it was out of my sight. Suddenly, I was alone in the Himalayas. Feeling exhilarated and nervous at the same time, I turned and ambled back towards the ashram, wondering what adventures would await me next.

That morning, I moved my belongings to a single room on the ashram's top floor, right at the end of a narrow corridor. Like the other rooms, it was sparse, but actually quite nice. With a grubby Western-style toilet and a sink, something I had not seen in a while, I felt as though I had been allocated the Hilton's luxury suite. And the view out of my barred window towards the snow-covered Himalayas and the river below was spectacular. Yes, I thought, I could stay here for a while.

The room was dirty, though, and looked like it hadn't been properly cleaned for months, if not years. In a desire to make my new abode homely, I tried to acquire some cleaning materials from two ashram boys who were squatting outside the kitchen, scrubbing vegetables. With my virtually non-existent Hindi and their absolutely absent English, this was slightly tricky.

Using arm gestures and hissing sounds, I tried to imitate the movement of a mop. Confused, one of the boys handed me a broom. '*Thik hai*,' I smiled, and indicated that I wanted to use a cloth – circular and rapid hand movement – to clean the bathroom, too. Now the boy was at a loss and called a colleague.

They both watched my pantomime performance with a mixture of amusement and concern, and again pointed at the broom. '*Nahi,*' I shook my head, '*cloth!*'

On hearing the commotion, an old Bengali professor I'd previously met at the *aarti* limped from his room and gazed at me over thick horn-rimmed spectacles. 'What is the problem?' he asked solemnly with a furrowed brow. Squirming, I explained that I was trying to obtain a cloth and a cleaning product of some sort. He translated my predicament into Hindi. The boys innocently pointed towards a bucket and shrugged their shoulders. *What's wrong with this? What else does she need?* they seemed to wonder.

As I found out later, the ashram's method of cleaning consisted of sweeping the floor with a broom and throwing a bucket of cold water across it later. Thus, the staff possessed no cleaning products whatsoever, no 'liquid soap', no cloths, not even dust pans. Defeated, I clambered up the stairs towards my room. The negotiation had taken about an hour.

Five minutes later, a mighty knock against my steel door caused me to jump. Outside, a beaming boy stood and proudly offered me an old T-shirt and a little sachet of shampoo. I was thrilled. With the enthusiasm of a challenge overcome, I began to clean away the layers of grime and dust that had accumulated on the room's surfaces. As a final touch, I built a little altar on the small wooden table beneath the window with incense, candles, postcards of Shiva and Parvati, and other devotional items I carried around with me.

After that, I walked to the big, yellow school building that was just a few hundred yards away from the main ashram.

'Come to the school at twelve o'clock,' Rudra had said just before I'd moved rooms. 'Ask for Swami-ji in the office. They will fetch me and then I will introduce you to the children and the teachers.'

I already caught a glimpse of his saffron-colored robes through the open door of a classroom before I even reached the office. As if on cue, he turned his head and waved at me. 'Come, please,' he called out to me. I walked down a flight of stairs into the small classroom. About a dozen children in bottle-green uniforms ran around excitedly.

'*Shaant*,' Rudra addressed the children, 'quiet! Sit down and say Good Morning to Ma'am.'

The children did as they were told, sat down at their tiny desks and peered at me through big, round eyes.

'Please take a seat, too,' Rudra said to me. I squeezed behind one of the desks to sit on a little wooden chair.

'This is Tiziana-Ma'am,' Rudra said to the children with a nod in my direction. 'Ma'am comes from Canada.'

'No,' I interrupted, 'actually I am from England.'

'Really?' Rudra looked confused. 'I thought you were from Canada.'

'No, Swami-ji. I am half-German and half-Sicilian, but I live in England. MJ is from Canada.'

'Ah. Sorry,' he smiled apologetically. 'So you are from England. Well, welcome. We are very pleased that you have come to help us.'

Today, Rudra behaved warmly, but utterly professionally towards me, which dispersed any doubts I still carried after yesterday's seemingly ambiguous conversation in the temple.

'Let's start right away then,' he said. 'Children, show Ma'am your exercise books. She will check your homework.'

Shyly, the children, who must have been about eight years old, lined up and, one after the other, placed their books in front of me. As I checked the spelling of simple English sentences in shaky children's handwriting, they studied me quietly. White-skinned, freckled foreigners with curly red hair were sparse in these parts.

For the rest of the lesson, I watched Rudra teach. He was strict with the children when needed, but equally patient, humorous and warm. Apart from his Indian accent, he spoke English almost immaculately, and I loved the sound of his soft, deep voice. Every time he looked at me from the front of the class – and he did so often, sometimes asking 'Is this corrrect?' after he explained an English word to the children – my heart jumped and I smiled at him.

The Universe was clever, I thought ironically to myself. It motivated me to do my *karma yoga*, my selfless service for the world, by placing a drop-dead gorgeous man in my path.

As I walked home from school, I pondered the concept of *karma yoga*. I'd become acquainted with the practice a few months ago in the young yogi's ashram. *Karma yoga* was the yoga of action. Altruistic work that is carried out without self-centered desires or attachment to the fruits of one's deeds is meant to generate good karma, purify the mind and ultimately lead to *moksha*, liberation.

It was an interesting idea. When I was in a cynical mood, I could see *karma yoga*, which was practiced arduously in many ashrams, as a clever way to get cheap labor. Karma yogis worked hard. They cleaned and cooked and built, and didn't receive compensation of any kind, other than the promise of karmic benefits somewhere down the line.

However, there was something beautiful and inspirational about it also. When I thought about it, much of my life to date had been pretty self-centered, in that I had more often than not followed my own desires. With my Western mind, I saw this, the following of my dreams and passions, as a positive attribute.

In India, it wasn't quite like that. Much importance was placed on *dharma*, one's earthly duty. *Dharma* was closely bound up with karma: in order to achieve good karma it was important to live life according to *dharma*. This involved doing what was right for the individual, alongside responsibilities towards the family, the community and also the Universe.

In the yoga ashram, we'd practiced a minuscule form of *karma yoga* for an hour every Sunday morning: we collectively cleaned the ashram. Much as I may have questioned it initially, in time, it had a profound effect on me. This was especially true in view of all the poverty I daily saw around me in India. I started to think about others more, how I could contribute to their lives, what I could do to bring joy and prosperity to those less fortunate than me.

In some instances, my attempts were clumsy, in that I gave away comparatively large sums of money to the many beggars that lined the Indian streets that were in turn probably just used to fund the criminal gangs that put them out there in the first place. On other occasions, my actions felt rewarding, for example when I, together with a group of ashramites, took big pots of food to the poorest areas at the Ganga.

Despite my many resistances, I tried to befriend and practice *karma yoga,* and aspired to perform one selfless or at least positive deed every day. It was hard sometimes, and I didn't always succeed, especially when I was in a bad mood or felt sorry for myself. But more often than not, it made me feel really happy. My new volunteering job at the *sannyasi's* ashram seemed to be the next step on the long ladder of *karma yoga* – at least that's what I hoped.

After lunch, I walked up the hill to the little village that surrounded the ashram. I strolled down the narrow lanes that were lined with mobile phone shops, tailors, fruit stalls, chemists and food sellers, most of them housed in little concrete enclosures resembling garages. When the shops opened after their afternoon *siesta* for the evening, I paused to have tea in the stall of the *chai wallah* with the grandiose moustache.

Sipping my sweet *chai* from a small porcelain cup, I watched the world slink by in the afternoon heat and felt stupidly, blissfully happy. What a strange twist of fate, I mused as I joyfully returned the inquisitive gazes of moustachioed men and broadly smiling, meditatively swaying women in saris. I was not sure how I had ended up in this Himalayan village, teaching English to a bunch of Indian kids and learning yogic practices from a *sannyasi*, but I could get used to the slow pace of life here. The setting was beautiful, and the people were welcoming and friendly.

My thoughts returned to Rudra. I liked him. He was so different from all the men I'd met before. My first impression of him sketched a picture of a man who knew what he wanted and was also adept at communicating it clearly. He seemed to be in control of his life. I was deeply impressed by how he had decided to live his life, and his dedication to Guru-ji and society.

I was equally struck by the intense energy that radiated from him. Beyond the fact that he was a *sannyasi*, he was a very attractive man, and Shakti, the all-encompassing life force, oozed from his every pore. I was still amazed that a lively man in the prime of his life – after all, he was only thirty-two – had decided to live as a monk in the remote Himalayas.

Especially in that austere ashram. Somehow, its ambience reminded me of my days of working in prisons. For my psychology degree, I had conducted my research for the final-year dissertation in a prison. I'd found it so interesting that after graduating, I took up a post as a 'pagan chaplain', a spiritual advisor for prisoners of pagan faith.

Much to Kassandra's amusement, whom I had once so taunted for her spiritual quests in the 'Third World', I'd begun to train as a Priestess of Avalon, a priestess of an ancient Goddess tradition, parallel to starting my degree. I'd always been fascinated with what is known as paganism, the 'Old Ways' of the witches, druids and wise women. I was drawn to sacred sites in nature, the cycles of the moon and the magic of healing herbs. Most especially, I was attracted to Goddess spirituality, a path on which God was seen as female.

Here, I found what had been missing for me in Catholicism: strong, life-affirming Goddesses who loved life and for whom the body and sexuality were not something shameful to be renounced. Instead, on this spiritual path, women were respected and equal; they were priestesses, seers and healers who honored and worked with, and not against Mother Earth. When I discovered that I could attend a course in the small Somerset town of Glastonbury to learn the ways of the priestesses of old, I signed up without a second thought.

So while the left side of my brain conducted scientific experiments, wrote lab reports and crunched statistics, its right side was involved in learning how to perform rituals to mark the changing seasons, build altars and make ceremonial tools. I began to live in a magical, parallel Universe that was inhabited by beautiful Celtic Goddesses and their power animals, ancient myths and glamorous ceremonial robes.

The Goddess path spoke to me so strongly that I gave up a prospective career as a forensic psychologist in favor of spiritual counseling in prisons and performing pagan wedding ceremonies in the community. Back then, I was on a quest. I wanted to bring the concept of the Divine Feminine into a very masculine prison environment. This, I felt, could help the men to reconnect with their feminine side that was so obviously wounded and buried under concrete-thick layers of abuse and violence. It was a transformational task, both for the prisoners as well as for me.

Most strongly etched into my mind is a springtime ritual I led in a sex offenders' prison in honor of the Celtic Goddess Brigid. During the ceremony, the prisoners held hands, knelt down before the image of the Goddess and asked her for forgiveness for the harm they had inflicted on women. Some even shed tears. Witnessing these men humbly connect to the energy they had tried so hard to destroy before touched me deeply.

The *sannyasi's* ashram reminded me of the dreary British

prisons. It had the same grey concrete rooms, barred windows and rigorous routines. Even the canteen, with its stainless steel trays and bland food, reminded me of prison. If one disregarded the religious focus, then the main difference between the ashram and a jail seemed that people were free to leave.

Funny, how I had again ended up in an exclusively male environment, so different from the feminine world of Goddesses that had become my life. When I thought about it, then there was nothing, absolutely nothing in the ashram that led me to believe that women existed in Guru-ji's world. From what I could tell, the ashram staff was made up exclusively of young men in their twenties and a few older men, such as the cook. Some of the teachers were female, but were drafted in from outside and didn't belong to the ashram as such. Maybe the tradition was more attractive to men than women.

Still pondering, I finished my *chai* and watched as the *chai wallah* prepared his tea in a small cast iron pot. I wasn't sure what the next ten days would bring, but I resolved to enjoy it.

1.9: Patterns in the Sand

Knowing that I'd have to get up at four am for my *sadhana* with Rudra, I tried to have an early night and went to bed straight after the evening *aarti*. But, as I noticed only too soon, sleep was hard to come by in this ashram.

With its constant influx of pilgrims at all hours, it never seemed to be quiet here. Large Indian families occupied the rooms next to mine, and in their holiday excitement, going to bed was probably the last thing on their minds. Doors banged, men shouted into mobile phones, gossiping women washed their saris on the landing, and children chased each other laughingly through the night. When I finally drifted off with ear plugs jammed tightly into my ears, it was past midnight.

During my time in India, I'd noticed that Indian people overall didn't seem to have much of a desire for silence and solitude. They were perfectly able to sleep everywhere, anywhere, at any time, even if it was next to a noisy road with trucks thundering by. It was a cultural trait I admired greatly.

In many ways, my new abode was my perfect nightmare – in particular because ashrams are traditionally tranquil refuges where one went to further one's spiritual practice. Most ashrams, including the one I had just left, maintained *mouna* (silence) in order to promote a contemplative, meditative atmosphere. As this place was really more of a pilgrims' hotel than an ashram, there wasn't even a remote chance of that. Though I lived on the ashram's top floor, it was hard to escape the noise.

My alarm clock mercilessly shocked me from slumber at four am. I was delighted to be greeted by an enchanting early-morning chorus of spitting, coughing, burping and throat-clearing resounding from the neighboring rooms. *'This is life – what can we do?'* I recited the words of Raheem, my Pakistani lover, ironically as I lay under a heap of blankets, for my room was drafty and freezing. More out of necessity than conviction, I tried to see the funny side of this chaotic situation and sent a highly expressive 'Good Morning from India' text message to Kassandra.

'Yes – it's the India tantrum. I know it well,' advised her instant reply.

Shaking my head, I crawled out of bed, brushed my teeth and shuffled down the corridor towards the temple. Rudra was already there. He was sitting cross-legged on the floor, quietly chanting *Om Namah Shivaya* to the sounds of his harmonium. When he heard me coming in, he turned towards me and smiled.

'Join in,' he invited me. 'The sooner you sing, the sooner you will learn it.'

I crouched down next to him. Feeling extremely self-conscious, I started to sing the hymn with him. I chanted hesitantly and so quietly that it was almost a whisper. If Rudra thought, as I suspected, *My God! How awful! She can't sing at all!*, he didn't show it. I was glad when it was over.

After the chant, Rudra got up to perform the *aarti*. I stayed where I was, prepared to watch him as usual. Not so. He took the 'Santa-Claus beard', the large hairy duster, from its place on the altar and handed it to me.

'Stand at the side of the altar,' he instructed, 'and wave this from left to right while I do the *aarti*.'

I did as I was told and stood sternly at the altar with the relic in my hand while Rudra chanted in quiet tones and anointed Guru-ji's sandals with ghee. I bit my lip when I imagined MJ's face. If she could see me now! She'd die laughing.

'What is this thing used for?' I asked Rudra after the *aarti*, when we were getting ready for our *pranayama* practice.

'This?' he asked and pointed at the duster. 'Oh. It is used to purify the air for Guru-ji during the *aarti*.'

Today was Sunday, and hence no classes were taught in school. It was also *havan* day, the day of the big evening fire ceremony. Rudra asked me if I would like to help him prepare the *havan* after breakfast. Eagerly, I accepted and we went to the temple, where he fetched a large tray filled with sand. With the help of contrasting colored powders and plastic templates, he began to create beautiful patterns in the sand.

'Let us be quiet now,' he said. 'This is the time when we will focus on our deity, on Guru-ji.' He pointed at the big portrait. 'We are creating this *yantra* for him. Through this act, we are inviting him to join us.'

I still hadn't found out much about Guru-ji, other than that he was no longer alive and had once taught a Hindu doctrine of some sort.

'What is a *yantra*?' I asked.

'A *yantra* is a kind of *mandala*. It's a geometrical diagram which we use to help us meditate. It comes from the Sanskrit words *yam*, which means to support, and *trana*, which means freedom. A *yantra* is the energetic form of a deity, the way they were seen in visions by the *rishis*, the seers of ancient India.'

Fascinated, I watched Rudra as he moved the colored powders to shape the intricate *yantra* patterns with careful attention. After a while, he looked up.

'Does this look crooked?' He pointed at the tray.

I moved closer towards the tray and perused the slightly wobbled shapes.

'A little,' I smiled, and looked up at him. 'But it's beautiful.'

He frowned and continued to form the pattern until it was completed to his satisfaction.

'What are you doing with this *yantra* now?' I asked.

'We will use it in tonight's *havan*. We are going to place the wood on this tray before lighting the fire. This is very powerful and auspicious.'

One of the ashram boys, wearing jeans and a T-shirt, entered the temple and began to clean the brass objects on the altar vigorously with a cloth.

'This is Parmod, my right-hand man.' Rudra seemed proud as we watched the young man absorbed in his task. 'I taught him the order of things, how exactly to clean these objects and why, where to put them. He knows everything now.'

The evening *havan* was again spectacular, complete with thunderous chanting, offerings of ghee, herbs and fruit, thick black smoke and violently coughing devotees.

'Why don't you hold the *havan* outside?' I asked Rudra afterwards. 'The ceiling of the temple is black, and people seem to be suffocating halfway through. I know they say that inhaling the *havan* smoke is auspicious, but this can't be healthy.'

'Do you think?' Rudra looked puzzled. 'But where else could we hold it?'

'Maybe on the rooftop?'

'No, that's too windy and dangerous. And besides,' he pointed at Guru-ji's portrait, 'where is Guru-ji going to sit?'

Yes, indeed, I smirked, where *was* Guru-ji going to sit? Did it matter, considering that he'd died almost a hundred years ago? Maybe he, or rather his portrait, could be carried outside too. He could even be covered with a blanket if he was cold.

My suggestion was met with dismay. I shrugged my shoulders. If Guru-ji, in whatever shape or form he still existed after his death, was as powerful and omnipresent as his devotees seemed to believe, then why was there a need for the picture at all? Wouldn't the Guru be everywhere? Surely he didn't live in the painting alone. I decided to let it rest and returned to my room.

Monday was my first full day at school. Today, my main task was to assist Rudra in class by marking homework. For the last time-slot just before lunchtime, Rudra asked me to tell the children stories about life in England. 'Sure,' I said. That would be easy enough.

What I hadn't realized was that I would be telling my stories not just to a handful of kids, but the entire school. Rudra had enthusiastically gathered all school staff and pupils together in order to meet 'Ma'am from England'. He saw my visit as a rare opportunity to improve their already very good English.

Slightly nervous, I entered the big room and encountered a sea of faces. Men, women and children sat cross-legged on the floor and looked at me expectantly. I quickly walked to the chair they had placed for me in front of the large blackboard and stood there hovering for a while. I had never taught children before, and felt completely out of my depth. I wasn't prepared in the slightest and had no idea as to what I would tell them. But there was no way I could back out now. With an overly enthusiastic smile, I turned towards my audience and greeted it.

'Good morning!'

'Good morrr-ning, Ma'am,' was the resounding reply.

'My name is Tiziana, and I would like to tell you about England.'

Round, long-lashed eyes continued to examine me. *Damn*, I thought, slightly desperate. What was typical about England? What would they want to know about? I resorted to the clichés: the red double-decker buses. Buckingham Palace. The Queen. Prince Charles. Fish and Chips.

Slowly, I began to tell the children a story. I asked them to imagine that Mr Chaudhari, the head teacher, had decided to take them on a class outing to London, as the Queen of England had extended an invitation to him. In their imaginations, I took the children to Delhi airport by bus, and had them savor the culinary delights of Indian Airlines on board of a Boeing 747.

After every sentence or so, I stopped to ask a question. 'Now, what sort of food do you think you can eat on an aeroplane?', 'How far do you think England is from India?', 'How are we going to get to Buckingham Palace from Heathrow Airport?'

The children jumped up eagerly after every question, chattering excitedly among themselves and raising their arms. 'Ma'am! Ma'am! I know, Ma'am!' they cried. I was relieved. It seemed that my story was working so far.

Rudra stood leaning against a table at the side of the room with folded arms and followed my narrative with a smile on his face. From time to time, I caught his eye and he tilted his head ever so slightly in support. I felt a warm glow. Just looking at him was a pleasure. I was proud to work with him, both in *sadhana*, spiritual practice, and in *seva*, service. I could almost see that renunciation was justified in his case. As a *sannyasi*, he seemed to be sharing his radiant energy with everyone, and not just a select few.

When the children became too rowdy in their excitement, he calmed them down and repeated my questions. By now I was enjoying the unfolding tale of traveling Indian children in London and decided to add a little humor to the narrative. I had the children drink tea from silver cups in Buckingham Palace and inspect the royal lavatories and bedrooms in great detail.

'Then you decide to take a bus. There is a drunken man on the bus and he smokes, although smoking is forbidden. What do you do?'

'Maybe you stay quiet in order to avoid a good thrashing,' Rudra interjected.

An energetic young boy with a mischievous face jumped up and raised his hand in the air, index finger extended.

'I know what you would say, Ma'am!' he cried eagerly.

'Yes?'

'"Stop smoking, you bloody fool!"' the boy shouted, beaming animatedly.

Rudra looked at me and we erupted into laughter. Slightly

bemused, the rest of the room joined us.

'So this is what you would say, Gopal, hmm?' Rudra smirked.

'Yes, Swami-ji!' the boy retorted with glowing eyes. '"Get away, you bloody fool!"'

Laughter rippled through the hall. Inwardly, I sighed with relief. I'd managed to wing it. After this, the rest of my teaching experience surely couldn't get any worse.

1.10: A *Sannyasi* Calls

Ready for an afternoon nap, I collapsed on my bed after an exhausting after-school tutorial with the pupils of Year 8 on the ashram's top-floor landing. I had to be on my toes with those kids, who certainly knew more about English grammar rules than I did. It was almost like they were giving me a tutorial than vice versa. Whenever I suggested something they deemed to be incorrect, they'd look at me with serious eyes and folded arms. 'No, Ma'am,' they'd shake their heads, 'this is not the correct form of past perfect.'

'They don't want to go home,' Rudra had told me during the break. 'They always ask me, *Please, Swami-ji, give us more homework! Let us stay longer at the ashram!* So I give them a tutorial every day, if I have the time.'

A mighty knock on my door caused me to leap to my feet. Curious, I stuck my head outside the door. To my surprise, it was Rudra.

'Can I come in?' he asked with his disarming smile.

'Sure,' I said, and let him pass.

Curiously, he inspected the room and my belongings, re-arranged his robes and sat down on one of the beds. I awkwardly took a seat on the bed opposite him. His eyes looked straight into mine.

Is this behavior appropriate for a sannyasi? a small voice in my head asked. I was confused. I'd heard that renunciates were not supposed to be in a room alone with a woman, because of their celibacy vows.

Oh, he's probably just trying to be friendly, another voice chipped in. *He wants to make sure you're alright.*

Hmm, maybe, the first voice chipped in again. My radar was hypersensitive after having to fend off unwanted advances from Indian men on an almost daily basis. At any rate, the door was open.

'How are you finding your time here?' Rudra asked, still smiling.

'Okay, thanks.' I nodded and shuffled around on the bed.

'Are you enjoying the teaching?' He raised his eyebrows.

'Yes, I am,' I said. 'It's great, although I'm really new to this.'

'You are doing very well.' He was still looking into my eyes, which caused me to smile nervously and look out of the open door.

Rudra continued to ask some general questions. Was I comfortable in my room? Did I have everything I needed?

'Give me your hand,' he suddenly commanded.

'What?' I replied, mystified.

'Give me your hand. I want to read your palm,' he said. He held out his right hand.

Reluctantly, I extended my left hand. He took hold of it with both hands and proceeded to study my palm with a look of deep concentration on his face. He traced my lifeline slowly with his index finger and nodded knowingly, as though he was reading an intricate map. My skin tingled under his gentle touch, but at the same time, something in me resisted it, too. Somehow, it didn't feel right. Amused, I wondered whether palm reading was part of his ashram training, or whether he had learnt this skill in the army.

'You are a person with strong determination and vision. You are very successful in your life.' He looked up at me triumphantly.

'Aha,' I responded with a hint of sarcasm. The unanticipated closeness made me feel uncomfortable.

'Yes, you are very determined.' He released my hand, shuddered slightly and gave me a coy look.

'You are the first woman I have ever touched,' he said quietly.

Right, I thought, and smirked. The uncomfortable feeling in my solar plexus had returned.

'You haven't even touched your mother?' I asked jokingly.

'Yes, but that is different,' Rudra said and crossed his legs.

'Aren't you tired?' he asked suddenly. 'Why don't you lie down on your bed? I can continue to talk to you, if you like.'

The situation was starting to feel surreal at this stage. I was totally confused about Rudra's intentions. Was he just being friendly, or was he trying to flirt with me, as my gut kept telling me? And if he really was flirting, then how did that fit in with his *sannyasi* vows? It was all a bit too complicated for me, and I wished it would just go away.

'No thanks,' I replied, and kept my sandaled feet firmly on the ground.

After some more chit-chat, Rudra got up. 'I have to go now, but I would like to spend some more time with you,' he said. 'Can you meet me tonight after ten o'clock? You can come to my room.' He turned towards the door.

'What?!' I asked. Had I misheard? To his *room*?

'Yes, I finish my ashram duties at that time. After that, I have more time to talk.'

'Forget it,' I said brusquely, 'I'll be long in bed by then.' I glared at him. 'And don't *dare* to wake me up!'

He seemed surprised.

'Okay,' he said. 'Never mind. See you for *pranayama* then.'

'Yeah. See you,' I murmured.

I followed the saffron-colored robes with my eyes as they wafted out of the room. Suddenly, I began to have serious doubts about my impulsive decision to stay in this strange ashram alone. Me and my crazy ideas, I thought – what had I gotten myself into again? Maybe I should leave. I could call Maniac and get him to collect me. I sank back onto my rose-covered pillow with a sigh.

Part of me was flattered, of course. I liked Rudra and wouldn't have minded his attentions in the slightest if he hadn't been a *sannyasi*. As things stood though, I felt uneasy about it. It was a bit like having a crush on a married man – all very well as long as it was just a fantasy, but too much when it actually happened. Something about Rudra felt phony, especially his dubious 'confession' that he had never touched a woman in his life before.

At the same time, I was aware that I had a tendency to ascribe bad intentions to men when this might not always be the case. It was an old pattern of mine, an old record from childhood that still piped up sometimes and told me that men were bastards who abused women and weren't to be trusted. It was about time I let that go.

Rudra was probably a really nice guy and just didn't know how to behave around women outside his culture. He was an Indian monk, right? He'd lived in the remote Himalayas for almost a decade. He was likely to be as curious about me as I was about him, and maybe he really just wanted to chat with me when his duties were over at night. And if there really was something developing between us, we could deal with it when it actually happened. *Chill out, Tiziana*, I told myself. *All is well.*

I took out my mobile phone and composed a text message for Kassandra. With a smile on my face, I told her about the flirtatious ex-army *sannyasi* who'd sat on my bed, his chubby Guru and the ominous knife dances. I also told her that I had a massive crush on him. Her reply came within minutes. To be honest, it threw me a bit.

'First woman. In the army. *Right.* He's probably a pathological liar who will get karmic detention. Take heed: if this is a man for whom nothing is sacred, neither monkhood, nor women, nor sex, nor you... then he is probably worse than the rest. Do what your nature desires, but please be careful: where lies and deceit are in the equation, things can get very dark indeed energetically. To look beneath a monk's robe is certainly interesting – but only for the ego.'

I pondered her words for a while. Kassandra was a very perceptive woman who had a knack of turning up in my life repeatedly as a sort of embodied voice of spirit in difficult situations. Could she be right?

To distract myself, I decided to make my way to the 'Moustachio Place', as MJ and I called the canteen across the road due to its overwhelming client base of moustachioed men. I was hungry and wanted to have dinner before the *aarti*. I felt nervous about this. In India, whenever an unaccompanied Western woman enters a restaurant entirely frequented and run by men, the whole place will stare at her incessantly from the moment she sets foot into it. This could be quite intimidating, in particular when I was feeling vulnerable.

At this point, I had learnt over time, I had two choices. I could sit quietly in the corner, try to ignore them and have an uncomfortable time as everyone continued to stare at me – or, I could make a big entry. Generally speaking, I had adopted the second option.

This evening, I chose my favorite strategy. Faking confidence, I entered the canteen slowly. With measured glances, I took stock of my surroundings, and looked straight at the Moustachio who stared at me most intensely. I, in turn, inspected him just as curiously, broke into a broad smile and complimented him on the beauty of his moustache. '*Sundar mooch!*' (Beautiful moustache!), I exclaimed enthusiastically into the round, tilting my head Indian-style. A confused silence ensued in the shack for about thirty seconds, before everybody erupted into hysterical laughter. The Moustachio in question, flattered by this unexpected attention, grew an inch taller. The ice was broken. It always worked.

I sat down at one of the wooden tables and the amused waiter was only too happy to bring me an assortment of delicious *dhal*, *sabji* and *rotis* in little stainless steel bowls. Some of the men continued to stare as I had my meal, but quickly averted their eyes when I returned their looks. Maybe they weren't sure if they wanted to be complimented on their moustaches as well.

'You're crazy!' my ex-travel companion Hee from Korea used to laugh whenever I played the staring game.

'What am I supposed to do?' I'd reply. 'The only way they will stop staring is if I stare back at them, and they realize how funny that is.' That wasn't always the case, but more often than not, at least it resulted in laughter from both sides.

Over time, I would get to know the staff of the 'Moustachio Place' well, and enjoy their sweet *chai*, *paranthas*, and other delicacies on a daily basis. To visit them in the morning school break and enjoy a *chai* with them became one of the highlights of my day. They'd examine my school books, ask questions, and ensure that I got excellent service. Surprisingly, the price for a main meal, a mere forty-five rupees (about fifty-five pence), became steadily cheaper with time, too.

Jokingly, I gave them devotional nicknames: the owner, a large man with a thick moustache resembling eyebrows became 'Uncle Mooch' (in India, all older men are addressed as uncle); the young *roti* maker Dinesh became Ganesh; and the youngest cook transformed into Gopala, the child-like form of Lord Krishna. They, in turn, called me Pooja (worship), because I always prayed before my meals.

A stifling, stagnant heat suffused the canteen, which opened out towards the road, and we were surrounded by a huge cloud of fat, black flies. Like a buzzing swarm of sunbathing tourists at the Riviera, they complacently sat in my meal, on my glass, my head, my hands. In this battlefield of hot food consumption, they were in an overriding majority, and they were everywhere. There was nothing I could do but surrender.

A quiet, slender man asked if he could join me. He had handsome, chiseled features with prominent cheekbones and kind brown eyes. His short hair was well-cut and oiled. I felt an instant rapport with him.

'Sure,' I said, and gestured at the empty seat opposite me. He sat down and unpacked a lunchbox.

'This is my mother's cooking,' he smiled, as he started to eat greasy samosas with his hands. 'I like home-cooked meals best.'

'You look like my father,' I blurted out. 'Really! When he was young, he looked exactly like you!' I was amazed at the resemblance.

Amused, the man looked at me for a moment. 'And you look like Mona Lisa,' he replied. He stretched out his hand. 'My name is Kavindra. I live in this village.'

'Hi,' I grinned and shook his hand, 'I'm Tiziana. I've just started to teach English in the ashram across the road.'

Kavindra was an NGO worker who lived in a nearby house with his wife and children. In his spare time, he also freelanced as a tourist guide. Not that there was much work for him to do, for few foreign tourists ever passed through the village, and the Indians generally knew where they were going. His English was good and I liked his calm, serious manner, so I took his number for a possible joint trip to nearby temples. It would be good to have a friend outside of the ashram.

On my way back to the ashram, I bumped into Rudra, who was standing near the entrance. I nodded curtly and attempted to walk past him towards the temple.

'Excuse me!' he called out to me. 'Could you come to the office for a moment, please?'

'Sure,' I said. *What does he want now?* I wondered as I followed him up the stairs. He gestured towards one of the chairs by the barred window. I sat down and waited. From behind his large desk, Rudra addressed me ruefully.

'I feel ashamed,' he said with a pained look on his face. 'I should not have asked you to come to my room at night. What impression do you have of me now? Maybe you find this objectionable.'

Dumbfounded, I stared at him.

He continued. 'Maybe you are thinking, *This man is only interested in my body. He has bad intentions.* I assure you that this is not
so. What I meant to say is that ten o'clock is the only time of the
day when I am free.'

My head was spinning slightly. Suddenly, the brown desk in
front of me became extremely interesting.

'I am sorry,' he continued, wringing his hands. 'I have been
feeling guilty all day. Please don't mind it.'

'No problem,' I mumbled, and got up to leave the office. So
maybe he hadn't been trying to flirt with me after all, just as I
thought earlier. I was relieved. Still, I was confused, and couldn't
stop thinking about Rudra all through the *aarti*. It was a
ridiculous situation: I'd primarily come to the ashram because of
him, but I didn't think that things between us would become
complicated, at least not so soon. Whatever it was, I sensed a
connection between us, and that something was developing
almost of its own accord.

'Can you talk to him, from person to person, with respect and
dignity?' Kassandra asked via text. 'Desire is nothing bad – on
the contrary, it's godly. What you do with it is what matters. But:
if you're looking for love, find somebody with a warm heart, not
a messed-up monk.'

I resolved to talk to Rudra in the morning and address the
energy between us openly. Too exhausted and puzzled to delib-
erate the issue any longer, I crept into bed to have an early night.
Sleep evaded me, however.

1.11: Entering the Cave

I met Rudra as usual in the temple for the morning *aarti*. After we'd solemnly worshipped the Guru's sandals for thirty minutes, he turned his head towards me. 'Please will you come to my room?' he asked. His voice was soft, shy almost. 'I need to talk to you in private.'

My curiosity and desire to clear the air between us got the better of me. I knew it was probably a bad idea, but I really wanted to see where and how a Hindu *sannyasi* lived. Besides, I was well used to my incurable curiosity getting me into bizarre situations, but took comfort in the fact that, for the most part, I was pretty good at getting myself out of them again.

'Okay,' I said, and followed him through the dark, deserted corridor into his office. Confused, I looked around. Where *was* his room?

'Wait,' he instructed, and disappeared behind the large steel cupboard near his desk. I heard keys rattle, followed by the clanking of a metal door. Rudra re-appeared from behind the cupboard and walked back onto the landing, looking cautiously from left to right.

'Go inside the door behind the cupboard and wait,' he said quietly. Wrapping my blanket tightly around me, I did as I was told. Rudra was closely behind me and motioned for me to walk through the door. To my surprise, there was a secret room behind the ashram's office. Stepping over the dim threshold reminded me of the hidden doorway in *The Lion, the Witch and the Wardrobe*, and I half-expected to end up in a Himalayan Winter Wonderland. Instead, I entered the mysterious world of Rudra's private room. Or cell, as it appeared.

The room was only marginally bigger than a large wardrobe and contained a bed draped with woolen orange blankets, a small table and a shelving unit. Thick blankets covered the windows, and a big, cracked picture of Guru-ji hung crookedly on one of the walls. The room was cold and messy. Money, Ayurvedic medicine bottles, books, papers, clothes, and documents bundled into plastic bags were strewn all over the surfaces. Small, concealed and dark, it felt like a cave. There was also a little en-suite lavatory with a grimy Indian-style squat toilet, a bucket and a sink. He lived like *this*? I was fascinated and repelled in equal measures.

'Please sit down.' Rudra pointed towards the bed.

I looked around the room. There was nowhere else to sit, so I rested cross-legged on Rudra's bed. He sat down opposite me in the same position. Looking into my eyes, he took my hand and held it gently in his. We sat in silence for a while.

'When I am with you, I'm at peace,' he said finally.

My body tensed, and I shifted around uncomfortably, unsure of how to respond to this intimate statement.

'I was very... *disturbed* about our conversation yesterday,' he continued in the peculiar, stilted English I liked so much. 'Please do not think badly of me. But I have not been able to sleep all the night. I was in turmoil. I was thinking about you the whole time.'

He continued to look at me with a smoldering intensity, his face only inches away from mine. I held my breath in a feeble attempt to stop my heart from beating so loudly.

'I haven't been able to sleep either,' I confessed quietly.

'I tried to get you out of my head,' Rudra continued. 'I was thinking of my Guru-ji all the time, concentrating on him, doing my *japa, japa, japa*' – he pointed at his *Rudraksha mala* – 'but it did not help. All the time, thoughts of you were coming.' He paused. 'We are on the same frequency. Some connection is there. I don't know...' He trailed off and continued to look into my eyes. I returned his gaze, not knowing what to say or do.

My mind buzzed and I was more confused than ever. Peculiar as the situation seemed, it was as though I'd known Rudra for a very long time. His clear, strong voice sounded so familiar, and when he spoke, I sensed it deeply in my body. It felt completely natural to feel the soft touch of his hands, to look into his unfathomable brown eyes and talk to him on such intimate terms. How could this be? I'd only just met him.

'You know you're playing with fire,' I said, as though I was speaking a prophecy. 'You're going to get burnt.'

The grasp around my hand tightened; Rudra's gaze intensified.

'I don't care,' he replied passionately. 'For you, I'll gladly burn my whole body.'

'Let's not go there,' I responded feebly. He merely continued to hold my hand.

I have to admit that by now, two conflicting parts of me were vying for my attention. My naive, romantic self loved the intensity with which Rudra spoke; the other, more savvy me thought it was a bit too dramatic. These words seemed so unlikely to come from an ascetic who'd spent the last decade living in the Himalayas and probably had very little experience with women. Overwhelmed by the strength of my attraction, I overrode my doubts.

All too soon, six am approached, and it was time for me to leave. I got up from the bed and waited for Rudra to unlock the door. Before he did so, he cheekily asked me what Western people did when they parted.

'They might hug,' I played along with an amused smile.

'Can we do this?' he asked. He was so close that my body almost touched his.

'Why not?' I said, feeling myself being sucked into the blackness of a gorge.

He pulled me into a gentle, yet strong embrace. Rudra was only marginally taller than me, but well-built, with a broad chest and big forearms. I smelled a slight scent of incense and soap. Disappearing in the folds of his saffron-colored robes, I thought how strange it was to be hugging an Indian monk. And yet, it felt so natural. He kissed me softly on the forehead. Feeling a bit dazed, I left the secret cell and went up to my room.

After this clandestine morning meeting, I was even more confused. What was happening between us? Was this a beautiful meeting of kindred spirits, or was Rudra really a sleazy, pretend monk who wanted to get off with a foreign woman, as Kassandra seemed to think? I had no idea. And did I want to take this bizarre situation any further?

Thankfully I had school to distract me. I looked at my watch and saw that I had about half an hour to get to my first class. I pulled out of my backpack the embroidered green *shalwar kameez* I had bought in Nepal, and dressed. I liked these comfortable suits. They looked feminine and stylish, and yet were so comfortable and practical. Maybe this was the reason that most Indian women wore them.

I looked into the mirror and draped the *dupatta* around my shoulders so that it covered my breasts. Even though I didn't really have body issues, living in Pakistan and India for almost six months had made me self-conscious. Women didn't show much flesh here, and many covered even their heads. If they didn't do this, relentless staring and hassle would be the result. This had not left me unaffected. By now, I felt naked when my arms weren't covered.

I picked up a pile of grammar books and a bottle of water and locked the door of my room behind me. As I left the ashram to walk the few yards towards the school, I stopped for a moment and took in the early morning glow over the mountains. I still wasn't used to being so deep in the Himalayas.

'*Namaste, ji!*' the boys of the Moustachio Place cried as they saw me walk past.

'*Namasteeee!*' I replied and waved back at them.

At school, I couldn't stop thinking about Rudra all morning. Part of me wanted to run away. I was scared of falling in love with him and having my heart broken by an impossible affair. I still remembered how painful my break-up with Steven had been, and didn't want to repeat the same mistakes by getting involved in another complicated situation.

But at the same time, I was almost paralyzed. And intrigued about our unlikely connection. Was there a deeper purpose to our meeting? And could he be The One, the soul mate I had been looking for all along?

A mighty thunderstorm brewed up over the mountains in the afternoon. The sky darkened with thick clouds, and a violent wind howled ominously outside my room, causing the shutters of my window to bang violently against their frames. In my drafty room on the ashram's top floor, I felt as though I might take off any minute, just like Dorothy in *The Wizard of Oz*.

The storm reflected how I felt on the inside. Hiding under thick duvets to escape the cold breeze that surged through the glass-less windows, I mulled the situation over in my mind. Quite clearly, Rudra and I were both attracted to each other, and yet, because of his vows, we faced a conflict. It was typical, I thought as the wind sent my altar objects flying across the room, that I had finally met a man who seemed to tick all of the boxes, apart from the small detail that he was a monk.

Maybe it was a test. Maybe, I reasoned, the obstacle of his monk's vow meant that we'd get to know each other on a mental and emotional level, rather than jump into bed with each other. Things had started to happen between us already and we'd crossed boundaries, but, as Kassandra had said, it was up to us how we handled the situation. Maybe this was the true meaning of Tantra: channeling and transforming sexual energy, the life force, into something transcendental and ultimately more powerful. But would we have the strength to acknowledge but not act on the desire that clearly consumed us both? Maybe it was wiser to disappear from Rudra's life before it was too late.

1.12: The Love-Secret

There was a knock on my door after the evening *aarti*. 'Can we meet to talk more?' A somber Rudra stood on the landing. He looked nervously over his shoulder and raised his voice when two men emerged from the room next to mine. 'I need to discuss tomorrow's school plan with you.'

My mind had doubts. *Don't do this!* it instructed. *Stop it while you still can.*

My heart objected. *Go. Talk to him more.*

'Sure,' I said. 'When and where?'

'Please come to the office at ten pm.' Rudra nodded curtly and turned to leave.

When I arrived at the office at the agreed hour, Rudra asked me to go into an empty guest room next to the office. 'Quiet!' he whispered. The corridor was dark and deserted. With a shawl over my head, I sneaked through the half-closed door of the room, feeling like a naughty schoolgirl. Rudra followed me swiftly and shut the door behind us.

We sat down on one of the beds, cross-legged, and faced each other. In the darkness, I could only vaguely make out his features at first. Like vigilant wild-cats, we sensed each other in silence for a few moments.

'Excuse me,' Rudra's velvety voice emerged gently from obscurity, 'I have to finish some *japa* rounds.'

As a *sannyasi*, he had to repeat a mantra with his *mala* several times a day to keep his mind focused on Guru-ji. He closed his eyes and silently recited the mantra while he moved the dark, jagged *rudraksha* prayer beads between the fingers of his right hand in count. I tried to meditate, too, but failed dramatically. Instead, I opened my eyes from time to time to look at him.

This is fantastic! I thought excitedly. *Finally a man who meditates!* My previous boyfriends had not been particularly interested in spirituality, which meant that I did most of my rituals, meditations and visits to sacred sites alone or with other priestesses. I had often wished for a man to share my spiritual path, somebody who understood where I was coming from. It seemed that my prayers had been answered, though right now, I was more mesmerized by Rudra's beauty than the act of meditation.

After Rudra had finished his mantras, we held hands and talked, hesitantly, sparingly. It was almost as though words were superfluous, and we communicated on a different level altogether. Like children, we were spellbound by the unexpected magic that was starting to unfold between us. We didn't quite know what to do, and so we sat.

Desire and curiosity danced intimately with a biting conscience and the unspoken question of, 'Should we...? *Could* we...?' Again I was struck by how familiar we were with each other, as if I'd known him forever. Like Rudra had said this morning, we were on the same frequency.

After an hour or two in each other's company, we parted by the door with a hug and a timid kiss. I buried my head in the soft cotton robes and held on tightly. Arms around my waist, Rudra showered my face and hair with light kisses.

'You're such a sweet girl,' he mumbled, 'such a spiritual girl. I can't believe I found you.'

Then he kissed me softly on the mouth. I felt it burn into my soul.

Another kiss followed, this time slow and lingering. His smooth, full lips were gently enveloping mine. Every time I pulled myself away to leave, Rudra drew me back into his embrace to kiss me some more. We stood by the door in the dark room for a long time.

'This is endless,' Rudra murmured and laughed, and finally let me go. My mouth found his for a last time and then I slunk through the metal door onto the hushed corridor, up the stairs, into my silent room.

I tossed and turned all night with the exciting glow of new, unfolding romance. Every time I woke up from my broken sleep and memories of Rudra flooded into my consciousness, I felt a fire spreading through my belly. My head was a jumble, but any doubts I still had were swept away by the exhilaration of having met a man I liked, of being kissed and held again. I replayed the sensations of Rudra's strong embrace, his light kisses and the way he stroked my hair, over and over again in my mind, until the early morning throat-clearing choir reminded me that it was time to get up.

I walked towards the temple with mixed feelings, not knowing how to behave towards Rudra after last night's intimacy. I needn't have worried. When he saw me enter, Rudra smiled warmly and motioned for me to sit next to him to sing Shiva's song. We performed *aarti* and practiced *pranayama* with the same focus as usual, though from time to time we glanced at each other timidly. When it was time to leave, Rudra lingered at the doorway for a few seconds.

'See you at school,' he said. 'And please come to my office after lunch so that we can talk more.'

'Sure,' I replied and returned his smile.

When I came to the office in the afternoon, he ushered me into his secret room. Before the door was properly closed behind us, he pulled me towards him and kissed me passionately. He slammed the door shut with his foot and pushed me gently onto the bed behind us. Not able to resist any longer, I flung my arms around his neck and kissed him back with the same intensity.

'I love you,' he whispered. 'From the first moment you've come to this ashram, I've loved you.'

His hands caressed my hair and my face. I held his strong, muscular body close to mine and closed my eyes. The skin of his hands felt like velvet.

'I love you, too,' the beat of my heart sang. 'I love you, too.'

Our mouths found themselves over and over again until it was time to go to the temple for *pranayama* practice.

Our romance developed at a breathless speed from that point onwards. At *aarti* and *pranayama* time, which we continued to practice sincerely every morning, we settled for glances and shy smiles. In school, our smiles grew bolder and we gazed deeply into each other's eyes across classrooms and corridors. When we thought nobody saw us, we quickly touched hands or brushed up against each other. And whenever Rudra had a free moment, he'd call me on my mobile phone and I'd sneak into his secret room, where we fell onto his bed and kissed. I often stayed there until the early morning hours. Only an idiot wouldn't have noticed how smitten we were with each other.

During these afternoons, we'd sit or lie on the bed in his tiny, dark room, illuminated sometimes by a little neon light or a candle. This room became our microcosm in which we got to know each other – far removed from the world that lay behind the woolen blankets that covered his window, a world that contained sunshine, wind, rain and people.

I was in a state of bittersweet bewilderment, convinced that I had found the man I'd been looking for all my life. It was as if Rudra's memory was written in my blood and I found myself immersed in a past I couldn't remember. Our connection was timeless – there was no beginning and no end. He was me and I was him, and the whole Universe consisted only of us. When he smiled or touched me just lightly, electricity currents ran through my body, and my heart started to sing uncontrollably. I was mesmerized by his beauty and couldn't take my eyes off him. It had been a long time since I'd been in love – three years in fact. As if to make up for lost time, I threw myself into the affair with extra fervor.

1.13: A Perfect Match

'How long have you known me?' Rudra asked me playfully, head propped on one hand, as we lay on his bed. His dark eyes were sparkling. I melted into his gaze.

'Oh, I don't know... years? A lifetime? Millennia? It seems like a very long time,' I replied with a smile. In truth, I felt there was never a time I did not know him.

'Yes.' He suddenly grew serious, and a dark shadow flitted across his dreamy brown eyes, like a ripple on a still summer lake. 'We're connected by birth.'

Indeed, our connection was astonishing. Within the short amount of time we spent together, we became attuned to each other rapidly. There was an understanding of incredible depth between us akin to seeing each other's souls to the very core. We soon reached a stage during which we almost didn't need to talk anymore, because we could read the other's thoughts, emotions and motives, even when we were not in the same room.

'Tell me about Varanasi,' I asked while tracing the contours of Rudra's face with my index finger. Rudra's birthplace was believed to have been founded by Lord Shiva around five thousand years ago. It was the holy city of death, and I'd heard that people went there specifically to die. 'Why do Hindus go to die in Varanasi?'

Rudra took my hand and kissed it. 'Because Hindus believe that if they die there, they will not be reborn. All their sins will be washed away by the Ganga.'

'What is it like in Varanasi?' I asked.

'Oh, it is beautiful. Very atmospheric. But the air can be quite thick with the smoke of corpses from the burning *ghats*.' He laughed.

'Do you miss it?'

'Not really. I was involved in many negative things there. Fighting. Drinking. Street crime. Going back reminds me of all that, of the life I left behind when I took *sannyas*.' He played with the small tuft of hair at the back of his head.

'You were involved in street crime before you came here?' I asked. This was the last thing I expected to hear. 'Really?'

'Yes,' he sighed. 'But I was lucky. My Swami-ji saved me. Yes, I had a good job in the army, but there was a lot of violence, too. At the weekends, some of the fellows and I were always up to no good.'

'Wow. You had quite a shift then,' I mused. I'd seen these transformations from a life of crime and drugs to religion in my prison work from time to time. Hardened criminals who saw the light sometimes turned into devout Buddhist monks or joined other religious organizations.

'I used to be a woman-hater, too,' he confessed. 'I'm not anymore now, but recently, Mrs Chaudhari asked me if I had something against women. She said, *You are always ignoring us. Don't you like women?* I don't know, maybe she expected me to be more caring or something.'

My heart sank when I heard this. I hadn't expected this from Rudra, and his admission uncomfortably reminded me of some of my ex-boyfriends, who'd had a deep-rooted hatred of women. They'd hide it, but ultimately, it would come out in some way. One boyfriend, who was in an Industrial band, recorded a song in which a woman was raped by a drill; another secretly devoured hardcore pornography in which men had violent sex with bound and gagged women. I was the exception, of course, they'd say. I was different, not like the bimbos they hated. They loved me. Unsurprisingly, none of these relationships lasted. How did I always end up with these guys? I wondered now.

Rudra's background matched my own in originality, I

thought. He was an ex-street fighting, ex-woman hating, Guru-loving *sannyasi* from India; I was an ex-Black Metal, ex-man hating, Goddess-loving priestess from Europe. Our life stories were remarkably similar. It was as though they had run in parallel, just waiting for the right moment in time to collide. He had started training as a *sannyasi* in India in the exact same year I had begun my priestess training back in the UK. Our family backgrounds were equally dysfunctional, and it seemed that we had both been involved in a fair share of mischief before we found our spiritual paths.

Yet, as misogynist as Rudra claimed to have been in the past, he certainly didn't behave like one now. He seemed to adore me, often massaging and kissing my feet and gazing at me with the same intensity as I was at him. When he lay with his head on my thighs during the afternoon and I stroked his face, he'd look up at me smilingly.

'I am in the lap of the Divine Mother,' he'd say, and 'You are my Parvati' – a reference to the love story between Shiva and Shakti, the myth we both loved.

Many Indian people lived and breathed the Hindu myths, and more serious devotees even aspired to embody them. For example, male devotees of the God Ram sometimes dressed up in women's clothes, imagining themselves to be Sita, Ram's beloved wife, in order to feel closer to him. Likewise, male and female devotees of the God Krishna would imagine themselves to be *gopis*, the cowgirls that played with Krishna when he was a boy, in their meditation to mentally partake in Krishna's pastimes.

A lot of modern Indian love stories are therefore modeled on the myths of famous divine couples: Sita and Rama, Krishna and Radha, and Shiva and Parvati. It was like that with us. We delighted in imagining that Rudra was Shiva, the Himalayan ascetic who didn't care about women and only wanted to meditate; and that I was Parvati who'd prayed to meet Shiva for countless years and traveled all over the world to find him. And now that we'd met each other, we were in bliss.

'Darling,' he laughed, 'women were the last thing on my mind. Really. And now you came to the ashram, and you've turned my life upside down!'

'What about your mother?' I asked him. 'How did she react when you became a *sannyasi*?'

'She was very upset,' he sighed and leaned back against the wall of his room. 'Very upset. She still calls me and cries, and asks me to come home. These days, I actually don't take her calls anymore.'

'What?!' Incredulous, I looked at him. 'You don't take your mother's calls anymore? Why? Can't you just talk to her?'

'You don't understand. She is... crying. She is not just anyone. She is *my mother*.' Rudra looked troubled.

'But maybe it would be easier for her if you talked to her and reassured her that you're okay and happy at the ashram?' I suggested.

'I tried that. And besides, it is against the rules of *sannyas*. As *sannyasis*, we have to cut all contacts with family members. We leave everything behind. We even perform our own funeral rites.' He paused.

'My mother is always trying to get me to come home. She is even offering me money. She said she would give me ten *lakh* (one million rupees) if I leave the ashram, and that she is saving it for when I don't want to be here anymore. So it's best not to talk to her at all. She just wants me to leave my path. Besides, I have a brother. He can take care of her.' Rudra turned his head to look at the picture of Guru-ji, as if asking for reassurance.

I knew that in Indian society, it was custom for the family's eldest son to continue living with his parents even after marriage, to help look after them in old age. For some, often the wives, this could be challenging. Life could turn into a nightmare if the woman didn't get on with the in-laws, because it was expected that she worked alongside her husband's mother in the household.

Yet, Rudra was dismissive about the Western lifestyle and the fact that most children left home at some point to live their own lives. Most of his knowledge came from the newspapers he regularly read, and he often ranted about how corrupt our society was with its lack of family values.

'You people do not take care of your parents! You put them in old people's homes!' he'd say, evidently appalled. When I pointed out to him that he had not exactly remained at home to take care of his mother in old age either, he said that this was not comparable.

'I am following the will of God. I'm a *sannyasi*. Besides, as I told you, I have a brother.'

'So why is your mother so adamant that you have to come home, if you have a brother?' I asked.

'She says he is a criminal, and wants me to live with her instead. But I will not. Too many *sannyasis* leave the cloth, because of outside temptations and pressure from the family. *This* is why we break off all contact, so that we stay on the path. It is not easy. Our path is a hard one.'

'*Sannyas*,' he added slowly, 'is like living your own death.'

1.14: How Rudra Lost His *Dhoti*

My days at the ashram blurred into one. Even though I only slept about four hours a night, I hardly had a free moment. In the mornings, after *aarti* and *pranayama* with Rudra, I'd walk down to the ashram kitchen, where two or three smiling boys would squat on the floor and roll out dozens of *rotis* before deep-frying them into greasy *puris*. They'd serve these with thick lentil *dhal*, something I found hard to stomach at seven am. I consequently asked for the *rotis* before they were fried and ate them with honey and bananas in my room, often in the company of an enormous orange monkey.

I was stunned when I saw this monkey for the first time. I'd been in my room, sorting through some papers, when I suddenly noticed a big, hairy hand appear on the lower part of my barred window. A second hand followed, and within seconds, two eyes peered over the windowsill. The monkey's body was the size of a small child. Like a prisoner, it'd cling to the bars outside my window and scrutinize me relentlessly. After my initial surprise – after all, I was on the seventh floor of the building – I got used to it and even started talking to the animal.

School began at seven thirty am, and before long, I was teaching five English classes a day. Rudra was relieved to get some time off to go to the bank and attend to other pressing issues. I frequently felt out of my depth, but ultimately didn't manage too badly. At least the children were all fluent in English and I kept them busy with stories and exercises from school books.

Before too long, I started to enjoy my days with the children immensely. They were bright, cheeky and eager kids, with a natural curiosity about everything and everyone around them. If I asked a question, they'd rise excitedly from their seats and scream each other down to get my attention. This could also be taxing. Like hawks, they picked up on everything I said, did or wore, and commented upon it instantly.

'Ma'am, we saw you talking to a man yesterday!' they'd pipe up in their melodious sing-song voices.

'Ma'am, this morning, you were hanging out washing in front of your room!'

'Ma'am, some of your hair is white!'

'Ma'am, you are wearing Indian dress today!'

They wanted to know which books I read, what I wrote into my notebook, how much water I drank during the course of a day, and where I got the water from. There was no stopping their excitement when one day they saw a tattoo lurking out from underneath the sleeves of my *kurta*.

For the first few days, I followed Rudra's instructions and taught English grammar according to the books he had given me. I soon grew bored of syntax and grammar though, and, feeling more confident, began to add my own flavor to the curriculum. I started to teach creative writing and used Hindu mythology to make the dry grammatical sentences more interesting. Most of all, I tried to challenge the children into using their imaginations.

One morning, as we read the story of Excalibur in Year 7 and I could see that the children didn't retain anything they read, I asked them to act out every single sentence after we had read it. Much laughter ensued as two boys pretending to be knights fought each other with broomsticks, while another boy playing King Arthur lay unconscious on the ground. We also worked on rewriting a scene of *Macbeth* into an Indian setting, complete with Maharajas and tigers. Rudra would occasionally pop into the class and be delighted with my progress.

My flock consisted of three classes, Year 6, 7 and 8, with children between the ages of eleven and fourteen. Class numbers were small. The maximum number of children was ten, and most of them were boys. Although school attendance was free, many villagers didn't find education for girls necessary.

'They think, what should we send our daughters to school for?' Rudra told me. 'They are going to marry, have children and work on the fields. They do not need an education.'

The few girls that did attend school were bright, industrious and eager learners that often outshone the boys. The three girls in Year 8, Abhaya, Radhika and Sananda, were inseparable. During lessons, they sat tightly huddled together on one bench and did everything else collectively, too. I often saw them running laughingly through the school corridors, holding hands and causing mischief. My red hair, bleached lighter by the relentless Indian sun, was an object of endless fascination for the girls. 'Ma'am, your hair is like golden,' they used to yell and laugh.

The boys in my classes were more bold and feisty than the girls. Small and thin, they didn't look like their fourteen-year-old contemporaries back home in England. Though they were naughty, too, they appeared more child-like, and there was a certain fresh-faced innocence about them. These children lived in a small, sleepy mountain village that had so far managed to avoid most modern world trappings. Their world didn't include internet, mobile phones and computer games. Instead, they played ball on the slopes beneath the school and roamed around in the hills. I often met them on my early evening errands, and in no time at all, they had told everybody in the village that I was the new ashram school teacher from England.

I particularly liked Gopal, the slight, mischievous boy in Year 8 who had come out with the 'bloody fool' comment in my English class. He had a handsome, oval-shaped face with a dreamy, wistful look in his dark, liquid eyes. In creative writing assignments, Gopal was generally the one who came up with the most bizarre, hilarious story lines.

I once asked the children to write a fictional biography of their teacher, Swami Rudra. Gopal gleefully penned a fantastic story in which Rudra lost his *dhoti* during *sannyas* initiation and had to hide naked in the bushes in order to risk losing face in front of

Guru-ji's other disciples.

Afterwards, Rudra stopped me on the school corridor. 'What was that assignment you gave Class 8 today?' he asked with mock outrage. 'The children just told me. Me, naked, without *dhoti*, behind a bush? Terrible!' He shook his head but failed to hide the smile that manifested on his face. I laughed. I found these essays delightful. Apart from amusing me, they gave me a legitimate reason to talk and read about my beloved Rudra even in school.

In another assignment, which centered on the love story between Shiva and Parvati, Gopal dressed Shiva in black leather, positioned him on a fast motorbike and had him fight a duel with the devil in order to win Parvati's love. I often watched Gopal as he wrote, with the enthusiasm of an inspired artist pouring from his young face. He would lie on the floor, chuckling to himself, trying to keep up with a pen that raced over the blank pages of his exercise book as if by its own volition. He reminded me of myself when I was a child. As soon as he had finished, he'd run up to me excitedly.

'Please can you check this, Ma'am?' he asked with a glowing face. 'And can you sign it, please?'

Another remarkable character was Chandresh, a tall and strong boy. He was much bigger than the other boys in his year, and always looked slightly disheveled. His kind, heart-shaped face often held a startled expression. Chandresh would incessantly moan and complain in class, yawn, and generally try to get away with working as little as possible. Outwardly, he could be mistaken as lazy, but once I got to know him and in particular his work, I saw that he actually possessed a lot of depth and thought intensely about the things that concerned him.

'Ma'am,' Chandresh once pleaded after I had reprimanded him for not completing his work, 'I always have to do things differently because I *am* different.'

The children loved Rudra without reservation. Many of them

had known him since they were toddlers. To them, he was not only a teacher, but also brother, father, uncle and friend. Just how much the children adored him came across in the assignment I gave the children about Rudra's life story in one of my English lessons.

'He sacrificed everything to teach us,' Abhaya wrote. 'He left his family and friends, and he is unmarried.' Being unmarried, in India, was comparable to saying 'He's got cancer' in the West. To bear the cross of bachelorhood voluntarily was an act of heroism in the eyes of many.

The other teachers in the school were Indian, and very kind and courteous towards their new *angrezi* colleague. Some of them were retired school teachers and Guru-ji devotees from Varanasi who spent term times in the Himalayas as an act of selfless service. Among them were the Bengali professor and his wife, alongside Mr and Mrs Chaudhari, an elegant couple in their fifties. It was usually Mrs Chaudhari and the wife of the Bengali professor who assisted Rudra during the evening *aarti* with the wafting of requisites in front of the altar. Mr Chaudhari acted as the school headmaster and assistant *pujari* in the temple.

Every day after school, I shared my lunch with Rakesh and Uday, two young male teachers, in the ashram canteen. They spoke a little English, and we'd enjoy simple conversations about religion, our countries and respective lives. They were sweet and respectful, often filling my steel tray for me with food and fetching me water. Rakesh and Uday were delighted that I liked India and in particular, the Hindu religion. For some reason, perhaps because I blessed my food before eating it with a Sanskrit mantra, they regarded me as a pious and virtuous woman.

'Ma'am, when are you coming back?' they asked me daily, for they knew I was only planning to stay for a short while. 'Please, you *must* come back for longer time! We can never forget you.'

'Yes, when *are* you coming back?' Rudra asked playfully when

I told him about Rakesh and Uday in one of our afternoon meetings. In denial about leaving the ashram, I had no answer to this question.

1.15: The Gift of *Tulsi*

I'd initially planned to stay at the ashram for a maximum of ten days. But on my fifth day in the school, something happened that changed everything again. When I came to the office to see Rudra for the afternoon, he ushered me to his room with a tense expression on his face. As I sat down on the bed, he said, 'Damn. Trouble. Something serious has happened.' Before he could tell me what it was, somebody banged on his door. Rudra jumped up, grabbed his keys and left the room. From behind the closed door, I could hear a mixture of arguing voices and crying girls.

'*Thik hai*, Abhaya? *Thik hai?*' I heard Rudra ask in a desperate tone of voice. 'Alright?' More crying ensued.

When Rudra finally returned, he told me that a male teacher had molested Abhaya, one of my students from Year 8. Abhaya and her two friends had been fooling around with the teacher, and suddenly the game had turned nasty. He'd pinned her to the wall and tried to kiss and grope her, the girls said.

I had a sick feeling in my stomach. Concerned, I took Rudra's hand. 'That's awful,' I said. 'What are you going to do now?'

'I don't know.' He ran his hand through his cropped hair and sighed. 'I will have to confront him. I have to send him back home. We can't keep a teacher like that. He'll leave tomorrow morning with the first bus back to Varanasi.'

'Who is this guy?' I asked. 'Do I know him?'

'Yes, you have met him,' Rudra said. 'He is the science teacher, the guy with the thick glasses who came to your class about England that day.'

I thought for a moment, and then recalled his face. He was a nerdy-looking middle-aged man. 'Really? That guy? Wow.'

Rudra absent-mindedly played with the *mala* around his neck for a few moments, then looked at me. 'Could you possibly stay longer?' he asked. 'We are desperately low on staff, and with him gone, I need to cover all of his science classes. Do you think you could change your flight and stay until the summer holidays begin?'

I thought for a split second. Although my flight to Germany was booked, I knew that I could change it for a fee.

'Yes, of course,' I replied. 'I'll stay.' How could I say No?

Although I didn't show it, I was thrilled. What a strange twist of fate. Obviously, my time with Rudra wasn't over yet. Apart from the dreadful circumstances, it felt like a gift from the Gods. Rudra and I were growing closer every day and our relationship felt magical at this stage. It would be madness to leave now. Through this unexpected turn of events, we'd get to spend more time together and ignore my inevitable departure for a while longer.

'I want to give you something.' Rudra suddenly interrupted my thoughts and pulled a small item from the little bag he carried underneath his robes. It was a *mala*.

'I feel to give this to you.' He gently placed it around my neck. 'It is made from *tulsi*.'

It was a delicate, hand-made *mala*, with irregular off-white beads that resembled minuscule tree trunks strung together on a red thread. I had never seen a *mala* like this before.

'The *tulsi* plant is very sacred in India,' Rudra explained as I curiously touched the tiny beads. 'It is believed to be the incarnation of the Divine Mother.'

As I found out later, *tulsi*, or holy basil, is a plant sacred to Krishna and Radha, the Hindu Gods who embody the ultimate tale of love, passion and devotion. The flute-playing, beautiful Krishna was Radha's divine lover when he lived among the cowherds of Vrindavan. Since childhood, Krishna and Radha were close to each other – they played, danced, fought, grew up together and wanted to be together forever, but the world pulled them apart.

Krishna departed to safeguard the virtues of truth, and Radha waited for him. He vanquished his enemies, became King, came to be worshipped as the Lord of the Universe, married other women and raised a family, and yet, Radha, though married herself, still waited for him. The two often met secretly at night time in the enchanting woods of Vrindavan to make love.

In relation to Krishna, Radha is acknowledged as the Supreme Goddess, for it is said that she controls Krishna with her love. It is believed that Krishna enchants the world with his beauty and flute playing, but Radha enchants even him with her boundless love.

When one of the *gopis* asked Krishna how she could meet him again in her next life, he told her to find something precious to offer him. Neither gold nor diamonds were good enough, Krishna said; only the gift of a *tulsi* plant would do.

Touched by Rudra's thoughtful gift, I used the *mala* daily for my mantras from then on.

Unsurprisingly, Abhaya and her two girlfriends were upset after the incident with the science teacher. They came to school the next day, but quietly huddled together on the bench with puffy eyes and whispered to each other all throughout class. I decided that it was best to leave them be.

'It'll take them some time to get over this. They're traumatized,' Rudra commented. 'One of the female teachers is talking to them. Abhaya came to me and she cried, *Swami-ji, I trusted him! I can't accept this from my beloved teacher!* And you know, I was feeling terrible, too.' He paused. 'Every time a child cries, it tears me apart on the inside. But I can't take them into my lap, because of the cloth.' He pointed at his robes. 'These children, especially Abhaya's year, I've known them since they were very small, since they were six years old. In many ways, they're like my own children to me.' He sighed deeply.

'They are very sad that he left, too. They loved him because he was a great teacher. And… I also told them that they have to become aware that they are not children anymore. They are growing into women, and still they are teasing men, even me! They need to be more careful.'

'I have told the girls to keep this quiet, even from their mothers,' he continued. 'We are going to be in a lot of trouble with the villagers if it comes out that such an incident has happened at the school.'

'Why? How can Abhaya keep this from her mother? Surely she'll notice that something is wrong?' I asked.

'Darling, you have no idea. Some of the villagers hate us.' Rudra gave a brief laugh.

'*Hate* you?' I shook my head. 'Why would they hate you?'

'They see us as a threat. We came from a different state and built a school here in their village. We are doing good work, and some of them, they do not like it. They think we are interfering. One time, some people even tried to kill me! They tried to break into the ashram at night! That is why my room is where it is, hidden behind the office – so that I can keep an eye on the ashram's entrance. I always have to be vigilant.'

He pulled the thick blanket that covered his bedroom window up slightly. Through the dirty window, I could see the ashram entrance below and the Moustachio Place across the street. 'Look,' Rudra said. 'I can see everything, but nobody knows that I am here.'

This worry was likely to be the reason that the science teacher was merely sent back to Varanasi and not reported to the police, besides the fact that reporting anything, particularly crimes against women, to the Indian police was hardly worth the effort, as I knew from my own experience.

When I was still in Rishikesh, a man in a car followed and tried to assault me one night as I was walking home from a friend's house. Watching hardcore porn on a flat screen TV in place of the rear mirror, he tried to lure me into his car. I shouted at him and carried on walking, though I was frightened because the street was deserted and I was alone. He continued to follow me, and at one point, got out of the car to expose himself.

More outraged than scared by now, I took down the car's number plate and reported him to the local police. What followed was a bizarre pantomime in which a gang of complacent and patronizing police officers first tried to convince me that I could decide what fate would befall the porn man if he was caught – *'No court necessary, Ma'am; as you wish, Ma'am, as you wish'* – and then began to flirt with me.

I was later told by my Indian friends that the police force was rife with corruption, and even had they made an effort to catch the man, it was likely that he would have bribed his way out of the complaint without much effort. I therefore wasn't too surprised at how Rudra handled the incident.

'How do you know that the teacher has really done this?' I wanted to know. 'What did he say when you asked him?'

'Not much,' Rudra said. 'But I could see it from his facial expression that he was guilty. Of course, he denied it, and said that he was a high-paid member of staff back in Varanasi. *Why did you come to work here then, in the Himalayas, this really tough place, where pay is low?* I asked him.' Rudra shook his head. 'It's probably likely that it has happened before. I just told him to stay in his room for the rest of the day and leave with the first bus tomorrow morning.'

'But can't he just get a new job there then? And do it again?' I asked.

Rudra shrugged his shoulders. 'What can I do about it? We have no evidence. In any case, he will not get a reference from us.'

I felt sick at the thought of this man simply taking on another teaching job and doing the same thing again. Had this been England he would have been placed on a sex offender's register and would never be allowed to teach children again. Here, they just sent him on his way: out of sight, out of mind. Compassion filled my heart for Abhaya, who wasn't even allowed to share this traumatic event with her mother, as though *she* was to blame. I found comfort in the knowledge that she could get support from her two girlfriends at least. But would the next girl be able to get away? I often contemplated this when I taught the girls from now on, and prayed that the teacher would not find a new job that involved children.

1.16: On Being a Pop Star in India

As new and exciting as it was, ashram life could also be exhausting. As soon as I'd stick my head out of my door, enthusiastic women would pull me into their rooms, stick sweets into my mouth and photograph me, usually through old-style film cameras, with every single one of their family members.

'Ma'am, photograph!' they'd cry animatedly. Sometimes, it took me twenty minutes to get down one flight of stairs. On the whole, and when I was in a good mood, I didn't mind. Rudra only smiled, when I, sometimes exasperated, told him why I was late. 'Let them,' he'd say. 'They know beauty when they see it.'

At first, I didn't understand the fascination the Indians seemed to hold for Westerners. Why did they, people I'd only just met and who didn't know me at all, want to photograph me all the time? And why did they insist on pretending that we were really good friends in the pictures? Friends explained that it was almost seen as a status symbol to know and befriend a Westerner in India, and that people took photos to prove it.

'Well, you know what the boys will do with your photograph,' seasoned India traveler Hee once remarked dryly. 'If you're lucky, they'll just tell their friends that you're their girlfriend or that they had sex with you.' She laughed. 'That's why I never let them take any photographs of me.'

Whatever the reason for this excessive attention was, I thought it best to surrender. I found it funny and endearing, especially when random children with bewildered expressions on their cute faces were placed into my arms from out of nowhere before the cameras began to flash furiously. I didn't really care what they did with the photos afterwards. But I've often wondered in how many Indian living rooms my image has ended up.

I compared my experiences in India, which could be intense at times, with those of a dark-skinned visitor to the UK. Back home, foreigners were ignored at best, or shot dead at worst. I pondered the many times I had been invited to a family home in Asia, fed, given lifts, and helped out through other acts of random kindness. People always talked to me on the street, and while this could be irritating sometimes, it equally provided me with much amusement and in some cases, great friends. Mostly, the attention I received seemed to be based on genuine curiosity. And was curiosity about other human beings not natural? Being half-Sicilian, I was a great onlooker myself. People fascinated me, and I was just as good at staring as the Indians, if not better.

When I wasn't with Rudra in his secret room, I often wandered around in the ashram. I was interested in everything that happened and in the people who lived here. It was so different from everything I was used to.

The ashram was certainly austere. There were few power points – usually one on every landing for which the pilgrims fought each other to charge their mobile phones that were sometimes stolen – and daily power cuts. Clothes were washed by hand in buckets and hung to dry on washing lines outside our doors, or draped over the railings.

All through the morning, cassette tapes reciting the *Bhagavad Gita*, one of India's holiest scriptures, would resound like a clarion call through the ashram via big speakers that were situated on every floor. I didn't understand much apart from the occasional word, delivered by a cheerful and didactic-sounding male voice, interspersed with glorious musical intervals, but it was soothing.

The kitchen consisted of a grubby, bare concrete room. Here Keshava, the bespectacled, moustachioed cook, prepared huge pots of *dhal* and vegetables on gas stoves that stood on the floor. A couple of shelves housed herbs and spices in plastic jars and a handful of aged, rudimentary kitchen tools. Next door, the ashram boys would squat and patiently roll out hundreds of *rotis* and fry them over a naked gas flame. Sometimes I joined them and together, we'd laugh at my lack of skill. The canteen was equally spartan and contained about a dozen long wooden benches and tables, alongside the obligatory portrait of Guru-ji.

Despite the rain that poured down almost daily, the ashram suffered severe water shortages, which was hardly surprising, considering the hundreds of dusty, weary pilgrims that visited it daily. Sometimes, Rudra instructed the boys to switch the water supply off for hours at a time, because the guests used it to wash their clothes, which meant there would not be enough left for the kitchen to cook the evening meal. 'Always keep two buckets of water in your room,' Rudra advised me. 'Like this, you can at least have a cold bath when there is no water.'

In India, a bath generally meant a bucket wash. You'd stand naked in the bathroom and use a plastic beaker to pour the water over yourself. If I was lucky, one of the ashram boys would lug a full bucket of hot water from the kitchen to my room, which would make the ritual a little more pleasant, especially when I wanted to wash my long hair. It was often so cold in my room that I'd actually stand inside the bucket to get my feet warm. Water was also used for one's after-toilet ablutions instead of toilet paper, which was hard to come by in the Himalayas.

The ashram's austerity was greatly contrasted by the friendliness of the staff, in particular the ashram boys, who were a highlight of my stay in the village. I loved those big, dreamy eyes that glowed with a curious mixture of adoration and awe. In their wonder at and enthusiasm for the simple things in life, these boys reminded me of the Sicilians. Amid their usual chores, they would always make sure that I had what I needed. *Chai* and food were delivered to me with broad, slightly embarrassed smiles that would make me feel happy for hours to come. Yet, their lives surely weren't easy: they were on call 24/7, and spent most of their days cleaning, cooking and looking after the pilgrims, as well as preparing for and helping with the *aarti*.

'Corrrrrect,' Rudra nodded when I complimented the boys on their friendliness. 'They'd die for me. They are so loyal! We were at a wedding one day, and I got into a fight.'

'A fight?! I thought *sannyasis* were peace-loving,' I teased him.

'Yes, well, somebody, actually, a taxi driver, was behaving without respect. He threatened me, so I had to do something, right?' He held up his hands. 'I couldn't just let him do this to me in front of all those guests. So I grabbed him by the throat, and this big, big fight started. And, I was so surprised... The boys all jumped in and defended me with their lives.'

I especially liked Anish, a quiet, slight boy with a gentle face and soft eyes framed by dark eyebrows that joined in the centre. I sometimes watched him as he worked in the ashram. He often gazed dreamily at the sky and sang gently to himself. Although we couldn't communicate with each other except through smiles, I adored him.

'They are actually very fond of you,' Rudra said when I complained once about relentless early morning banging on my door with water I hadn't asked for.

'Yes, I'm fond of them, too. They're lovely. Why don't you teach them English?' I asked him.

'They don't need to learn English,' he replied dismissively.

'Why not? It would be useful if they could speak to the foreigners passing through here, no?'

'Darling, they are ignorant, uneducated.' He shook his head.

'Well, then why not educate them? You came here all the way from Varanasi to uplift and educate the villagers in a different state, but what about your own people? What about uplifting and teaching them?'

Rudra implied that I didn't understand. Things were as they were in India and everybody had their place in life. Who would cook and clean if suddenly, the lower castes began to learn foreign languages? To me, this inequality in education was simply upholding the social control and injustice of a redundant caste system, and I said as much.

India's hierarchical caste system, in which social classes were defined by hereditary groups and dictated the work one carried out in life, still existed sporadically in rural areas of India, especially in the North. This system meant that certain people, notably of the Dhalit caste, were considered impure and often worked as rubbish men or cleaners. Social change was coming, but slowly.

I thought of Caitanya Mahaprabhu, a *bhakti* yogi and social reformer who lived in Bengal in the fifteenth century. Caitanya Mahaprabhu believed that *kirtan*, the chanting of the holy names of God, was the quickest way to purify the heart and attain auspiciousness. He consequently traveled all over India, chanting the divine names of Krishna constantly and ecstatically.

Moreover, he mixed with and defended India's so-called 'Untouchables', Hinduism's lowest caste. Whereas high-caste Brahmins were horrified when as much as the shadow of an 'Untouchable' fell upon them, Caitanya Mahaprabhu preached that there was no difference between them – what mattered was that they chanted the 'Holy Name'. Belief made them equal in the eyes of God. His radical philosophy had evidently not made it into many Indian ashrams.

I had witnessed this inequality several times, even in Westernized yoga ashrams. Whereas Western students often paid thousands of dollars to train as yoga teachers in a month, the ashram cooks and cleaners were on a meager Indian wage that meant they often had to struggle to support their families. I was surprised that these hierarchical structures existed in spiritual communities that paid lip service to equality and the Oneness of all.

1.17: One Loin Cloth and Two Chapattis

On the morning after the assault, I walked towards the temple and heard Rudra play a song I didn't know. '*Sita Rama Rama Ram, Sita Rama Rama Ram*' was the mantra. It was a joyful, energetic chant.

I stopped by the door and watched Rudra for a few moments. His eyes were closed and he was swaying gently to the rhythm of the chant as he played the harmonium. Because it was so cold, his body was wrapped in a saffron-colored blanket.

I loved Rudra's singing; his clear, deep voice possessed infinite passion. When he sang *kirtan*, he was completely absorbed in the moment and lost in the magical worlds of the Hindu pantheon. It stirred a hidden part in me, and tears would sometimes roll down my cheeks just from listening to him.

After a while, he turned around and smiled when he saw me. He waved me towards him. I walked through the temple, acknowledged Guru-ji briefly and sat down next to Rudra on the floor.

'That was a beautiful song,' I said. 'You have such an amazing voice. You should record it sometime. Make a CD, you know?'

Rudra looked embarrassed. 'No, no. Singing is just a hobby for me.'

'What was the song about?' I asked and looked over his shoulder at the harmonium. A sheet with Sanskrit writing on it lay next to it.

'Oh, this was a *kirtan* about Sita and Rama. Do you know their story?' His eyes lit up.

'Not really,' I replied. I remembered that our yogi in Rishikesh had often used the mantra *Sita-Ram*. I knew that they were a divine couple, but that was about it.

'It is a wonderful story,' Rudra said with a dreamy look on his face. 'Rama was a king, and in India we say that he is the perfect man. He has *all* the good qualities – honesty, strength, courage, morality, and so on. He had a wife called Sita, and their famous love story is told in a book called the *Ramayana*.

'One day, Rama is banished from the kingdom of his father for twelve years. He has to leave and Sita insists that she is coming with him. So together with Rama's brother Lakshman, they leave the palace to begin an austere exile in the jungle.

'For a while, they live there very happily. It is beautiful in the forest, you know? And they have no duties there. But one day, the demon king Ravana kidnaps Sita. He saw her and he desired her, because she was so beautiful. He wants to marry her.

'Rama and Lakshman search for her for many, many months. Finally, they meet Hanuman. He is the king of the monkey army and an incarnation of Lord Shiva. He offers to help them and finds Sita on the island of Lanka. They fight a great battle, and Sita is rescued after Rama kills Ravana with a golden arrow.'

There was a glow on Rudra's face.

'And you know what the best thing about this story is for me?' he asked. His mind seemed far away. 'There was an army of monkeys who threw stones into the sea towards Lanka, where Sita was prisoner. They had written the name "Rama" on every single stone. These monkeys had such faith and loyalty. People who saw them ridiculed them for this. *Why are you doing such a foolish thing?* they asked. But the stones floated on the water and created a road. And so Rama and the monkeys could walk to Lanka to rescue Sita.'

'This is pure *bhakti*,' Rudra said. He put his right hand on his heart and looked at Guru-ji. 'Pure devotion. Whenever I sing this song, I cannot stop my tears from flowing.'

Touched by his passion, I remained silent.

'And I tell you about another song,' he continued enthusiastically. 'In this song... wait, I will sing it to you. It goes "*Ekta kapon, duto rot.*" It is an old Bengali song.' He sang the lines.

'It means *One loin cloth and two chapattis*. And do you know why? Because the song is about a *sadhu*, a *sannyasi*. It talks about his life. All he needs, apart from his faith in The Almighty, are one loin cloth and two *rotis*. Nothing more. He left everything else. Such great trust!' he said.

'You really love this asceticism, don't you?'

I felt a twinge of sadness. When Rudra talked like this, I remembered who he was. It reminded me that we weren't just lovers who'd met somewhere in the Himalayas and would live happily ever after. He was a monk and had been so for almost a decade.

'This austerity, it saved me,' he nodded. 'I was nothing before I came here, only involved in negative things. Now my life is different. It has purpose now. I never forget that.'

During my yoga practice, I thought about his words. Certainly, Rudra's life had changed drastically when he left Varanasi for the Himalayas. Suddenly, he had shouldered enormous responsibilities, and at the mere age of twenty-three had been teaching and thus co-raising a whole generation of children. He was needed and saw the positive impact his actions were having on others first hand. People revered him, served him and bowed down to him.

Rudra in turn was conscientious in carrying out his ashram duties. He was compassionate and patient even when pilgrims arrived late at night and woke him up for the fifth time, which meant he hardly ever got a full night's sleep. 'We are here to serve. This is our duty,' was his mantra.

I sometimes wondered what would have become of him if he had remained in Varanasi. *Sannyas*, for many Indian men, offered a way out of rigid societal structures in which a lifetime of marriage, work and children was the only other alternative. In the more conservative areas of India with their strong cultural and familial values, it was considered shameful to disobey one's parents and lead an independent, single life or marry a person of one's own choice outside one's caste. And although many arranged marriages worked well, alcoholism or even suicide were sometimes the answer to cope with the frustration that came with living a lie, in particular for gay people or those trying to forget the lovers they were unable to marry due to caste restrictions.

I recalled an encounter I had with a young man while visiting a Durga temple in the mountains. 'Ma'am,' he addressed me as we climbed down the temple's many steps, 'has God ever appeared to you in a dream?'

'Yes – why?'

'Well,' he said, 'every day I pray to God, but God does not help me.'

'What are you asking for?' I asked.

He turned to look at me. 'Ma'am, the girl I love… she's from a different caste than me. This means I can't marry her. Her parents won't accept me.' He paused. 'So I came here today to ask the Divine Mother to help me, to appear in her parents' dream, to tell them to let me marry my love.'

Moved by his story, I told him to keep praying and make offerings. As he disappeared around the corner, I wished him Good Luck. His fate did not appear to be uncommon in India, as I learned during my time there.

At least, as a *sannyasi*, one gained respect. To leave one's family and renounce the pleasures of married life was considered to be a big sacrifice, made for the attainment of spiritual wisdom and the betterment of society. For that reason, Indian society was geared up to support holy men and women on their quest. It was considered highly auspicious to feed a *sadhu* and generously donate money to ashrams and temples. Notwithstanding rapid economical and technological growth, spirituality was still India's biggest treasure.

1.18: Intimacy

'Look at us,' Rudra said proudly. It was late afternoon, and we stood embraced in front of his bathroom mirror. 'If people would see us together on the street, they would say that we are a perfect match. *Perfect.*'

I contemplated the image in the dusty mirror. A dark-skinned man in saffron-colored robes with smoldering brown eyes next to a pale, red-haired woman in a green *shalwar kameez*. We looked like day and night, like Shiva and Sati. And yet, the happiness on our faces was the same. We held each other close, as if posing for a photograph, my head resting in the nape of his neck. I liked what I saw.

Rudra lightly placed a kiss on my cheek. 'Meeting you has shown me,' he said quietly, 'that all those things I thought mattered – race, color, language, time, distance – are not important at all.'

I smiled. How strange my life had turned out to be since my fated encounter with Rudra mere weeks ago. It seemed like I had been here for months. When I allowed myself to think about it, it was mad and overwhelming. Therefore, I preferred not to think most of the time and just flow with the current that was growing in rapidity daily. Though certainly intense, our relationship was still fairly innocent at this point. We spent much time in Rudra's room kissing and caressing each other, but we had not ventured further than that.

Every night, I slithered like a Succubus from our veiled realm into the dark, quiet hours before dawn to catch whatever sleep was left before I had to get up again for school. Rudra accompanied me through the dark office to the staircase which led towards my room. I'd climb up the stairs while he watched me, smiling. Our eyes would remain connected until I disappeared around the corner.

Much later, when I lived in an ashram in England and partook in early morning rituals that included an enigmatic dance around a *tulsi* plant, our parting would remind me of that of Hindu Gods Krishna and Radha. As described in the chants of the *Mangala Arati* practice performed by Krishna devotees all over the world, the illicit lovers stole into the deep forests of Vrindavan at night to enjoy their passionate love amid fears of being caught, and reluctantly separated at dawn to return to their respective lives and duties.

Did I have qualms about having an affair with a *sannyasi*, a Hindu monk who'd sworn an oath of celibacy and renunciation? Of course I did. As enamored as I was with Rudra, and as much as I desired him, I was never comfortable with the secrecy and the deceit. I wanted to shout out my love from the highest peak of the Himalayas, or at least from the ashram roof, but instead I had to sneak around dark ashram corridors at night, ever fearing to be caught.

It was a risky business. Whenever I was in Rudra's room, one of the ashram boys would knock on his door to request one thing or another.

'*Swami-ji!*' they'd shout while banging vigorously on the metal door. '*Swaaami!*'

Then Rudra would jump up, straighten his *dhoti* and exit the room with a papal expression on his face. I often wondered whether the workers knew of our relationship. If we could hear them outside Rudra's room, surely they could hear us, too? The ashram was a small place, and it only took one person to see or hear me to realize what was going on.

Besides, I felt like a hypocrite. In one of the yoga ashrams I visited, I'd witnessed a love affair between a yogi and an older married woman who used to sneak off in the middle of the night for secret meetings in the meditation hall. At the time, I found it disgraceful that a spiritual man, a yogi who prided himself on his celibacy, would do such a thing in an ashram. After all, ashrams were a place of spiritual repose, not carnal affairs, right? How could people be so dominated by their desires and break the ashram rules? Why didn't they go elsewhere? And now, through a bizarre turn of events, I had suddenly become involved in a similar situation. Without a doubt, the Gods were having a good laugh at my expense now.

However, overall, I didn't feel that my love affair with Rudra was wrong. Much as I tried, I failed to see how something as beautiful and delicate as a growing connection between two people could be wrong. How could the Gods be against love, or even sex, the mere act of creation? How could they condemn the greatest gift they had given us?

What Guru-ji instructed his *sannyasis* to do – the self-control, renunciation and abstinence he advocated – was a different matter. The way I saw it, these rules were man-made and denied an essential part of human life: celebration of the sacred union between man and woman. The austerity and physical self-denial in Indian ashrams reminded me of the Catholic Church. I didn't agree with it, but what nudged my conscience from time to time was that Rudra had made a vow that I only too gladly helped him break.

'How come you let yourself become involved with a woman as a *sannyasi*?' I asked him that afternoon, when we lay on his bed. 'What changed?'

'Well... I don't know. In recent months, I started to think about women. I was thinking, *If* I had a woman, then she would have to be like this, and that, and I was imagining what it would be like. I think it's my age.' He rolled over on the bed and wrapped his arm around my waist. 'And then you came. I started to have impure thoughts when we did *pranayama* together, those first mornings.'

'Really?' I thought back to that fateful day when I'd first arrived here with MJ. My first *pranayama* session with Rudra. It seemed so long ago.

'Yes, I thought, *Beautiful girl, beautiful body*, you know, things like that. In the end, it became something I could not control any longer.' He kissed my fingertips, one after the other.

I never failed to marvel at the irony of destiny. *If you want to make God laugh, then make plans*, the age-old saying goes. Rudra had avoided women with all his might, first by joining the army, and then by becoming a *sannyasi* in an ashram in which no women lived. In the end, the Goddess of Love drew him in anyway.

'You know, I... I have never done this... thing,' Rudra said. He had the look of a small boy on his face.

'You've never done what?' I asked.

'This thing...' he lowered his voice, 'sex. I have never been with a woman before you.'

'You have never had sex?' I asked incredulously. 'Come on!'

'No.' He shook his head firmly.

I just laughed. 'Get real,' I said. 'Do you expect me to believe this? You're thirty-two!'

But Rudra remained serious. 'How could I have done this? I am not married. I joined the army when I was very young, and there were no women. After that, when I was twenty-three, I took *sannyas* and came to the Himalayas. And,' he paused, 'I have never met a woman I liked. I was not interested in women.'

I didn't believe him. Maybe it was my cynical Western mind, but it seemed too unlikely to be true. With his smooth and flirtatious behavior, Rudra lacked the timidity of the sexually inexperienced. He was a boisterous man, full of initiative, vision and confidence, accustomed to knowing – and getting – what he wanted. And he was too attractive.

I still found it hard to take my eyes off him. He radiated beauty. It wasn't just the way he looked, with his smooth skin and a smile that had the ability to light up a room. Neither was it solely his strong, supple body and the intriguing contrast it created with the soft flowing robes he wrapped it in. There was an almost otherworldly gracefulness about Rudra. He glowed from the inside.

Sometimes, I would relish just sitting in the back of one of his classes, observing him. In those moments, merely being in his presence was enough for me, and I felt blessed to have not only met, but also won the love of such an exceptional human being. In addition, Rudra had a great sense of humor, and we laughed a lot. With a charismatic personality like that, it was only too likely that there had been women in his life before.

'Look,' I said and rolled over on my back. 'Your virginity doesn't impress me. It's not like I'm a virgin myself. It's okay. Just tell me the truth.'

'I am telling you the truth!' he retorted in a rush of passion. 'Maybe in *your* country it is impossible to still meet a virgin man. Here in India, it is not. I tell you, you are getting a *brahmachari*'s body.'

'Don't misunderstand,' he added. 'Many people tried. I never succumbed. But eventually,' he lifted his head and looked at me sharply, 'somebody had to crash through the barriers.'

'*Really?*' I raised my eyebrows.

'There was a girl from Austria once. A very beautiful girl, fantastic really. She came here with her father. When I showed her to her room, she basically made it clear that she wanted to have sex with me. *You're alone here?* she asked. *I'm alone, too.* I ran.' He laughed.

'You didn't take her up on the offer?' I asked, skeptical.

'No!' He shook his head vigorously. 'I thought, Oh, this Western girl, who knows how many men she has been with. There may have been dozens. Maybe she has AIDS. So I did not do it.'

He continued. 'There were other girls, too. Some foreign ones, and also Indian ones. One girl came to me for medical treatment, and she fell madly in love with me. She then came back with her mother, and both were crying. Terrible! The mother, imagine, the *mother* begged me to marry the daughter.' He shook his head with disdain. 'They said that we could produce a spiritual child, and that, if any union would have to be made, then it should be this one.'

'But how come she fell in love with you in the first place?' I asked.

'She was infatuated. I was treating her, and maybe she was impressed with my knowledge. I know a lot about women's periods, women's bodies, and so on. I told her that she had developed a fixation with me like a pupil does with a teacher. It would pass.'

'Did she believe you?'

'No. She cried more.'

'And then, what did you do?'

Rudra laughed. 'I ran away to the school. Women's tears, that's not for me. I can't deal with that.'

'I never had such desires until recently,' he confessed. 'I just did not have any sexual thoughts. Not even masturbation.'

I found this unfathomable. 'What? You never even masturbate? How can this be? Surely that's not normal.'

'I was never interested in it. When I was a child, a boy told me that you could get pleasure from touching yourself... down there. He told me how to do it. So one day, I tried. But after a couple of strokes, I gave up. I did not see the point.'

'Wow,' I said, 'that's unusual.'

'Yes, it might seem strange,' Rudra responded sullenly. 'But for me, *they* are strange, doing this.'

'Darling, remember I used to be a woman-hater,' he added with a smile. 'For most of my life, I thought that women are below me. Why would I want to associate with them? I kept well away. Yes, we used to watch porno movies when I was in the army, a lot of them, every weekend. But secretly, I always felt sick inside when I saw that stuff.' He frowned.

My relative openness about my body and sexuality was in stark contrast with Rudra's shyness and rigidity. The more I got to know him, the more I uncovered the confusion he harbored about sex. On one hand, he felt its pull and desired it. 'You will teach me, yes?' he asked, eyes glowing with keen excitement.

On the other hand, he saw sex as a shameful weakness, something that needed to be overcome and controlled. Much of this ambivalence was certainly influenced by his training in the *sannyas* tradition. Like many Eastern spiritual masters, Guru-ji advocated a strictly celibate lifestyle. Lust and passion were seen as enemies, and loss of semen equaled loss of power and *prana*.

His views on sex were also strongly conditioned by the society he grew up in. As I rapidly and harshly found out in my first weeks in India, sexuality was deeply repressed in the East. Sex before marriage was taboo, which led to an unhealthy over-sexualization in males that resulted in leering, harassment and the general perception that foreign women were sexually free and thus, fair game. This was mainly due to the great popularity of Western porn movies.

Indian men seemed to love and resent this in equal measures. They wanted to experience and enjoy sex, but deep down, some saw us as harlots that deserved to be treated with contempt. 'Honey, we're *casteless*,' laughed Korean Hee one afternoon. 'That means we're worse than untouchable to them!'

I'd seen these double standards over and over in my father's native Sicily: the men sowed their seeds generously with the droves of foreign women who lined the beaches every summer. Ironically, most of them had Sicilian girlfriends, too: girlfriends that were expected to remain virgins and stay at home with their parents until they married. If a Sicilian woman rebelled, she was regarded as crazy, loose, immoral – a slut. Although I was used to these concepts, I just didn't think to apply them to India. It never failed to amaze me how similar Italy and India, Italians and Indians, were.

Unfamiliar with this mentality and how deeply it ran in the national psyche, I crashed into Rudra's world with my enthusiasm for free love and sacred sexuality, a world that was as alien to him as his was to me. I simply presumed that he thought along the same lines, because he was Indian and worshipped Lord Shiva, who was the God of Tantra and the erotic consort of Shakti after all. Back then, I believed that all Indian men were masters of Tantra, breast-reared with the knowledge of the *Kama Sutra* and no hang-ups about the divinity of lovemaking whatsoever.

1.19: An Ideal Husband

'Darling, could you imagine settling down in India? Move over here, live with me and get married?'

My body stiffened. The question shocked the life out of me. Even though it was all I had wished for, all I could think of since I'd met Rudra, when he asked me that question, I had no idea how to respond. *Oh, he doesn't mean that,* my mind piped up. *He's only saying that in the moment.*

I stared into space and remained silent. The moment passed. I still don't know why.

I sometimes thought that Rudra would have made an excellent husband. Every evening during the *aarti*, I watched him intently from my place in the temple at the right side of the altar. The tender way he looked at the huge portrait of Guru-ji during the *aarti* spoke volumes. While he carefully cleaned and anointed the Guru's wooden sandals, he lovingly gazed up from his kneeling position at Guru-ji towering above him, as if conversing with him in a secret language. It was clear that he adored the idol and would have done anything for him.

Despite his outwardly stern demeanor, Rudra had a loving and passionate nature. He cared deeply about the children he taught, the pilgrims, and the villagers he treated. Yet, because of the robes he wore and the restrictions they signified, he couldn't overtly show his care, especially not physically. Hence, his love poured out twice daily through his ritual act of worshipping Guru-ji in the *aarti*. This devotion and surrender, in a marriage, could have been hugely transformative – or suffocating.

Of course, a relationship with a dead Guru who could not talk back surely was easier than engaging deeply with an actual person. Or was it? Maybe the challenges were just different. I was often amazed how Rudra could perform the same ritual and the one same song twice daily every day, 365 days a year, and still manage to do so with presence and passion. He always seemed fully focused and engaged during the *aarti*. It would have driven many others, including myself, crazy after three months, let alone eight years.

When I watched Rudra's communion with Guru-ji, I was reminded of certain strands of Tantra, in which one is encouraged to see one's partner as an embodiment of God/dess, and treat him or her accordingly. Wasn't this ultimately what life was all about – to recognize that we were all aspects of the Divine, that we *were* the Divine?

Even though *sannyasis* claimed to lead a life of detachment, this seemed only partially true. Great love and devotion often existed between master and disciple, and although the relationship was platonic, it carried challenges similar or sometimes even greater than that between husband and wife. *Sannyasis*, like the rest of us, were always in relationship – either with a living Guru, or a dead one, to whom they were completely surrendered, at least in theory.

Rudra was so devoted to Guru-ji that it was impossible to talk about religion with him. Where it concerned his spiritual path, he was a self-professed fanatic. All that mattered to him was Guru-ji – not even the Hindu Gods could reach his status.

'I don't care about the Gods,' he once confessed. 'Not about Shiva, not about Parvati – none of this means anything to me. Just him.' He pointed at the crooked picture that hung on his wall. 'Just Guru-ji.'

I never knew how to react when he said things like that. Sharing my Beloved with a dead Guru was strange, especially because I still hadn't warmed to Guru-ji. His portrait continued to give me the creeps. I was comforted by the fact that he was dead. And at least Rudra didn't love another woman.

I couldn't relate to this obedience to a Guru. I hadn't grown up in a Guru tradition and was somewhat suspicious of them. I knew that some Gurus carried out amazing humanitarian and spiritual work, but ultimately, I found the concept of human deities that were revered even before God alienating. In India, it was common for people to have a Guru, a spiritual teacher. The Guru signified a Supreme Divinity that shed the light of knowledge onto the darkness of ignorance. Not only could the Guru impart important spiritual practices, s/he also was there to help you to rise to your highest nature and thus become self-realized. In return, complete surrender and unquestioning loyalty was key.

The concept sounded intriguing, but friends' disillusioning experiences of harsh tests and abandonments the Gurus employed to test the disciple's devotion and 'purify' them had left me wondering whether this power could not be abused. Some of the pot-bellied, seemingly mercenary Gurus I had met during my stay in India did not exactly strike me as examples of supreme enlightenment.

With a smirk, I recalled a meeting I had with a 'tantrik full-fledged Guru', who, after an initial meeting to see whether I wanted to take yoga lessons with him, sent me amorous e-mails adorned with roses and hearts. And I was familiar with the dark tales of sexual abuse, corruption and alcoholism that surrounded some well-known Gurus such as Sai Baba and Chogyam Trungpa.

Yet, I had trained with a spiritual teacher in Glastonbury for many years and it had been an invaluable experience that propelled my life to different heights. I just wasn't sure whether harsh treatments by Gurus could really strip devotees of karma and whether it was not simply an excuse to control insecure people that were desperate to escape an unhappy life.

Rudra dismissed all of my questions about Guru-ji. 'Please don't say anything about my Guru,' he warned me. 'I love you, but I love my Guru-ji, too.'

Instead, he handed me a little book that had been written by a disciple. It gave an idealized version of Guru-ji's life. The book told me that Guru-ji advocated the virtues of manliness, virility and a form of self-sacrifice that bordered on the heroic. Like many of his Vedic contemporaries, he condemned sexuality, and his teachings were based on a strict set of morals and ideals. Why exactly he'd been deified was beyond me. Yes, he'd set up some ashrams and uplifted poor communities, but did this make him a Saint? Reading between the lines, my uncomfortable feelings about him remained.

'You know, Guru-ji appeared to me one time,' Rudra confided. 'One night, I could not sleep because it was all getting too much. I was sitting outside on the ashram landing, praying and despairing. I had no idea how I could keep going. We did not have enough money, there was no water, and we were extremely understaffed. Suddenly, I had a vision. Guru-ji appeared, and he was *huge.*'

Rudra paused in awe as he remembered the apparition.

'He was bigger than the ashram, and I saw him holding the building in his arms. *You think* you *hold much?* he asked me. *Do you see how much I can hold?* This brought me to my senses. And do you know what happened the next day? Some people came to the ashram, and they said they came from an organization that awarded grants to *sannyasis.* So they gave me a lot of money in cash for the ashram, and it was exactly the amount of money that I needed to get us out of trouble. The water returned at the same time. I never doubted again after that. Life can get tough here, but Guru-ji is always looking after me.'

I wasn't surprised. I had experienced such synchronicities myself various times in my life, although, of course, they were not related to Guru-ji. Prayer and belief were powerful forces.

It was at this point that it dawned on me how much the boundaries between religion and spirituality could blur in India.

When we in the West think about India, we often think about spirituality that is somehow different from organized religion. I remember how exotic it all seemed to me when I first arrived in Nepal and later, India. I was completely charmed by the sight of young men placing their right hands on their hearts and bowing their heads devotionally when passing temples, and the overt display of the manifold Hindu Gods everywhere, from shop windows to rickshaw dashboards and bedrooms. I loved the way spirituality seemed so entwined with mundane life, even in the younger generation.

Hee, whom I had taken to calling Korean Kali because she was ever intent on shattering my illusions, educated me once again. 'To most Indian people, all this *puja* is just like drinking *chai*! They grow up with it!' she remarked when I enthused about a young Indian man's devout activities. And, when I thought about it, would I find it so enchanting if I was in Europe and saw young men making the sign of the cross and carrying pictures of Jesus around with them everywhere?

To the average Indian, reciting the Vedic mantras and appearing for *puja* seemed to mean little more than what reciting 'Hail Mary' and attending church on Christmas Eve might mean to a notional Christian in the West. Worshipping a dead Guru-ji's painting and wooden sandals was therefore not all that different from praying to Jesus on the cross and taking Holy Communion. Ultimately, a lot of Vedic knowledge had been institutionalized and confined into organized religious groups that in reality often acted in ways that were quite removed from the wisdom they preached.

1.20: Emerging Shadows

With all my experience in affairs of the heart, maybe I should have known that our untainted bliss couldn't last. One afternoon after school, I was on the ashram's landing with half a dozen girls who were waiting to have their homework checked when my mobile phone rang. It was Rudra.

'I love you, I love you, I love you,' he whispered. 'Please come and meet me now. I am in the room next to the old professor.'

'I'm checking homework,' I said. 'I'll be with you shortly.'

When I was done, I walked down the stairs and stopped abruptly when I spotted Rudra. With nothing more than a *dhoti* wrapped like a big nappy around his pelvis, he stood barebreasted in the corridor, looking like a wrestler before a fight. The door of the room in which we had agreed to meet was wide open.

This being India, I was shocked. If somebody were to see him standing there like this, with me in his vicinity, they would quickly catch on. In addition, his energy was boisterous and aggressive. When I approached him, I could see that his eyes were clouded and bloodshot.

'What are you doing?' I hissed. 'Why are you dressed like this?'

He looked at me defiantly. 'Today,' he responded grimly, 'I want to go the whole way. I want to live.' His eyes darted wildly from left to right. I'd never seen him like this before.

We entered the dimly lit room and Rudra closed the door behind us. My instincts rebelled. Something was very wrong. As so often, I ignored them. When Rudra hugged me, I noticed a strange smell. My nostrils recognized the pungent aroma, but my brain didn't connect. It made no sense. Rudra kissed me urgently. I tasted his mouth with my tongue. Again, that familiar smell. Now it was mixed with a bitter taste. I pulled away and looked searchingly into his eyes.

'Do you... *smoke*?' I asked.

His eyes widened. 'Smoke? No, of course not.' He shook his head.

'Strange,' I said, 'you smell of smoke.' I was sure that that's what it was. Or could it be particularly strong incense?

'Oh, must be from the pilgrims,' he mumbled and averted his eyes.

We lay down on one of the beds and embraced each other. Today, Rudra was like a different person. When he touched me, he did so roughly, almost aggressively, and he spoke to me harshly and impatiently.

'I'm cold,' I said.

'Well, dress yourself properly then,' was his indifferent reply, and he pulled at my top. 'Look at what you're wearing.'

'Scratch my back,' he commanded suddenly. 'Now. Come on.'

I scoffed. 'Forget it. Not if you talk to me like that. What's the matter with you today?'

He exhaled with irritation and pushed me. Not violently, but enough for it not to be a game. I looked into his eyes and was surprised to see fury in them.

At this point, I got up from the bed. I didn't know what was going on with Rudra, but I didn't like it.

'Where are you going?' he demanded. 'Lie back down.'

'I'm leaving,' I said and walked towards the door.

'Don't go out now. Somebody might be in the corridor!' he said quickly.

'Well, go and look and let me out then,' I replied. 'I'm not staying a minute longer. I don't know why you're acting like this today.'

'Acting like what?' he asked. 'What do you mean?'

'What do I mean? You know exactly what I mean. You're so aggressive today. I don't know what got into you. You talk to me like I'm a slave, you push me, you look at me in that way...' I trailed off.

We stared at each other for a moment.

'I'm sorry,' he said. 'Please don't go.' He walked towards me and took my hands.

'I am going. I don't want to be treated like this. Have I done something to upset you?' Tears started to well up behind my eyes.

'I'm sorry. Please stay.' He hugged me.

I was confused. What had happened to the sweet Rudra I knew? Why was he behaving like this out of the blue? Had I done something wrong?

'I'm sorry, darling,' he murmured into my ear, still holding me tightly to his chest. My body was rigid, resisting his touch. I tried to pull away.

'I am just tired. I have hardly had any sleep. Every time I fall asleep, somebody knocks on my door. *Swami-ji* this and *Swami-ji* that, all the time they come with problems. Pilgrims arrive in the middle of the night, one after the other, and every time I have to get up and show them their room.' He sighed. 'And they have no gratitude. All this, and they still complain and argue about the price of the room.'

I relaxed a bit. Maybe he was really just stressed and sleep-deprived. I surrendered to his touch and hugged him back.

'I am still going to leave though,' I said. 'I want to go and rest.'

He held me to his body. 'So much anger, and so much love,' he murmured. 'One minute, you are so angry, and then you are loving again. You are so sweet. So sweet and so innocent.'

He let me go and opened the room's steel door a crack. He looked from left to right, then indicated that the path was clear.

'Nobody there,' he said, 'Go. See you tonight.'

With a sinking heart, I slid past him and left the room.

The strange mood between us continued. Tired after the evening *aarti*, and still hurt and confused about what happened in the afternoon, I lay down on my bed and fell asleep.

At ten thirty pm, I was woken up by urgent knocking on my door. Drowsy and barefoot, I tapped across the cold concrete floor to open it. Rudra frowned at me from the dark landing, his robes wrapped tightly around his upper body.

'Where are you?' he demanded, urgently.

'Sorry, I must have fallen asleep,' I mumbled, rubbing my eyes. 'Come in.'

'No, I can't come in! Don't you understand?' He looked impatient. 'I am waiting for you badly! Get dressed and come to our room.'

He walked off resolutely. Rudra's bossy tone annoyed me, but I decided to let it go. I threw my Tibetan blanket over my shoulders, slipped into my sandals and followed him down the stairs. In the room, I lay down on the bed.

'How can you fall asleep?' he challenged me. That harsh tone of voice again. 'The best man of your life comes along, and you fall asleep!'

Still drowsy, and irritated, I shrugged my shoulders and curled up on the bed beside him. After some unsuccessful attempts to wake me, Rudra accepted my tiredness and we called it a night.

1.21: Secrecy

Rudra's behavior became more erratic over the next days, and I responded in kind. He was increasingly possessive and dominant. He tried to tell me what to do and when, and planned my time for me without consulting me.

'We will meet this afternoon at three o'clock,' he'd say brusquely.

'And what if I have other plans?' I'd ask, incensed. 'Does it not occur to you that you could ask me if I want to meet you at three o'clock?'

Being used to unlimited freedom, I found Rudra's assertiveness difficult and intrusive and was often confrontational in response. The more he told me to do something, the more I reacted and did the opposite. Our relationship increasingly resembled the power struggle of two control freaks.

'Who do you think you are? Not even my own father tells me what to do! Do you think *you* can?' I'd challenge him.

Rudra found this puzzling. 'Darling, I'm not trying to boss you around,' he'd say, 'really. You misunderstand.'

'Well, it sure sounds like it. You are the one who's trying to call the shots all the time. You determine when we meet, and for how long, and now you even want to tell me where I have breakfast and with whom. I mean… *please!*'

I was still annoyed because that morning, he had instructed one of the ashram workers to deliver breakfast to my room, though I cherished going to the kitchen myself every morning to have a talk with the boys.

Rudra couldn't understand my indignation. In his world, men were used to telling women what to do, and this was seen as protective and caring, not controlling. He could not understand my strong reactions when, in his mind, he simply wanted to look after me and make sure that I was alright. In his case, it was probably amplified because as the ashram head, he was used to giving orders and having people follow them without question or backchat.

The secrecy and pressure that surrounded our relationship didn't leave me unaffected either. The discordance often made me sarcastic and provocative, as though it was all his fault. I was raging against fate in a desperate attempt to control the uncontrollable, because I felt deep down that our story was doomed to end before it even had a chance to begin properly.

I tried to stay centered. I knew that rough patches in relationships were normal, but it threw me that they had emerged so soon. Time distorted, contracted and expanded here in the Himalayas; we lived through the different stages of our relationship in days rather than weeks or months.

Yet I loved Rudra and wanted to stay calm during this difficult time. And for that, I needed to keep up my spiritual practice and get enough rest. Maybe we were just tired from the lack of sleep and bewildered by the speed at which things had developed between us.

And it wasn't like the sweetness had left completely.

'Please can you come into the office and see me after the *aarti*?' Rudra asked me before I left his room that afternoon.

'But why?' Evenings were his busiest time, and the office would be crowded with eager pilgrims jostling to book rooms, ask questions and complain. He had no time to talk to me then. Was this another attempt to boss me around?

'Just briefly,' he said. 'It gives me energy if I see you even for a moment.'

My heart melted into a puddle.

'Really?' I asked. 'Okay. I'll come by. But for what? I mean, I should have at least a reason. Otherwise, what will the people think if I just loiter around the office?'

'Invent something,' he suggested.

I was touched by Rudra's request. I was convinced that he didn't notice me when I went back to my room after the evening *aarti*. He was always so serious then, negotiating with the pilgrims until late in the evening.

As it turned out, I was wrong. He saw everything. He'd even recap what I was doing during the *aarti* – how I sat, what I wore, at what point I had gone to the altar and whether eager Indian pilgrims had pushed me out of the way – although I had no idea how on earth he could see this when his eyes were firmly fixed either on the harmonium or on Guru-ji.

From that evening on, I'd invent little reasons to come to the office, such as borrowing matches or a pen. He found this endearing; I felt self-conscious. Perhaps I was paranoid, but I was convinced that people suspected us of having an affair. Our conduct around each other was too familiar, and I spent a lot of time in the office, sitting opposite Rudra on the low chair in front of his desk. Sure, we were surrounded by school books in order to pretend that we were engaged in planning classes, but I still had an inkling that people knew, especially those that lived in the ashram.

I was particularly sure that the old bespectacled professor from Bengal knew. Brows furrowed, he would regard me seriously, and I believed, suspiciously all the time, even during the *aarti*. When I was in the office with Rudra, he would appear as by magic and sit with us, and to make matters worse, his room was right next to the one in which Rudra and I sometimes met at night. 'This is too risky,' I would protest. 'What if the professor sees me going in or out?' It could easily happen.

Rudra wasn't worried. He would openly have intimate conversations with me in English when other people were around, presuming that they did not understand us. Once, he pressed his leg against mine when we jointly tutored some children on the landing; another time, he made suggestive comments about our pastimes in a classroom with a group of students surrounding us. I always admonished him when this happened; not so much for my sake, but for his. I figured that one revealing, overheard remark could seriously compromise his position. I would only face ejection from the ashram and perhaps a little embarrassment, but for him, much more was at stake.

He was careless around the ashram boys as well, such as during one afternoon, when we sat in the temple at *pranayama* time after an argument. Rudra wanted to discuss our relationship there and then, while two of the ashram boys cleaned the altar.

'I don't think this is the appropriate place to talk about these matters,' I said quietly and motioned towards the workers.

'Oh, don't worry, they don't understand,' Rudra brushed my concerns aside.

'They may not understand the language, but they will pick up what we're talking about anyway. These people are not stupid!' I protested.

He merely laughed. 'Darling, they are ignorant. They are uneducated boys. What are you worried about? They do not know anything.'

I wasn't convinced.

One of the boys in particular, Parmod, Rudra's right-hand man, had started to flash me a shrewd smile whenever I passed him, whereas previously, he had ignored me. A couple of times I had encountered him late at night outside the office when I crept out of Rudra's room. I didn't think that he had ever explicitly seen me coming out of the room, but he had to be wondering why I wandered around in the dark ashram at two am with a *dupatta* around my head.

In addition, the ashram's water tank was on the roof right opposite my room. The boys spent a lot of time up there to check the water supply, and would frequently see that my room was locked from the outside with a padlock until the early hours.

Eventually, Rudra began to listen. He told the boys that 'Ma'am' had come to his room to use the bathroom. I didn't think that they bought these stories. First of all, I had my own bathroom, and secondly, a *sannyasi* was not allowed to be alone in a room with a woman. Everybody knew this, and Rudra's secret bedroom was especially out of bounds.

'You know Indian culture so well,' he purred admiringly after I warned him once again that we had to be more careful. 'You understand it perfectly. Outwardly, you may be loud and boisterous, but inwardly, you are quiet and you love peace. You are ninety-five percent Indian, five percent European.'

Maybe this was so, but it wasn't so much that I wanted to preserve an outward appearance of virtue and piety, as implied by his remark. I didn't believe in Guru-ji's views on the evils of carnal desire, but I was uncomfortable with the secret meetings and the constant fear of being caught. I knew how much the ashram boys, the children and the pilgrims respected and loved Rudra.

Rudra became aware of it, too, when, one day, he returned to our room with a pensive look on his face.

'God,' he said, 'these people love me so much! This old man, out there just now, he praised me for leaving my family, gave me some money because he knows I have none of my own, and he touched my feet. And here I am… with a girl in my room. If he knew…' His uneasiness was visible beyond the smile on his face.

I knew what he meant. Fair or not, the rules were as they were and Rudra had chosen to live the *sannyas* life that was, after all, based on celibacy and renunciation. Was risking all this worth it? Was it selfish and immoral of me to engage in this relationship, knowing what was at stake for him? Should I, should we be stronger and support each other in honoring his vow and the commitment he had made? Or should we just accept things as they were and make our own rules? It was a dilemma that never ceased to haunt me.

1.22: The Blue-Eyed Hermit

That evening, I climbed up a hill near the ashram to the site of a little temple dedicated to Shiva and Parvati. I needed some time by myself to reflect. A tiny, dusty path led past the mud hut of an elderly hermit who looked after the temple. Al Pacino had originally introduced me to the old sage. He'd often sit in the hut as I passed by, tend his sacred fire, and invite me in on occasion to share a cup of *chai* with him.

The hermit had long white hair and an even longer beard, and possessed the clearest eyes I had ever seen. Of a color reminiscent of Mediterranean skies, they were so deep they seemed to continue for miles. Looking into his eyes was like embarking on a journey. The expression I found inside of them was so pure and compassionate that it convinced me that he truly was a Saint. He spoke little and seemed content with quietly caring for the temple and engaging in spiritual practice.

The site overlooked the hills and their platformed fields, all the way across to the Himalayas. The sunsets could be spectacular, drenching the hills in a golden light. The temple housed a big Shiva *lingam* and various stone statues, as well as a trident in the center. Sometimes I longed to stay there with the hermit and live the simple life of an ascetic in quiet contemplation of the beauty of nature; away from the complicated entanglement that was currently unfolding in mine. Being here was like visiting a secret fairytale world, so different from the reality I knew. I sat down on the little stone wall that surrounded the temple to observe the horizon and contemplate the vastness of the Himalayas.

Further afield, village women in colorful saris carrying wicker baskets on their backs worked on the layered fields from dawn to dusk. I heard their voices tinkling like chimes in the evening stillness. When they saw me, they called out to me laughingly and I waved at them. The women looked graceful and feminine even on the fields, adorned with headscarves, bangles, jewelry and make-up. Yet, like the Goddess Kali, they also carried sharp sickles and knives for cutting the plants.

There were even tigers roaming in the village. I never saw one, but we frequently heard reports of their nightly tearing of buffaloes, and I was warned not to go out after dark.

What awed me most about the mountain village was its stark colors. Everything looked and felt so richly vibrant: the bright red, yellow and blue flat stone houses, the blossoming trees, the fragrant purple flowers, the vivacious people, and the razor-sharp contrast of the Himalayas against the brilliant sky. Sometimes I felt like I was looking at a photoshopped version of reality. Surely this wasn't real? Everything seemed magnified. Or was it simply that I lived more intensely?

I turned towards the altar and watched the hermit as he swept the floors of the temple with a battered straw broom. I reflected on what had happened in the last couple of days. I was upset at how things had developed with Rudra. Why was he behaving like this all of a sudden? Everything had been great between us, and now he had turned into a control freak. I wasn't happy with how I handled the situation, either. Why did I let him provoke me, and why did I react so strongly? Couldn't I just laugh it off and ignore him?

I couldn't. Maybe I was over-sensitive, but Rudra's bossy manner hurt me deeply. I thought we'd live happily ever after, but my old, unhealthy relationship pattern with men had reared its head again. I recognized these power struggles from my other relationships and knew how hard-headed I could be, too. But whereas previously, I'd usually been the antagonistic one, now suddenly the tables had turned. Why did it always have to be that way? Why was there always some drama? And why couldn't I just be in a normal, respectful relationship with a man? Perhaps I should just forget about relationships altogether and live a simple life, like the blue-eyed hermit, who now carefully poured water over the Shiva *lingam* to clean it.

I sighed. As disappointed as I was, I didn't want things with Rudra to end. I was too much in love with him by now; hooked on the passionate, magical moments we'd spent with each other. I knew he was The One, the man I'd been waiting to meet for so long. I wouldn't let those little clouds ruin our love. Maybe he was just irritated about something else and his behavior would revert back to normal soon. Yes, that was probably it. I'd just ignore it and carry on as normal.

Stubbornly, I pushed my intuition, which tried to tell me a different story, out of the way.

I got up to take a stroll to the market. As I slowly wandered up the mountain road, I smiled at the beautiful, fragrant flowers that grew on the side of the path. Suddenly, my eyes widened. To my left was a deep gorge filled with a mountain of discarded plastic bottles and bags. Hundreds of them. I scowled. As remote as the village was, it had not stopped plastic from getting there. I'd seen this in Rishikesh, too, where the Ganga was so littered that a *sannyasi* took initiative and founded a recycling company called 'Clean Himalaya'.

'Why is this so?' I once asked a fellow traveler. 'How can anyone litter such a magnificent landscape?'

Apparently, he said, plastic was an evil that Western civilization had brought with it. Indians previously had reused everything and were still not used to the concept of non-biodegradable, non-reusable objects. But was this really so? I found his response a little patronizing, and considering that we faced similar problems in the West decades after the introduction of plastic, it did not ring true. Surely, anyone could see how unsightly these heaps of rubbish were. Even the ashram entrance was littered with empty bottles, crisp bags, and other rubbish.

Disturbed by this sight, I planned a litter-picking outing with the students to teach them about environmental awareness. Perhaps some discussion around plastic coupled with practical action would be a start.

'Do this outside of school hours,' Rudra suggested when I told him about my idea. 'It's not in the curriculum. And besides, we have a cleaner who tidies up outside the ashram.' I could see no evidence of it, and started to pick up bits of rubbish myself in the school breaks. It made little difference.

In the market, I ran into Kavindra, the friendly NGO worker. Together, we walked along the main street and I was glad for the company. Despite the turmoil I was experiencing with Rudra at the moment, I still adored my new life in the village. Most of all, I loved the villagers. They were quite different from the people I had met elsewhere in India: open and friendly without being pushy, and there was a certain pride about them. The village was well-kept, and although poverty existed, it seemed that it was taken care of within the community.

Mod-cons were scarce, which only added to my feeling of having landed in a different world. It was possible to buy what one needed, but there was little variety. Food consisted primarily of a limited range of vegetables, generally potatoes and cauliflower; fruit meant bananas and oranges. Luxuries like contact lens solution, which I needed, did not exist in the mountains.

'Indians are not good with contact lenses, Ma'am,' the friendly chemist laughed when I asked him for it. 'We prefer spectacles!'

Internet was hard to come by, too. There was one expensive computer and telephone shop, run by the studious Manoj, a middle-aged man who spent more time outside than inside his shop due to the frequent electricity cuts, but it was not worth using. It took about half an hour to load a page and, if you were lucky, another thirty minutes to send an e-mail.

My little shopping excursions to the village could sometimes be highly amusing. Tonight, I was on a quest to buy some eye make-up remover. This turned out to be an arduous undertaking, as nobody seemed to understand what I wanted, despite Kavindra's helpful translations into Hindi. 'But how do Indian women remove their make-up at night?' I asked. *They* all wore eye make-up. Surely they needed to remove it, too. The moustachioed men that manned the shop counters shrugged their shoulders. Such matters did not concern them.

Kavindra seemed confident that this challenge could be overcome. Together we wandered from shop to shop, hunting for the elusive eye make-up remover. Soon, once the strange request of the *angrezi* lady had made the rounds, half the village was on our trails, eager to advise me where I could obtain the object of my desire.

One lady suggested sweet-smelling rose water. Another pointed at a bar of soap. A third one thought that facial cream might do the trick. In the end, I settled for a small bottle of baby oil.

I loved these little adventures. An act as mundane as buying a cosmetic item could turn into an exciting and highly amusing event in which I'd meet new friends and learn more about the foreign culture I had landed in.

1.23: Spiraling Deeper into the Cauldron: The Awakening

Back at the ashram, I deposited the newly acquired baby oil in my bathroom and looked into the mirror. I grimaced. The combined stresses of teaching, lack of sleep and my secret relationship with Rudra were beginning to have a visible effect on me. My pale face contrasted with the dark circles beneath my eyes, and I was losing weight rapidly.

I also noticed it in school where I found it increasingly difficult to stay cheerful, alert and patient while teaching five or six classes every day. The children were perceptive like sharks. When I was calm and in a good mood, they would be as meek as the infant Samuel at prayer. If I showed any weakness, such as tiredness or impatience, they'd pick up on it instantly and make my life hell. They'd be unruly, inattentive, talk and fight in class. I had to make sure I was in top form.

To regain some equilibrium, I told Rudra that I wouldn't meet him any longer at night. Instead, I would try to go to bed at nine pm so that I was able to offer my best teaching. Surprised, he looked up.

'You're so professional,' he said, not without admiration. 'You're even compromising your love life for your teaching!' He tried to change my mind, but seeing that I wasn't to be swayed, gave in eventually.

I began to realize what being part of Rudra's life really meant. Unable to show affection openly, our relationship consisted of stolen moments here and there. His life was filled with duties to the ashram, the needs of the pilgrims, school, and his patients. There was no space for a woman.

I started to question myself whether being with him was worth it. In the precious time we spent together, I was convinced that it was. My attachment to him grew daily. A smile, a word from him was enough to lift my spirits on a stressful day. Relationships, I thought then, were challenging, but when you found your soul mate, you did what it took to be with that person. And despite the difficulties in our relationship, I had no doubts that Rudra was my soul mate. We understood each other too well for it to be otherwise.

And after being with Rudra for some time, I noticed a strange shift in my personality: for once, I was giving without reservation. I was giving love, time, energy and commitment without necessarily expecting a return. This was quite unfamiliar territory to me, for whom relationships had thus far primarily consisted of unspoken contracts: 'I do this if you do that'.

Previously, everything had to be on my terms. Here, I found myself surrendering. I could live with and accept the noise in the ashram, the austerity, the bland, greasy food, the big hairy spiders and bugs that crawled across the ceiling of my room, the cold-water bucket washes, the four am starts and lack of sleep. All these outer circumstances didn't matter because of where I was, because of who I was with, because of the magical energy that existed between Rudra and me. I still had my inflammatory temper, but I noticed a gradual softening happening inside of me.

In the midst of my stay in the ashram, I was as usual sitting cross-legged on the bed in Rudra's semi-dark cave, where nothing but he and I existed. On this day, Rudra left the room to attend to some pilgrims. Waiting for his return, I surveyed the tiny space with my eyes. What a strange existence he lived, I mused. I looked at the ever-present crooked picture of Guru-ji, swathed in his flowing orange robes; the stacks of rupees that sat in a cardboard box on the small table; the water jug; bits of old food; the muddle of papers and random objects.

There was also a small, flat glass bottle on the table. It was facing the wall so I couldn't see its label, but it looked like a whisky bottle. Curious, I leaned forward to pick it up. 'Gin', the label read. *How did this get to be here?* I wondered. Maybe somebody left it at the ashram. I opened the bottle and smelled it. Yes, it was gin alright.

Bemused, I placed the bottle back on the table, and as I did so, noticed a wastepaper basket on the floor next to the bed. It was crammed full of empty gin and whisky bottles, interspersed with empty cigarette packets. I had to close my eyes and look again. No. Surely not. This could not be. Dumbfounded, I sat back down on the bed.

That moment, Rudra entered the room and tried to kiss me. I recoiled and looked at him. 'What is it?' he asked. 'Are you alright?'

I took a deep breath. 'Can I ask you a question?'

'Sure,' he said.

I pointed at the bin. 'What is this? Why do you have a bin full of whisky bottles and cigarette packets in your room?'

Rudra avoided my gaze. 'Oh... the pilgrims left these behind.'

'Really? So why do you collect them in your room?' I frowned.

'I also use the alcohol to mix into my Ayurvedic remedies.' His eyes darted from me to Guru-ji, and back.

'Really? Why?' I edged forward on the bed and picked up one of the bottles.

'I have to do this. The pilgrims don't believe that the medicine works otherwise.' He was now looking straight at me. I held his gaze.

I thought it unlikely that this amount of alcohol was needed for the minuscule preparations but remained silent. Sensing that I was not convinced, Rudra became defensive.

'Are you accusing me of being an alcoholic?' he asked brusquely.

'No,' I retorted. 'I'm just asking you a question.'

Eventually, Rudra admitted that sometimes he drank little bits of alcohol. But really, eighty percent of it belonged to the pilgrims. After a few more minutes, he confessed that yes, he had an alcohol habit, an unfortunate hangover from the time he spent in the army.

I couldn't believe it. Was this a bad joke? *Sannyas* and the yogic tradition were based on renunciation. One of its conditions was to abstain not only from sex, but also from all intoxicants. *Sannyasis* lead a very simple life, with the aim of purifying body, mind and spirit to loosen the attachment with the material world. The theory is that by living this lifestyle, the spirit becomes very refined, enabling more subtle spiritual practices which in turn could facilitate the path to enlightenment.

In my naivety, it had not even entered my mind that a *sannyasi*, especially one of Rudra's standing, could be indulging in intoxicants. Neither did I think that, knowing the impact intoxicants could have on one's spiritual progress, he could be interested in doing so. Obviously, the Universe was intent on shattering my illusions.

'Are you insane?!' I asked, glaring at him. 'You're a *sannyasi* and you drink hard liquor? Are you kidding me?'

He remained silent and started to pace around his little room.

'Haven't you tried to stop this?' I asked after a while.

He exhaled sharply. 'I tried many times, *many* times, to leave this habit. But I cannot. Even my medicines have failed me.'

Quietly, I continued to look at him.

'You know, and sometimes, I cannot sleep. There is always stress, noise, pilgrims, and I get fed up with this. And then... I drink.' He burst into tears.

Let me wake up from this nightmare, I prayed. *Can this get any more surreal? I'm having a love affair with an alcoholic* sannyasi *in the Himalayas? Surely I'm dreaming this.*

'Please don't leave me because of this,' Rudra implored me. 'I don't want to lose you.'

I felt numb and betrayed – not only because my illusions were shattered and because he had kept his addiction a secret from me. Most of all, I felt deceived by fate. How ironic all of this was. *Finally a centered, spiritual man,* I had thought when I first met Rudra. *A religious man who lives only for the good of others and for his spiritual practice.*

With the scars of growing up with an alcoholic mother still etched deeply into my psyche, this discovery was a double slap in the face for me. I thought that after my chaotic relationship with Steven, I'd cured myself of my fascination with troubled men. Evidently, this was not the case. Paradoxically, like Sleeping Beauty, I had met what I tried to avoid the most.

Now what?

I needed to get some fresh air and process these new developments that were unfolding in the drama of my life.

'Please don't go,' implored Rudra and grabbed my arm. 'Don't leave me.'

'I just need some time to think about this,' I said, now more softly. I got up and turned to leave. 'I want some space. We'll talk later.'

Looking dejected, Rudra opened the door and I left.

I grabbed my journal and a pen and left the ashram to find a spot in nature where I could sit quietly for a while. As I left the ashram, I ran into Kavindra, who attempted to walk towards the village with me. However, I wanted to be alone now. Where could I go and be undisturbed? I asked him. He pointed towards a nearby hill. If I climbed it, he said, I would find a nice, quiet place to sit. I said I'd call him after I was done so that we could eat together and visit the evening *aarti* at a nearby Shiva temple.

I sat on the hill overlooking the valley for a long time. Different thoughts and questions swirled around in my mind as I stared into the distance from my elevated nature seat. My feelings were a mix of disillusionment, hurt and empathy. How could this have happened – again? How could I let myself get involved with an alcoholic? An alcoholic in disguise at that. And how could I not have noticed sooner? It just wasn't fair.

Yet, part of me related to the 'holes' in Rudra's character. They made him more human and reflected the interplay of light and dark that made up all of us. Perhaps, I wondered, when there was so much light in a person in that he performed so much good work for others, maybe this light had then to be balanced with facets of extreme darkness? After all, there was no day without the night to contrast it; good could not exist without a concept of evil. And ultimately, were not these differences all in our minds?

Maybe the *sannyas* lifestyle that expected Rudra to be 'holy', good and perfect all the time had to take its toll somewhere? Maybe the pressure to perform was too much for young men who lived in the slums one minute and were elevated to super-human status the next.

Whatever it meant, this was the moment at which I began to see Rudra for the person he really was. I began to see his compulsions, insecurities and hypocrisy, as well as his strength, idealism and beauty. It was interesting to notice this after such a short amount of time, something that could take months or years in other, less intense relationships. And somehow, I liked the challenge of sharing his darkest secrets and seeing him fully naked, stripped of all illusions, and loving him regardless.

My trust was bruised, however. But hadn't it been obvious right from the start? Did I really think that a *sannyasi* who only too readily invited me to his room and did all he could to seduce me could truly be committed to his spiritual path? Had the red flags not been there all along? And had I not ignored them only too happily?

And what was Rudra doing in the clothes of a *sannyasi*, wrestling with his demons? Guru-ji strongly advocated self-control, abstinence and honesty, yet Rudra didn't fare too well on any of these counts. I wondered what kept him here. Why did he squeeze himself into such a rigid framework if he was not convinced about its relevance or strong enough to follow through? And how was it possible for a *sannyasi* to buy alcohol and cigarettes? It wasn't exactly like he could go to a shop and buy them in his renunciate's robes. Did he have an accomplice?

Frustrated, I picked up a stone and threw it towards the ashram that towered beneath the hill I sat on. What should I do now? Leave? Stay and see how things developed? I had no idea. Maybe I needed to sleep on it. If only Kassandra was here! She'd know what to do.

My instincts told me to take a step back. There had been talk about marriage and my moving to India, but now I felt again that I wanted to transform the romantic feelings we had for each other into something stronger and ultimately more sustainable. There was a lot of emotion between us, but what was it actually based on? On a human level, away from a deep feeling of spiritual and intuitive connection, we hardly knew each other.

And, I reasoned, I wanted to go back to Europe after all. Perhaps I could come back to India in the winter and see how we viewed the situation then. If our feelings for each other were still strong, then we could see what to do about them. Maybe, I thought, trust really needed to grow slowly.

After some more brooding, I decided to make my way to the village to meet Kavindra. In the midst of all this turmoil, I felt blessed to have a friend outside of the ashram.

After a pleasant evening with Kavindra in the village, I returned to the ashram ready for an early night. Just as I was about to retire, Rudra came to my room and asked if we could talk. I still felt too distraught and wanted to sleep on it, so postponed the meeting to the following day.

I felt more centered the next morning after my yoga practice.

Rudra slunk around with hanging shoulders and repentant eyes. We agreed to meet in the afternoon after school. In the convoluted conversation that followed, filled with questions, accusations and apologies, he promised me that he would stop drinking. Today. *Now.* Rudra was convinced that Guru-ji had sent me to the ashram so that I could point out and correct his shortcomings.

'Right,' he said. 'This is it. From this moment, I will not drink anymore. It's in the past. You give me the strength to do that. This is my wake-up call. I will be a good *sannyasi* from now on.'

He asked me to chide him to keep him on the right track. 'A good wife does this,' he reminded me with a raised index finger.

'Does she?' I replied wearily, suppressing a sarcastic comment about good *sannyasis* not having wives in the first place.

'Please don't leave me in the ashtray,' he pleaded. 'Please help me to overcome this addiction.'

I was doubtful. I didn't want to play the role of rescuer. I had tried this before with my mother, then with several men, and it had never worked. I knew the begging, bargains, disappointments and manipulations of a co-dependent relationship only too well.

'What can I do? Only you can decide to stop drinking. I can't do this for you,' I finally said.

'You could say that you will leave me if I don't stop this.' Rudra pointed at the bottles that were still in the waste basket.

I shook my head. 'I'm not going to do that.'

'Please give me another chance.' His eyes searched mine.

My head was spinning as I experienced a range of conflicting emotions. Some were of a compassionate nature, but mainly, I was consumed by self-righteous anger. Part of me could not fathom how Rudra could have been ordained at the ashram for almost a decade despite breaking most of its rules. For all of these years, he had been deceiving his Swami-ji, and all of the people that respected him as a noble *sannyasi*.

When Rudra saw that I was not to be swayed, he threatened me with suicide. He could hang himself, he said, and if I didn't believe him, I'd see the consequences by the next morning. At this point, I had enough. What *had* I managed to get myself into, and more importantly, how could I get myself out of it again?

My remaining reason was rapidly vanishing into quicksand. I wanted to run, and yet experienced a strange sense of loyalty, a hook that kept me rooted to the spot with a strong urge to resolve and fix the problem. It felt like a matter of life and death.

I should have just left. Instead, I stayed, and ultimately, unfathomably, spent too much time with Rudra that afternoon. At some point, I made the mistake of touching him, and all my resolves of dissolving the relationship melted away. Hormones and need, a desperate need to make it all come alright, took over. I took his hand and looked at him for a long time, tears filling my eyes.

'You have no idea how much I love you,' I said, and meant it. My mind was horrified. *Where is* that *coming from?!* it asked. My heart shrugged its non-existent shoulders.

Dejectedly, Rudra looked at me, then averted his eyes and shook his head slightly. I suddenly felt humiliated. 'What is she doing?' his eyes seemed to say. 'After all this, she *still* wants to be with me?' It appeared that, as soon as my resolve to remain distant had faltered, his respect for me had dropped. Trying to make my words come undone, I talked, justified myself, asked questions, but Rudra remained sullen and silent. Eventually, I got up to leave and we parted without saying goodbye.

1.24: The Confession

I felt dreadful the next morning. I saw Rudra from afar on my way to school. He stood on the rooftop as the children were doing their morning exercises. Our eyes met briefly, but neither of us smiled. In the morning break, I took my breakfast alone at the Moustachio Place. Rudra was nowhere to be seen. I tried to be cheerful, but felt sick with worry and confusion on the inside. Were things between us over?

At the end of the school day, I walked slowly towards the ashram with a stack of books in my arms. I hadn't spoken to Rudra all day. Suddenly, my heart jumped. He was hovering outside the ashram gate.

When he saw me, he frowned. He looked away and I thought he was going to walk away. My heart sank. Would he tell me that it was all over and that I should leave? I'd reached him by now and wasn't sure what to do. My eyes sought his.

'Do you want to meet after lunch?' he asked me quietly, lips barely moving. His eyes scanned the Himalayas.

'Yes,' I replied, relieved.

I walked past him to the ashram canteen. I had lunch with Rakesh and Uday as usual, but felt distracted. As soon as I had cleared my tray, I made my excuses and left.

Rudra was already waiting for me in his office. I slipped past his desk behind the wardrobe and into his unlocked room. He followed me and locked the door behind us.

'I'm sorry,' he said and kissed me. 'I am sorry about this situation. And I am sorry about not telling you earlier.'

'It's okay,' I said, though I didn't mean it. My stomach still felt like a thousand ants were crawling around inside it. After what I'd found out the day before, I didn't really want to be here – and yet, I was relieved that Rudra seemed to want me still. I felt like a death row prisoner whose execution had just been averted.

'I thought about what happened yesterday,' he said. 'I am happy that you found out. It will encourage me to stop these habits. Guru-ji sent you. I am convinced of that. He wants me to amend my ways and he has brought you here so that you can help me and point out my shortcomings.'

Even though I was relieved that we were talking, I was still angry and confused. I'd been ruminating about the situation for the past twenty-four hours, and thought that maybe I'd found a solution.

'I don't judge you for your addiction,' I said slowly. 'Everyone makes mistakes. But you have to get yourself out of this mess.'

'I know,' Rudra said and took my hand. 'And you are going to help me with your love.'

'Do you know what I think you should do?' I continued. 'You should tell your Swami-ji about the alcohol. It's only fair.'

'Oh, no, no,' Rudra said quickly with a shake of his head. 'He is too busy. He has many things on his mind. I can't bother him with this.'

'But it's the only correct thing to do! Rudra, you've been deceiving him for almost ten years! You run this ashram by yourself and you have a raving alcohol problem! Do you see the irony? You're a renunciate! Renunciates don't drink and smoke! It's only a matter of time before it comes out anyway.'

Rudra shifted around awkwardly.

'Why don't you confess and let him decide what to do about it?' I pushed on. 'Maybe he will help you. He is your superior, after all. I'm sure he has enough compassion to offer his help. How else are you going to get yourself out of this mess?'

He picked up a medicine bottle from the table, looked at it, and put it down again. 'Maybe when he is less busy. Right now, it is not possible.'

'This is ridiculous,' I spat. 'So what exactly are you going to do? Put your head in the sand and hope it all goes away?'

Rudra just shrugged his shoulders. 'Guru-ji will help me. I

trust in him.'

'Yeah, right,' I replied. 'Look, Rudra. You're a great teacher, a great *pujari*, and I'm sure you're a great Ayurvedic doctor, too. I respect you for all that. But this,' I tugged on his robes, 'this you don't deserve to wear. You're not a renunciate. You don't follow any of the *sannyas* rules, do you?'

Ouch. I could see the pain on Rudra's face. Had I gone too far? We lapsed into silence. I sat on one end of the bed, staring into space, Rudra on the other. After ten minutes of silence of which I felt every painful second, he shifted. His words seemed to come from out of nowhere.

'You know, my father killed himself. He committed suicide, because of me.' He paused. 'I never told you that.'

He leaned back towards the wall with his arms crossed. He looked up then with eyes so anguished that it sent a dagger through my heart. Not knowing how to respond, I just waited. We sat in silence for a while.

'Why because of you?' I finally asked.

'When I joined the ashram, my parents did not want to accept that I had left for good. My father continued to call me on my mobile phone. I was in *sannyas* training – a very tough, austere training – at the time, and asked him not to contact me anymore. It was against the rules. A *sannyasi* has to cut all contacts with his family for good.' Rudra ran his fingers through his hair and looked straight at me. 'What if it came out that Rudra, one of the best new recruits, was still speaking to his father? What would that look like? So I stopped taking his calls. And then… he killed himself.'

I was too shocked to speak. Instead, my body tensed when I tried to imagine the blow Rudra must have felt in his body when he heard that news. And the regret.

'I did not find out for over a year.' He shook his head despondently and looked towards the floor. 'The information reached the ashram, but they did not tell me.'

'They did not tell you?!' I sat up with a jolt. 'What?!'

'No,' Rudra sighed. 'They did not. They thought, *Rudra, he is a good man. We do not want to lose him. If we tell him, he might leave.* Do you know how I found out? I was in Varanasi one day, for training purposes. By chance, I met my brother there, and he told me. *You did not know?* he asked me. No, I did not. I did not even have the chance to perform my father's funeral rites, as is custom for the eldest son.' Tears filled his dark brown eyes. He blinked them away. 'He had predicted that.'

I edged forwards on the bed to sit next to him and took his hand into mine. He pressed my hand slightly as he continued.

'You know, one time I even ran away from the ashram to see my mother. I just had to meet her after that.' His voice trailed off. I hugged him tightly and together we sat on the bed in the darkened room. The words stayed in the room, like witnesses, resonating. We breathed them in and out.

Suddenly, I could feel the enormity of what Rudra was carrying. I began to see the agony, guilt and confusion that must have accompanied his decision to renounce ordinary life to become a *sannyasi*. I felt the conflict between his chosen path, his parents' wishes, and the rules imposed by his superiors. In Rudra's society, things were black and white. If you wanted to follow the path of God, you had to cut the ties. Unlike in the tantric tradition, on his path the separation between spiritual life and earthly existence was distinct. Detachment was paramount, as was self-sacrifice for the good of society.

A cold anger overcame me. How could they, the Gurus and holy ashram men, speak of love and compassion, the very qualities that were supposed to be at the root of all spiritual paths, and then impose such rules on their followers? How could it be right to conceal the death of a *sannyasi*'s father out of fear of losing a 'good worker'? How could this be truth, and how could it be based on free will?

I wasn't at all surprised now that Rudra was drinking.

I had absolutely no idea how to handle the situation. If I left the ashram now, I'd lose Rudra and leave him alone with a destructive addiction. That didn't feel right. But what would happen to me if I stayed? I didn't want to be with an alcoholic. I knew I couldn't deal with it.

It was a nightmare. I was damned if I stayed and damned if I left. Distraught, I churned it over and over in my head, prayed and wrote pages upon pages into my journal. I texted friends. I even called my mother for advice, who'd been so thrilled initially when I told her that I had fallen in love, even when she found out that Rudra was a monk.

Mum was shocked. 'So what are you going to do now?' she asked.

'I don't know,' I cried into the phone from my room. 'I have no idea what to do.'

'I can't tell you what you should do,' she said. 'But it might be best if you leave him to his monkhood. He will not change, at least not soon. And you mustn't talk him out of being a monk. Don't do this under any circumstances. This is his spiritual path and only he can decide what to do.'

I knew she was right. 'Yes,' I mumbled, 'maybe it's best if I just leave. I'll sleep on it.'

'I'll pray for you,' Mum said. 'Let me know what you decide.'

Bless her heart, I thought. I was happy that Mum and I had such a close relationship now and that I could tell her almost everything. Not long after I had left home, Mum had stopped drinking from one day to the next, without any external help. She'd just resolved to stop and has never touched alcohol since. I was proud of her for this. Maybe there was hope for Rudra to do the same?

But no matter how much I meditated and talked to others, I still couldn't make up my mind. My heart desperately wanted to stay with Rudra, and my mind told me to get the hell out of the ashram.

And so I did nothing. Our daily meetings resumed, with a slight shift in focus that now centered on alcohol, mainly through my challenging and confronting him about his use of it. Our relationship had entered a new dimension – more dramatic, more torturous, and ultimately, more honest.

Now that I shared his darkest secret, Rudra told me more about his life. Tales he had not confided in anybody for years, or perhaps ever, tumbled out of him in daily monologues. It was like he'd waited for this opportunity to be real with somebody for years. I'd sit and listen, ask questions, and comment from time to time.

'You are the closest of the close now,' he said. 'I am telling you everything.'

1.25: The Three Stooges

In the midst of all this, three *sannyasi* colleagues from Rudra's tradition came to visit the ashram for a few days. They were somber, middle-aged men with shaved heads who reminded me of the Three Stooges. Wrapped in the obligatory saffron robes, they peered at me curiously in the mornings during *pranayama* time, but otherwise remained distant and silent. The devout trinity often sat together in Rudra's office and conversed with him way beyond ten pm, which made our meetings more difficult.

Rudra was irritated by their presence. 'What are they doing here?' he complained. 'Can't they see that it's high season for us? No, they come here, occupy a room and of course pay nothing for it. And I can't even say no, because they're *sannyasis*, like me.' The trio even visited his room once, he said. Luckily, by now, he had removed all of the whisky bottles and cigarette packets that formerly graced his abode so conspicuously.

Nevertheless, Rudra was a gracious host, and put on a school display in honor of the three *sannyasis*. One morning, when I walked to school, the children all stood military-style on the landing, singing and drumming the Indian National Anthem like a band of skipjacks, while a solemn-faced Rudra, flanked by the Three Stooges, looked on. I smirked and placed myself behind Rudra.

'So you put on this performance for them?' I whispered in his ear. 'Impressive!'

'Yes, well,' he retorted, still with a deadpan expression on his face, 'we do need to make a good impression. They will go back to their ashram and report.'

The energy between us was still volatile. Good moments of intimacy and tenderness could change into torturous drama, usually accelerated by Rudra's intoxication and my reaction to it, from one minute to the next. We'd fight, make up, fight and make up. It was exhausting, to say the least, and reminded me of my parents' highly explosive marriage, in which the violence that took place every evening was replaced with apologies and silence the following morning.

Yet, I couldn't let go. Neither of us could. Somehow I thought that our connection was a karmic knot that we needed to work out. We were soul mates and had met for a reason. It was only a matter of time before we would overcome the challenges of addiction and *sannyas*, and live happily ever after.

Every day, I practiced the art of letting go. When I meditated or wrote into my journal, my heart opened and I could see the big picture. It was in these moments that I often felt peaceful and immensely grateful for what had happened. The Universe had brought me the man I'd prayed for, and though challenging, I had the sense that all would end well eventually.

Outside of this state of acceptance, it wasn't so easy. I tried to release my need for perfection and my ideas of how people and life should be, but weren't. Most of all, I tried to accept Rudra as he was. I realized how judgmental and insensitive I had been. His addiction had nothing to do with me and had been there long before I was. He would stop drinking when he was ready to do so – or he wouldn't. It was his choice, and not my problem to solve. Instead, I tried to overcome my own addiction to relationships with unavailable, volatile men.

It was hard. I recognized that I had always loved from a place of need and lack, rather than from fullness and joy. I sensed that it could be different, and daily, I read a quote by the Indian mystic Osho I had come across a few weeks earlier:

When your love is not just a desire for the other,

when your love is not only a need,
when your love is a sharing,
when your love is not that of a beggar but an emperor,
when your love is not asking for something in return but is ready
  only to give
– to give for the sheer joy of giving –
then add meditation to it and the pure fragrance is released.
That is compassion, compassion is the highest phenomenon.

I worshipped this quote. My soul desperately wanted to experience a higher form of love, but my mind didn't know how. I felt like a toddler who knew it was possible to walk but fell flat on her face time and again. Every so often I'd get a glimpse of insight and feel that I had grasped that all-encompassing love. Then I'd run to Rudra to apply my newfound knowledge, and something unexpected would happen, something that pushed all my buttons and which would completely pull me the opposite way again.

It had been like that the day after the Three Stooges arrived. I came to his room, excited and looking forward to seeing him. I'd just meditated on Osho's quote. I understood that love meant letting the other be how he was. Today, I'd be compassionate and accepting. I'd be the most loving woman on the planet. I'd show Rudra what true love was, how real lovers behaved.

I sat down on his bed with some homework I wanted to mark. He leaned over to kiss me. The pungent scent of cigarette smoke hit my nostrils. Irritated, I jumped up.

'Did you have to smoke? It's disgusting,' I snapped. 'You know how much I hate it!'

Rudra shrugged his shoulders. 'So? I just had a cigarette.'

His nonchalance infuriated me even more. 'I'm leaving. Kissing you is like kissing an ashtray.'

We stared at each other for a few silent minutes, neither of us wanting to give in. A quiet little voice in the back of my head informed me that I was acting like a brat. *You're ruining every-thing*, it said quietly. *This is crazy. You love this man. What happened to your compassion?*

The voice was shut up by another part of me that was stronger and actually didn't give a damn. That part was violent and controlling. It was hurt and outraged, too. All that seemed to matter to this part was to win, even at the cost of losing the man I adored. *I won't be seen as weak*, it cried. *He won't walk all over me!*

I knew this part well and actually, I hated it. It had often emerged in my other intimate relationships. It was destructive and unreasonable and I was powerless against it in situations like this. It was like there was an open, weeping wound inside me, and when it was touched even lightly, I'd erupt in a rage. This was mainly in circumstances in which I felt that the other had betrayed me.

Later, after I'd calmed down, I'd often see that the situation was entirely different from what I'd imagined, and that I'd interpreted things in a different way than they were intended.

I knew all this, and yet I still couldn't stop it. Being with Rudra was like a rollercoaster ride. I was forever running away and coming back to him. He was forever apologizing and disappointing me. Love was swiftly becoming my spiritual practice.

1.26: The Sacred Marriage Rite

During sunrise one morning, a few days after I had discovered Rudra's addiction, I felt unusually calm. Instead of going to the temple, I decided to meditate in my room. Sitting on my bed, I closed my eyes and focused on *ajna* chakra, the point between my eyebrows. I slowly and deeply breathed in and out through my nose for several minutes.

I smiled softly. I felt relieved, as though something heavy inside of me was dissolving. A warm glow and a sense of peace spread through my body, and my muscles relaxed. In my internal world of altered consciousness, where everything made sense, I was completely filled with divine love. It felt exquisite, so sweet that it almost took my breath away.

With my eyes still closed, I had a vision. I felt the presence of Lord Shiva behind me and saw beautiful Parvati, the Divine Mother, in front of me. Together, they held hands around me and surrounded me with so much light and compassion that I wanted to cry with happiness. Lord Ganesh, their elephant-headed son, sat on my lap and playfully made me laugh.

Suddenly, I clearly heard the following words in my mind:

Remember the spirit of love today, of surrender, of softness. You can't fight fire with fire, rock with rock. With flowing softness, move around the obstacle. In time, love softens the hardest of hearts.

Tears of understanding started to run down my face. I suddenly recognized that I had tried to block and control what I really needed to surrender to: the flow of love. I'd placed conditions and expectations on an energy that just was as it was; something that was unconditional and free. It didn't care about addictions, social status and cultural differences – it just was. Yes, Rudra and I were in a challenging situation, but who knew why? And who knew what the future held?

I resolved to enjoy the moment as a gift from the Gods. I

reasoned that it was they who had brought Rudra and me together, so they'd take care of the rest as well. I would trust from now on.

That moment, I heard more words in my mind:

What belongs together can't be separated by sheer will; and if it does not belong together anymore, it will part. Just let things run their natural course – don't block them.

I knew then that I was going to surrender. Tonight was the night; I wanted to make love to Rudra. I wanted to unite with him, become a physical part of him just as our souls had united who knew how long ago. We had talked about the possibility of making love, but I had not been sure if I wanted to take that final step, given how volatile things were between us.

Today, in the sweetness of my meditation, it felt right. Of course, my mind wondered whether it was a good idea.

Where is this coming from? it cried, outraged. *Are you crazy? You've only just found out that Rudra is an alcoholic, and now you want to make love to him?!*

But heart was not to be reasoned with. It didn't care what the circumstances were. It just wanted to love.

I physically desired Rudra more strongly than I remember desiring anybody else in my life. This potent physical attraction was mutual, and it kept us hopelessly entangled. Even though deep down I feared it might be a bad idea, the sexual chemistry between us was simply too strong. I was tired of doing the right thing. I wanted to live in the moment. Sod the consequences. Shakti wanted to unite with Shiva. Energy wanted to manifest.

'Okay,' I said to him that afternoon, 'tonight's the night. But please stay sober. I don't want alcohol to mix with the sacred energy of love.'

At this point, I don't believe I knew what I was doing any longer. I was in too deep.

When I entered Rudra's cave that night, small candles illuminated the room, and the sweet fragrance of sandalwood incense softened its edges. I was pleased to note that Rudra had honored my request to stay sober. His eyes were clear, and when I kissed him, toothpaste was the only thing I tasted.

Quietly, we sat absorbed in each other's presence for a while. Nervous anticipation danced in Rudra's dark eyes and united with the flames that flickered brightly in my heart. Tentative words and timid movements transformed into passionate kisses. Inquisitive hands freed smooth skin from rough fabrics. Hair brushed teasingly over limbs, tongues caressed delicately, teeth bit gently.

Time and space melted and wove new patterns in the intimate dance that ensued between Shakti and Shiva that night. We tasted and touched each other with awe, enchanted and overpowered by the archetypal energies that manifested themselves through our bodies. Our lovemaking felt monumental, and yet as familiar as the joining of two long-lost parts that had only been pretending to be separate.

In this ancient language of love, I gave myself to Rudra without reservation, heart and soul. All our human limitations and differences seemed a dream now that faded into insignificance. In the love that was the Source of all things, we were united beyond duality and separation – beyond male and female, light and dark, human and divine. Waves of gratitude leapt through my body. It had all been worth it.

After infinite whispered vows and tender kisses, we parted with great difficulty in the early hours of the morning. A soft, sweet energy lingered between us as I slipped over the threshold of our secret den.

'I will never forget this night,' Rudra smiled, eyes ablaze. 'Will you?'

Slowly, I shook my head, before I turned and floated up the stairs into my room.

1.27: The Curse of the Kali Priest

The next morning, Rudra knocked on my door at five am. Rubbing the sleep from my eyes, I opened the door and squinted at him questioningly.

'I just wanted to see you,' he smiled softly.

Tenderly, I returned his smile. Memories of the previous night flooded my consciousness and made my body tingle.

'It's so nice to see you,' I said. We dived into each other's eyes for a few moments and he turned to leave. My gaze followed him until he was out of sight. I stretched, closed the door and crawled back into my warm bed. Life could be so blissful.

A couple of hours later, I got up and dressed. I would have liked to stay with Rudra and relish the glow between us all day, in particular as it was Sunday and neither of us had to work. Yet, perhaps foolishly, I had arranged to visit a nearby Kali temple with Kavindra. I thought of canceling the outing, but then considered that it might be good to have some distance and fresh air after this powerful experience. I also didn't want to let Kavindra down. So, even though I didn't really want to, I left the ashram. Rudra made no objections and wished me a nice time.

What followed was a strange and somewhat dark day. Kavindra and I spent an eternity in the village's marketplace, trying to catch a jeep to the next town. This task seemed near-impossible. I still carried the energy of the previous night within me, and felt incredibly tired because I had only slept for two hours. Exhausted, I sat down on some steps and apathetically watched Kavindra as he hailed down jeeps and rickshaws whose drivers shook their heads and shrugged their shoulders. Eventually, he secured us two spaces in a crammed jeep. Squashed between women, men and children, we slowly drove down the winding mountain road towards the next town. There, we looked at bustling shops selling colorful fabrics and religious items, and visited an evocative water temple dedicated to Shiva and Parvati.

After we had eaten some lunch of *dhal*, *rotis* and *sabji* in a small canteen in the market, it began to rain heavily. We ran across the street and sought shelter in a *chai* stall. Two tall, stylish *sadhus* kept us company. With their smooth, near-aristocratic features, immaculate robes and glistening ornaments, they seemed more suited to the pages of Indian *Vogue* than to the hardships of a wandering ascetic life. Their curious, alert eyes expressed great interest in my garnet jewelry, which however was no match for the chunky crystals, rings and silver bangles they had adorned themselves with.

Once again, I was fascinated by the different facets of *sadhu* life: what could be better than to wander through India, wild and free as the wind, with your best friend in tow? I imagined the two dandy *sadhus* traveling from village to village, not knowing where they would rest their heads that night, meeting new people and living different experiences all the time. With their mischievous grins and sharp savvy eyes, those two reminded me of daredevil Casanovas that smuggled jewels through the Rajasthani desert and had a different girl waiting for them in every town. My traveling soul yearned to join them.

Two young women from South India sat nearby with an assortment of necklaces, bangles and earrings spread out on the table in front of them. This was probably what had brought the two dandy *sadhus* here. With not much else to do, I started to browse through their wares, and finally bought two matching necklaces with red and white beads, symbolizing the male and female energies; red for Shakti, white for Shiva. In Tantra, these colors stood for the menstrual blood of the woman and the semen of the man – both were revered as sacred because they contained the life force. I wanted to give one of the necklaces to Rudra when I left.

Finally, Kavindra spotted a shared jeep that was headed in the direction of the Kali temple. '*Chalo, chalo!*' he urged me on from the other side of the road, and obediently I trotted through the rain to join him. As I was about to climb into the jeep, a young moustachioed man came charging at me from the right, pushed me out of the way and swiftly took a seat in the vehicle. Bewildered, I looked first at Kavindra, then inside the jeep. 'After *you*, Sir!' I finally addressed the Moustachio ironically, as I followed him into the jeep's interior. He responded with a blank look.

This discourtesy towards women was a phenomenon I had observed all over rural North India. Sometimes, I would stand in a shop, in the middle of being served, when an Indian man would enter and direct some Hindi phrases at the shopkeeper. Invariably, my custom would be forgotten and the man would be served before me. I generally tried to remain equanimous throughout these irritating incidents, but once lost it completely in a mobile phone shop when it happened one too many times. Alarmed, the shop boys called my friend Anand and asked him to calm the 'crazy foreigner lady'.

'Why do men treat women without respect in your country?' I asked Kavindra irately while glaring at the culprit, who sat opposite me. Kavindra shrugged and looked uncomfortable. He probably didn't know either.

It was still raining heavily when we arrived at the Kali temple. We jumped off the jeep and sought shelter at a tea stall, whose kindly owner asked me to sign his guestbook and lent me an umbrella. Kavindra and I scurried down the muddy path towards the temple complex, dedicated to Kali, 'the black one'.

Kali is a Hindu Goddess, symbolic of dissolution and destruction. She is often portrayed wearing a necklace of severed heads and yielding a sickle in her hand. Although sometimes misrepresented as dark, violent and merciless, she is generally understood as the compassionate Mother Goddess of Time and Change. Devotees believe that Kali helps them to let go of what is no longer needed in life, similar to a mother who takes a harmful object out of her incomprehensive child's hand. We might not understand or like it when things come to an end in our lives, but with hindsight, when we see the big picture, we often realize that it was for our best and that our greatest learning occurred through loss. Viewed metaphorically, what Kali really destroys with her sickles are the demons of ignorance and ego. Nevertheless, in some places, older incarnations of Kali prevail, and in those temples weekly animal sacrifices performed to appease her still take place.

Unsurprisingly, this Kali temple was an eerie place. The octangular outdoor shrine was painted the color of blood and housed a large icon of Kali in the center. Despite the gloomy weather, a large number of pilgrims were chanting and praying to the Goddess on their knees. Devotees offered flowers, coconuts and incense to the priests that mingled among them and conducted small *puja* ceremonies by reciting mantras and giving blessings – for a fee. A tall, moustachioed *pujari* made a beeline for me and asked where I came from. After some pious small-talk, he scribbled down his address and telephone number, so that we could 'write to each other'.

When I first noticed how blatantly religion is intertwined with commercialism in many Indian places of worship, I was taken aback. The relationship between deity and devotee here is very practical, based on 'give and take'. You have a wish, and the deity grants your wish if you pay the priests for it. It's as simple as that. I thought back to how I once visited the banks of the Ganga in North India. I had purchased a little flower boat from a girl with the intention of floating it down the river with my prayers. Just as I had lit the incense and candle and was about to immerse the flower boat in the water, a warden accosted me and asked for money. I asked him to be patient as I was in the middle of performing my ritual, but he continued with his mantra-esque requests for money – '*Ma'am, donation for Ganga, five hundred rupees, Ma'am'* – until I sent him away rudely to continue in peace.

It wasn't that I was averse to contributing to the upkeep of temples or river maintenance – it was the insensitivity with which these requests, and often demands, would be carried out. Without fail, the priests always approached right at the moment of prayer or ritual and often interrupted me crudely, even when I was obviously chanting mantras or meditating, and would not relent even when I politely asked them to wait until I was finished.

There were of course exceptions, but as a whole, it was all long lines of pilgrims with rupee notes, coconuts and flowers in hand, most of which would be tossed carelessly onto a huge mountain of offerings that had built up behind the priests. 'Don't give them anything,' my friend Sanjay advised me whenever we visited a temple. 'They are just greedy. Prayer is enough. You come to God with an open heart and you bring offerings if you want, but what matters is your heart, not your money.'

The rain did not stop, so we decided to wait in the *chai* stall opposite the temple. My new *pujari* pen pal joined us. It was cold and wet, and, instead of showing signs of stopping, the rain became torrential. A big thunderstorm brewed, and soon the earth shook with fierce roars. I shivered in my thin *kurta* and stared listlessly into the rain. This whole trip had been a bad idea from the start, and I wanted to go back to the ashram.

By now I was cursing myself that I had forsaken a cozy Sunday afternoon with Rudra for this soggy nightmare. As so often in the mountains, my mobile phone had no reception and I could not even call him. My mood did not lift when news reached us that there would be no jeeps back to the ashram because of dangerous landslides caused by the weather. A little earlier, we had joked that the Kali priest had invoked the storm because he did not want me to leave. Now our joke of having to spend the night at the temple had become a real possibility.

To distract myself, I thought back to the first time I became aware of Kali. Many years ago, a boyfriend gifted me a framed picture of the fearsome Goddess on the battlefield. Naked, eight-armed and blue, she stood on the lifeless body of Lord Shiva with her long red tongue outstretched. A garland of severed men's heads dangled from her neck, while she yielded a large blood-stained sickle in one of her hands. She looked utterly terrifying. Who was this awesome Goddess, I wondered, and why was she dancing on the corpse of another God? Why did Shiva look so blissed out as he lay beneath her feet?

As intimidating as I found the image, something intrigued me about Kali in equal measures, and without knowing much about her, I kept the picture in my temple room for years. It was not until much later, in fact, until I wrote a play about Kali in the form of a female suicide bomber from Palestine that I began to understand the transcendental meaning of the myths surrounding her.

In one of the stories, powerful demons have taken over the realm of the Gods. Despairing at the havoc these creatures cause, the Gods ask Shiva, the most powerful among them, to intervene. Born from his wife Durga's brow, an angry Kali springs forth and begins her battle against the powers of evil. She is so powerful that nothing can stop her, and ultimately gets carried away in her killing spree.

When all the demons are dead, she starts destroying everything else in sight. To stop her, Shiva goes to the battlefield and calmly lies down beneath her. Shocked by the realization that she has trampled on her husband, Kali sticks out her tongue in astonishment, and her homicidal rampage comes to an end at once. Thus, by surrendering to her at the height of her rage, Shiva manages to pacify her.

There are many interpretations of this myth. In some of the Tantric texts, the Goddess is naked because she is beyond all illusions, and her red lolling tongue represents the passion and creativity of nature. She stands on the lifeless corpse of Shiva and awakens him. Without Shakti, the feminine life force, Shiva is inert. Shakti is the 'i' in Shiva, without which he becomes *Shva*, meaning corpse. Yet, the interplay is mutual: Shakti equally has to combine with Shiva, consciousness, for creation to take place.

Eventually, the rain became lighter, and a number of Indian families who had been fidgeting restlessly in the shack decided to brave it and venture outwards. Kavindra and I followed suit. There was so much water on the road that we had to take off our boots and roll up our trousers to wade through the newly formed, muddy river.

By now, I was laughing. What else could we do? The situation was too bizarre. As we had been told, there were no vehicles whatsoever. So, to keep our spirits up, we began to walk barefoot along the road, trying to avoid the rocks that had tumbled from the mountains as best we could. After about an hour's hike, a jeep appeared on the horizon. Like the drowning shipwrecked, we started to wave our arms wildly to hail it down. The driver just shrugged his shoulders apologetically and drove on – the vehicle was full. So we continued to walk. Dusk set in. We crossed more puddles the size of small lakes and tried to forget that new landslides could hit us at any moment.

Eventually, after what seemed an eternity, somebody gave us a lift back to the market town where we had eaten our lunch. From there, it again took many failed attempts to find transport back to the ashram. In the end, we half-walked and half-hitch-hiked, with long frustrating waits on dark, cold roads. Exasperated and frozen to the bone, I arrived at the ashram late in the evening.

The Sunday *havan* fire ceremony had already started. Although I had been really looking forward to it, I did not have the energy to go to the temple. Instead, I crawled into my bed and covered myself with as many blankets as I could find, and listened to the congregation's chants from my room. I was annoyed with myself. Why did I go on this stupid trip in the first place? Why had I not stayed here, enjoyed a relaxing day with Rudra, and participated in the fire ceremony? I pulled a blanket over my head, yet failed to warm my icy limbs.

Eventually, I dragged myself out of bed to have some dinner in the canteen. I was still freezing and arrived wrapped in my Tibetan blanket with a hood pulled over my head. The canteen was packed with hungry pilgrims who eyed me curiously. For once, when my dinner arrived within minutes, I was grateful for the preferential treatment the ashram workers gave me. I quickly devoured my food and went to see Rudra in his office to tell him what had happened.

'Where *were* you?' he asked with concern when he saw me. 'Why didn't you call me?'

'Why didn't *you* call me?' I asked. 'It was raining. I had no reception.'

'Yes, we also had none.'

We looked at each other for a moment.

'Did you miss me?' I asked playfully, after I had filled him in on the day's disastrous events.

'Not at all!' Rudra thundered authoritatively, and smiled disarmingly at the same moment. I melted.

In a moment of recklessness, I leant over the massive desk towards him and kissed him lightly on the cheek. His eyes grew wide.

'In the office!' Mock outrage and pleasure fused in his eyes.

Smiling, I stood opposite him. Looking to assess whether the air was clear, Rudra ushered me into his room and locked the door behind us.

'Have you decided how much longer you are going to stay?' he asked.

'Well, how much longer do you want me to stay?'

'Stay until the end of the month, until your visa runs out,' he suggested.

That was another two weeks. I wasn't sure if I wanted to stay that much longer, given how volatile things had recently been between us. And I was afraid of falling even deeper in love with Rudra and thus having a harder time leaving later on. I called the airline company but delayed making a definite decision until later.

Something in Rudra was changed since this morning. He appeared happy to see me, but once we were in his room, he refused to kiss me. Instead, he started to give me a sermon about the dangers of physical love. Sex, he said, caused only attachment, jealousy and possessiveness. This was not exactly what I expected to hear after our passion-filled night and the arduous day at the Kali temple.

'You know,' he said, standing by the door of his room while I sat on the bed, 'all my life I was curious to experience sex. What is this thing that everybody is talking about? I heard people speak about it, but I could not relate. And now I can.

'Now, my curiosity is satisfied. I know what these people are talking about. And I ask you: is this, *this*, what people are hungry for?' His eyes were challenging me. I was beginning to feel nauseous.

'These urges,' he continued, 'they will not come again now for a while. My mind was polluted with sexual thoughts.'

My stomach started to cramp. Devastated by what I was hearing, I was unable to respond. Was this all our beautiful night meant to him? A satisfaction of his curiosity?

'Guru-ji teaches that we are not just the body,' Rudra said and pointed grimly at the Guru's portrait. 'He is right. This body of flesh and bone, it will decay. It does not last.'

This was enough. I jumped up from the bed. 'So this is what last night was for you?'

He didn't answer and remained standing by the door. Furious, I pushed past him and stormed through the deserted office into my cold room.

1.28: Sinking Deeper: Uncomfortable Truths

The following morning, I saw the situation with more perspective. Men always said the most stupid things and women took them too seriously and got hurt. Did Rudra really mean what he said the previous night, or was I taking it out of context and hearing it the way I wanted to – as a confirmation that he did not love me and used me for his own ends? What had really happened, and what was merely in my mind?

Nevertheless, after being so open with him – I had let him into my heart and my body after all – his words, intentional or not, hurt me. The atmosphere between us was still cold, and I was letting it be so. Not only was I tired, but I was also beginning to feel that part of me was addicted to the painful dramas that played themselves out between us.

I didn't go to see Rudra after school because I wanted to give as well as have some space to avoid an eruption of another dramatic scene. And of course, I was also too proud. Instead, I retreated to my room to write and ponder. Insights started to pour in, and as so often, I saw myself reflected in Rudra. Most of all, I could relate to his volatility.

Like me, Rudra was a person who had kept his heart closed for a long time. 'Always keep your heart open,' I often said to him, not quite knowing where these words were coming from. During our magical night, I felt his heart opening for a fraction, timid and hesitantly like a shy woman at first, then vastly, fully, and the resulting surrender was a beautiful sight. But between the veils of time and space, I also saw a man who was overwhelmed by the intensity of emotion and thus closed his guarded heart as quickly as he had opened it.

When I told him this later, he smirked and shook his head slightly. 'You know me, my mind so well. You know me better than my mother does, and she gave birth to me.'

'I think that nobody should give one's heart to anybody,' he added after a pause.

'Why?'

'Because it hurts.'

'It only hurts when you resist it,' I responded. 'Love, real love, doesn't hurt.'

Yet, true as I believed this to be, I also knew from my own experience that if one's heart had been closed for such a long time, it was often not possible to open it again without tremendous emotional pain. It was fear that had kept my heart closed for many years, fear of being hurt and disappointed, and I suspected that it was similar in Rudra's case.

Never mind traveling alone to dangerous places and working in high security prisons – it was *this* fear, the fear of intimacy and exposing a vulnerable heart that was the toughest thing to face and overcome. I was familiar with the dreaded terror of dependency, of losing myself, the panic of losing control that kept many hearts imprisoned behind barbed wire. And I also knew that when these tough walls we erected around ourselves crumbled, they often exposed a wounded, needy being that we would much rather keep hidden away.

Was it a wonder that men like Rudra, who had spent most of their life in a patriarchal society and possessed little experience of women, felt shell-shocked when confronted with such intense closeness and female sexuality? In his encounter with Shakti, the feminine principle, he found that apart from love and passion, she could evoke feelings of need, jealousy, possession and dependency, too. And of course there must have been also the guilt about breaking his vow of celibacy, which might explain the many references to Guru-ji the previous night.

In the midst of my reflections, a big, hairy orange hand appeared on the green bars of my window. A second hand followed, and soon I was again perused by the relentless eyes of my monkey companion. I sighed and hurled some scrunched-up paper at it. The animal disappeared as rapidly and silently as it had appeared.

Ultimately, I figured that Rudra's feelings about love and sexuality were ambiguous at best. 'I am losing energy through sex,' he'd said. 'It makes me feel drowsy and tired.' Unlike me, he didn't believe in the tantric way, of transcending the sexual energy to take it up into higher realms. Sexual urges were to be suppressed and eradicated completely.

In one of our discussions about alcohol, he had asserted that he did not want to stop drinking because he feared becoming addicted to 'this thing', to sex. It reminded me of a conversation I once had with a friend, who said she could not stop smoking because it prevented her from becoming bulimic again.

All addictions were the same, I mused, whether they were to nicotine, alcohol, sex or food. They were all desperate attempts to fill what I called 'the black hole', a deep existential wound that we were too terrified to face. And so we buried it under layers of chocolate and whisky, temporarily numbing and hoping to kill the monster that reared its head over and over again, begging to be seen. 'Get down!' we cried. 'You don't exist!' But time and again it surfaced, and time and again we numbed it with our drugs of choice.

How would it be if we released the suspected monster from the recesses of our unconscious mind? What would we find? And, I asked myself, never mind Rudra and alcohol – what was *my* addiction? Maybe I was like an alcoholic, too, who, although dry, needed to stay away from alcohol for the rest of her life. My drug of choice wasn't alcohol, but emotionally unavailable men with addiction problems.

This time, I had outdone even myself. Rudra was the epitome of unavailability: an alcoholic Hindu monk who was a self-professed misogynist. What was I trying to prove? That I could melt the heart of the toughest men and thus confirm to myself that I was lovable?

My unpredictable relationship with Rudra had dragged my hidden monster rapidly out into the open. Maybe it was time I took a closer look at it.

I resolved not to take Rudra's words personally and use the time to take care of myself instead. I would trust and let go, and appreciate the happiness I'd had, should it indeed be over. If he loved me, he'd come to me. If he didn't, then all I could do was to let go.

It was easier said than done. The question that posed itself over and over again was: would it be better to stay, or leave?

Distraught, I tried to calm my mind with repetitions of the *Maha Mrityunjay* mantra, the Vedic healing mantra I had recited thousands of times during a five-day *havan sadhana* in the yoga ashram.

Om Tryambakam yajamahe
Sugandhim pushti-vardhanam
Urvarukamiva bandhanan
Mrityor mukshiya mamritat

translated as:

OM. We worship and adore you, O three-eyed one, O Shiva. You are sweet gladness, the fragrance of life, who nourishes us, restores our health, and causes us to thrive. As, in due time, the stem of the cucumber weakens, and the gourd is freed from the vine, so free us from attachment and death, and do not withhold immortality.

I chanted the ancient words under my breath as I moved the *mala* through my fingers. I meditated on the meaning of this mantra often, and particularly liked the latter part, in which the gourd is freed from the vine in due time. To me, it meant that there was really no point in frantically pursuing anything, especially not spiritual enlightenment – it would happen organically in its own time. I often sought comfort in the mantra, and today prayed that Rudra would come to see me before my round of one hundred and eight mantras ended.

Sure enough, he did. He stood outside my door and regarded me regretfully.

'Do you want to come to my room and talk?' he asked, while tears started to run down my face. As usual, all of my resolve to stay calm fell away when I saw him.

Once again, Rudra knew exactly what was going on for me. He had read my fears, my doubts, my distress, and had come to my room to disperse them. It always amazed me when that happened.

'Darling, do not take what I say so seriously,' he said. 'I talked without thinking. In fact, I over-talked. I did not mean it as it sounded.' He looked at me. 'All this suffering... for nothing. You know that I love you.'

Nevertheless, I continued to feel exhausted and irritable. I had had enough of the sleep deprivation, weird food times, teaching, and being in love with an unavailable man. I didn't know what was what any longer and my brain felt like it was made from cotton wool. It was time for a reality check.

1.29: Fight or Flight

Tired of the scolding that he'd asked for initially, Rudra carried on drinking and smoking, in particular when he knew that I was coming to see him. Like a child sticking up two fingers at his mother, he had taken on a 'What are you going to do about it?' stance. Whereas before he had begged me to help him overcome his addiction, he now not only seemed resigned to it, but also used it frequently to control me.

On one of the last days of term, Rudra and I had agreed to meet after school. After enjoying my lunch in the canteen with Rakesh and Uday, I was in a good mood, and was looking forward to spending the afternoon with Rudra. I was just on the way to my room to get ready to meet him when he stuck his head out of the office door.

'Excuse me,' Rudra called out to me.

I turned my head and smiled. 'Yes?'

'I just got busy. I cannot see you today. Please excuse me, yes?'

Startled, I replied 'Okay' and continued on my way. Rudra disappeared into his office. Although I feigned indifference, my heart sank. I had been looking forward to seeing him. Moreover, I thought I knew that the reason for his change of plan was that he wanted to drink. Deflated, I sat down on my bed. What to do now? As so often in the Himalayan afternoons, the weather was gloomy. I felt alone and disappointed.

Eventually, indignation took over. *How dare he let me down for the sake of a bottle of whisky!* I thought. After all, hadn't he sworn that he would stop drinking? Once again, the familiar feeling of betrayal descended on me like a vulture. Ignoring all objections from my mind that pleaded with me to remain calm, I stormed down the stairs, into the deserted office and banged on his bedroom door.

'Anish?' I heard Rudra's muffled voice from inside his cave.

'*Kya haal chaal hai?* What is the matter?'

I didn't reply and continued knocking on the steel door. Keys rattled, and eventually, a disoriented Rudra blinked at me from a darkened room.

'Is this what I think it is?' I asked.

'Sorry?'

'Did you say you were busy because you wanted to drink?'

He didn't need to reply. The pungent scent of whisky that penetrated my nostrils told me everything I needed to know. Disgusted, I turned to leave. He followed me to the landing. Another drama ensued. Again, I said I'd leave the ashram. Again, he promised this was the last time. Again, we made up after the fight.

Feeling utterly slighted, I became more reactive and hurtful. 'Back home, I don't even have friends like you,' I'd tell him. 'Not because I think it's bad, but I'm simply not interested in being around people that drink and take drugs. If you had told me that you're an alcoholic before you decided to woo me, none of this would ever have happened.'

'How could I know that you would find out?' he defended himself. 'I thought, she is only going to be here for a couple of weeks, so why tell her about it?'

'Still, you could have told me to give me a choice! I would have never let myself become involved with an alcoholic!'

'I knew that. You are just like an Indian girl. That is why I did not tell you.'

His indifference made me furious. And of course, I was also angry with myself. Why hadn't I been more careful? Why hadn't I listened to Kassandra? Why had I been so blind? And why was I still with him?

In a quest to stop him from drinking, I tried every tactic I could think of. I was in turn kind, angry, sulky, distant, manipulative, despairing and compassionate. I implored him to think about the children. None of them worked.

'If you respected your body, you wouldn't destroy it with toxins. Do you know what you are doing to your liver? What kind of Ayurvedic doctor are you?' I confronted him.

'Maybe I do not respect myself then,' he shrugged. 'Look, I cannot leave an addiction just like that. It would not be an addiction if I could. Anyway, what do you want? When I am ready to leave these things, they will fall away. Guru-ji will see to that.'

Bravado or not, I envied his trust and surrender. It was all so simple for him. Guru-ji had brought me to the ashram, and that's why it was fine to become intimately involved with me. Guru-ji supplied the means for alcohol and cigarettes, and thus it was okay to indulge in them. In Rudra's world, Guru-ji was the divine orchestrator of everyone's life, including mine. In this way, Rudra relinquished all responsibility.

'Do you know when you're finally going to learn?' I challenged him. 'When your whole life is falling apart and you've lost everything: your job, your status, the respect you enjoy now – that's when you'll wake up and sort your life out.'

He fell silent. I left the room.

Back in the cave the next day, he brought the subject up again.

'What you said to me yesterday really hurt me. And do you know why? Because it is true. You are right. I am sinking deeper and deeper into these negative things because I can. Nobody challenges me, apart from you. And if I do not stop now, what you said will probably come true. I will lose everything.'

'Hmm,' I said. 'And then what? Are you going to return to your mother's?'

He laughed. 'You are just like a tiger.'

'A tiger?'

'Yes. You are always getting me by the throat, just like a tiger holds its prey with its teeth. And you are always right, too, and that is why I have no choice but to tell you the truth.'

I had reflected on what we had spoken about the day before, too. Rudra was a grown man, and this was his life. He was old enough to decide what he did with his body, and I suddenly felt that I had no right to talk to him as I had done. It was actually none of my business.

And I was all too aware of my own hypocrisy, too. How could I chide him for his discrepancies, and yet assist him in breaking his *sannyasi* vow to satisfy my own needs and desires? I said as much and apologized. He disagreed.

'My love, you have every right to talk to me like this,' he said. 'You are the only person that is honest with me.'

I still felt I had overstepped the mark.

'No,' Rudra said while he held my hand. 'I know why you are doing this. I know that you want me to be a good *sannyasi*, and that you want me to overcome my shortcomings. You are the one person that really sees me and above all, loves me. You love me so much. Actually, you love me *too* much.'

He held my gaze.

'I once told my Swami-ji that I was having problems with liquor. You know what he said? The same thing you have said to me. That is how I know that your words come directly from Guru-ji. He, the Almighty, speaks through you, because both of you say the same thing. Guru-ji sent you into my life to save me.'

I wasn't so sure.

Besides, Rudra's addiction was probably an open secret anyway. Now that I knew him better, I could instantly see the changes in his behavior when he had drunk, and above everything, I could smell it before I even entered his office. Surely those that worked for him and knew him saw this also. But, even if they wanted to act, what could they do? He was their boss, and if they confronted him, they could lose their jobs. It was not part of the hierarchical Indian culture to confront one's superior, or one's parents. Jobs were rare and the population large.

When I later sat in my nature place on the hill to ponder and write, Kassandra called me on my mobile phone. She was of the opinion that it was high time to leave the ashram.

'Ms Stupia,' she said, 'listen to me. You've been the biggest signpost of his life. You did what you came there to do, and now it's time to go. You won't change this guy, but at least you've been honest with him. What he does or doesn't do now with his life is not in your control.'

She had a point. Maybe everything was perfect, after all, and I just didn't see it?

A gang of mischievous schoolboys that had played at a distance from me while I was talking to Kassandra crept closer and eyed me curiously.

'Ma'am, where are you from?'

'Ma'am, what are you doing here?' they probed me. As I got up to leave, the smallest one, who was about ten years old, pursed his lips.

'Ma'am,' he whined, 'one kiss please!'

I laughed and got on my way. 'Get lost. I'm old enough to be your Mata-ji!'

The boys followed me. '*One* kiss! Ma'am. *Pleaaaaaaaaase,* one kiss!'

The beseeching mantra followed me all the way to the ashram.

1.30: Final Oscillations

In my desperation, I vented my anger at organized religion. Why couldn't *sannyasis* marry? The way I saw it, Rudra could have performed all of his tasks just as well, and possibly better, with the support of a loving partner. *Sannyas* seemed to create a lot of unnecessary unhappiness. I thought of Rudra's parents, and the sad stories he'd told me about them. How much he must have shut down emotionally in order to survive this and stay on the path. Was such severe control really necessary to serve humanity and God? And why didn't he seek help for his alcohol addiction?

But maybe it wasn't that easy. I knew that unlike in the West, where Alcoholics Anonymous and other support groups are common, in India, an alcoholic has nowhere to go to get help. Counseling, psychotherapy and support groups are not the norm as they are in the UK, especially in the rural areas. Alcoholism is therefore often left untreated, and more often than not, swept under the carpet.

In Rishikesh, I made the acquaintance of a schizophrenic man who wandered the streets begging for money, so that he could afford to buy medicines. He, a highly educated, well-spoken man, told me about the challenges he faced due to his mental illness, and the difficulties in getting adequate psychiatric care. Likewise, in some of the rural areas, women who refused to fit into traditional roles were often seen as 'possessed' and brought to priests by their families for an exorcism.

Yet, I also had to admit that perhaps, Guru-ji did have a point. I could see how sexual desire muddled my thinking, and that it was for this reason that I had ignored all of the warning signs about Rudra. Because I wanted it to be different, I failed to see things as they really were.

Things had spiraled out of control and, like me, Rudra desperately wanted to get back to some kind of normality. He tried the moral route.

'There are certain rules and regulations in this ashram, and I have to keep them,' he addressed me sternly in the cave. 'This is haunting me.'

'*Really*,' I retorted sarcastically. 'Rules and regulations in the ashram, yes? You mean like the ones that forbid drinking and smoking? And all of a sudden, it's haunting you? Now *that's* interesting!'

But I knew that he was right. We couldn't continue like this. The secrecy, combined with our other problems, was too taxing for both of us and it proved almost impossible to keep up appearances in front of the staff and children.

More than once, we resolved to keep our relationship strictly platonic from now on, only to fail miserably every time we were together in his room, to 'talk' or 'translate mantras'. Mother Nature in her guise of desire, lust and passion was too strong a Goddess. We found it impossible to resist each other.

By the end of May, I couldn't wait to get out of the ashram. Everything revolved around Rudra and his addiction, and there were preciously few good moments left. I tried hard to let go of the need to control the situation, and accept that my beloved Rudra was an alcoholic, and that this was the way it was for now.

During the last week of my stay, when it all became too much, I tried to leave the village several times. A few days before my planned departure, Kavindra, alarmed by my vague reports of problems at the ashram, found a jeep that offered to take me straight to Delhi. I canceled it at the last minute. Likewise, I called, and recalled, Maniac who was ready to come and fetch me. Thinking that something would change and take a turn for the better, I held out – just for one more day.

Unsurprisingly, Rudra had grown cynical at my announcements of imminent departure. Every time we had an argument and things didn't go my way, I proclaimed that I would leave, only to come back to him later and say that I had changed my mind. I felt weak and inconsistent.

I remembered the many times my mother threatened to leave my father after he beat her, only to return to him for more abuse.

'This is it,' she'd say, jaw clenched, fury burning in her eyes. 'I am leaving. My bags are packed.' But she never even left the house. The bags remained, packed, in the spare room, into which she had moved many years ago.

'It's not so easy,' she used to say when I, not even ten then, pleaded with her to please leave and take me with her. 'Where will I go? I have no money, no job. How will we survive?'

I didn't care where we would have gone. Even a safe house would have been fine by me. All I wanted was to get away from this brutal situation.

I thought of a friend who had stayed with a psychopath who abused, beat and humiliated her for years. I'd always wondered why seemingly strong women lost their resolve around men that were so obviously not good for them. I still didn't know why, but I was experiencing first-hand the overpowering pull of a toxic relationship for the second time in my life.

I finally decided to leave sooner rather than later. I booked my flight out of India for five days after term end, which would allow me to catch up with MJ before going back to Europe. I couldn't imagine staying any longer in this turmoil. I wanted to get away and put it all behind me. I wanted to breathe again.

MJ agreed when I spoke to her on the phone to tell her that I was coming back to Rishikesh. 'Why stay?' she asked me, perplexed. 'What for? More of the same? Just get out of there!'

1.31: Swami-Ji's Visit

And with my departure date creeping ever nearer, I was preparing to get out at last. It was now Thursday, and I had decided to leave on Sunday morning. End of term was tomorrow, and I hoped that we'd manage to remain peaceful over the next couple of days. Yet, as so often, life had different plans for us.

The Three Stooges had left the ashram, but we were to receive another, much more important visitor from the *sannyas* tradition. Rudra pulled me to one side after school.

'Tonight we're not going to meet. My Swami-ji is coming,' he informed me solemnly. This was big news. Swami-ji was not only the official head of the ashram and this branch of *sannyas*, but also the man who had turned Rudra into a *sannyasi*. I was curious, as well as apprehensive to meet him. He was of Guru-ji's lineage, after all.

In the evening, I half-heartedly made my way to the temple for the *aarti*. From my usual place at the wall, I spotted a white-haired elderly man in orange robes sitting cross-legged on the floor. This had to be Swami-ji. He appeared frail and, I hated to admit it, quite likeable. The congregation gazed at him in awe, shuffled around and elbowed each other in the ribs.

At seven thirty pm on the dot, the *aarti* began. This time, it was led by Swami-ji, who slowly swayed to the rhythms of the chants and thoughtfully anointed the wooden sandals with trembling hands. Rudra assisted him quietly in the background.

Halfway through the *aarti*, just after the martial drums had set in, I was suddenly overcome with an uncontrollable anger. I wasn't sure why, but the feeling manifested rapidly and rose inside my belly like a cobra. Was it because of Swami-ji's presence? Whatever the reason, I was overwhelmed by what I perceived to be a display of blatant religious hypocrisy.

I became more furious with each line of the Sanskrit chanting.

I stood in the temple, diagonally right to Guru-ji's portrait, and looked firmly into his eyes. Impassively, almost derisively, he looked back at me. 'What?' he seemed to ask with a self-satisfied smile.

My anger grew and seemed to drip out of my every pore as I continued to stare at the idol, forgetting all that was around me. The chanting and drumming and ritual offerings faded into the background as I entered a parallel universe with Guru-ji. I shouted at him in my head, challenged him, accused him and judged him.

'What are you teaching these young men?' I screamed silently. 'You take them away from their families, you deny their bodies, and as a result they turn to so much despair that they start drinking. Do you think that's right? Or spiritual?'

He didn't even blink.

'Can't you see what you are doing? Can't you see that these men could live their lives and do what they are doing without your silly restrictions and guidelines for pseudo-manhood? Spirituality is not about ego, personality cult, cutting oneself off from loved ones, deceit, manipulation and control. Spirituality is love, unconditional love, and love alone. But your path is filled with dark energy, poisoned with corruption and power over others.

'Your organization is one big lie. If self-control and denial are at the root of health, happiness and peace, then why is there a need to numb out the pain? Release him!' I demanded.

'Is this love?' I continued my self-righteous tirade. 'Is *this* love?'

Guru-ji looked back at me dispassionately. 'Are you finished?' he seemed to say. 'And what about *your* hypocrisy? What are you doing in this temple if you don't agree with my ideas?'

Yes, what was I doing here, worshipping Guru-ji every evening during the *aarti* as though I was the most pious, devoted member of the congregation, dutifully bowing down and placing flower petals at his feet? It was a good question.

From the very beginning, I'd felt a nagging unease whenever I laid eyes on the enormous portrait of the Guru. And at this point, I detested him and all he represented in my eyes: the lack of the feminine, the mock austerity, the monotheistic Guru worship. Yet, still I made my way to the *aarti* every evening without fail.

Logic failed to reach me, however, at this point. I grew even angrier when the entire congregation, after placing their flower petals on Guru-ji's sandals, made a beeline for the old Swami-ji, bowed down in front of him and touched his feet with their heads. With a fatherly gesture, Swami-ji placed his hands on their heads and blessed them. I wondered whether most of these people that bowed down to him with so much devotion actually knew who this Swami-ji was.

Like a petulant child, I stood rooted to the spot.

'I'll be damned if I give one more single flower petal to you,' I spat towards Guru-ji, stopping short of giving him the finger instead.

'And I'm certainly not bowing down to *you*,' I continued, as I watched Rudra crouch down and lay his head on Swami-ji's feet. Eyes closed, he had a look of true *bhakti*, devotion, love and gratitude on his face. I tried to remain untouched. The flower petals one of the ashram boys had given me during the *aarti* remained firmly in my hand.

As I was about to leave the temple, Rudra called me over.

'Meet Swami-ji,' he invited me. 'He will be pleased to see you.'

Oh no. This was the last thing I wanted to do. I didn't have the strength to say so, though. So, quietly infuriated, I followed Rudra into the adjacent room, in which Swami-ji sat enthroned on a cushioned chair.

'Swami-ji,' Rudra addressed his superior. 'This is Tiziana, our new volunteer from England. She is a wonderful teacher and has been working with us for some weeks now.'

The old Swami peered at me. I eyed him just as curiously.

'*Namaste*,' I said casually. 'Nice to meet you.'

'*Namaste*,' he responded kindly in stilted tones. 'Thank you for serving this ashram and the mission of our Guru-ji. Are you enjoying your stay here?'

'Yes, immensely,' I mumbled.

I tried to act courteously, but my performance was poor. I felt utterly hypocritical to stand in front of this elderly monk and act the part of the virtuous volunteer teacher from the UK, when the reality was that I was having an affair with his disciple. 'Hello,' I wanted to say. 'I am sleeping with your *sannyasi!*'

Rudra interjected. 'She practices *pranayama* with me twice a day,' he nodded enthusiastically. 'And she comes to every *aarti*, too.'

The Swami smiled benevolently, as a long line of devotees filed into the room to pay their respects. Humbly, they fell to his feet and waited for a blessing, which he absent-mindedly administered while talking to me. He looked at me through kind eyes.

'You should come and live at the ashram for a longer time,' he suggested.

I sniffed arrogantly and remained silent.

He added: 'Do you *want* to leave?'

With a sideward glance toward Rudra, I responded: 'Right now I want to leave, yes. But I'll definitely consider your great offer in the future.'

Badly concealed sarcasm was dripping from my voice. Rudra stood by the table to my left and shifted around uncomfortably. I had broken etiquette by being the only person who failed to bow down to Swami-ji, and now I wasn't exactly behaving in a deferential manner either.

The part of me that was still rational felt like a spoilt brat. My negative mind had overpowered me again. I saw myself doing it but was unable to stop. Perhaps Rudra simply wanted to introduce me to the man who meant so much to him, the man who had changed his life and liberated him from drugs and crime. It was possibly a sweet, well-meaning gesture, but at the time, from the hurt space I was in, I simply could not appreciate it.

Frustrated and irritated, primarily with myself, I saluted the old Swami and went to bed. If our relationship had been terminally ill at this stage, then this had surely signed its death warrant.

1.32: Love's Duality

I woke to the sound of loud knocking on my door at five thirty am to find Rudra standing on the landing. He had a big smile on his face.

'What is it?' I asked, still in my pajamas and slightly annoyed.

'Nothing… I just had the urge to see you,' he replied.

Dawn was rising behind him. Eyes glowing and energized, he seemed a different man. It was as though a big shadow had been lifted from him. After one last lingering look, he turned to leave. Before he did so, he quietly said, 'I love you.'

This was totally unexpected. 'Wow,' I said, shaking my head in disbelief. 'Where did that come from?'

'I will tell you later,' Rudra replied excitedly and skipped down the stairs in his black plastic sandals.

I was thunderstruck. Did the passionate, heartfelt words I directed at Guru-ji the previous night in my head have an effect, I wondered? Had he listened to me? It seemed improbable, but this was strange… and auspicious.

I dressed and walked down to the temple, where Rudra was practicing *kirtan* on his harmonium. When he saw me enter, he stopped and beamed. As I soon learned, it was Swami-ji's visit that had so thrilled him.

'You know, every six months or so, clouds appear. I feel heavy. Then he comes, and everything changes. He gives me energy. Now I can carry on.' He sighed with relief.

Rudra's child-like joy was wonderful to witness, and I reconnected with the energy I fell in love with, the essence beneath the dark clouds of addiction, drama and need. I felt too tired and raw to express great enthusiasm myself, but inside, I was moved.

At six am, Rudra got up to leave, took my head into his hands and kissed me tenderly. Again, I was astonished: he had always insisted that we kept our distance in the temple. Something had truly changed.

'Today is the last day of school,' he said. 'Please come to my room after class and we'll talk more.'

My last day in school was easy and joyful. There was no formal teaching; instead, the whole school congregated for a *Gita* chanting class. I entered the assembly room slightly late, and my students, who all sat cross-legged on the floor, waved at me excitedly. I took a seat next to Abhaya, Radhika and Sananda, my girlie trio from Year 8, who giggled and elbowed each other when they saw me. After the first chant, Gopal and Chandresh waved me over to the far end of the room.

'Ma'am! Ma'am!' Gopal cried. 'Come over here! Sit with us!'

Amused, I obliged and joined the boys.

Rudra sat on the floor in the center of the classroom with his harmonium and taught the children a new *kirtan* about Lord Shiva. It was a song he had been practicing during our morning session. '*Har Har Mahadev, Shiva Shankara Tripuri*' was the mantra. Encouraged by Rudra, the children sang loudly and with great abandon. I looked over at Chandresh, who leant against the wall with his eyes closed, singing fervently. I could see the devotion on his face and smiled. This was the boy who fooled around in class and many believed to be lazy.

I turned my gaze towards Rudra, who commanded the crowd with ease. It was evident how much the children adored and idolized him; and how much they energized him in turn. More than ever, I was reminded of the impossibility of our being together fully under these circumstances. Those children needed Rudra: he was a beacon of stability and inspiration in their lives. And unless I was prepared to have a platonic relationship with him, or unless the rules of *sannyas* changed, we had to part ways.

We concluded the class with the Sanskrit *purnam* mantra. 'We sing this after our practice because otherwise we don't feel complete, yes?' Rudra explained.

Om purnamadah purnamidam

Purnat purnam udachyate
Purnasya purnam adaya
Purnam evavashishyate

Om. That is full/complete/perfect.
This is full/complete/perfect.
Perfection arises from the perfect.
Taking the perfect of the perfect, it remains as the perfect alone.

After class, I gathered the children of my classes together for a photo session. I had grown fond of them over the past weeks, and wanted to remember them as they were that spring. Posing eagerly, they crowded around me and were excited when I was able to show them the results instantly on my digital camera. 'Ma'am, will you send us the photographs?' 'Ma'am, please!'

I promised I would. Looking at those photographs now, some of which include me with my students, my image shows me an outer reflection of what was going on inside of me. My skin was almost grey, dark circles framed my eyes, and my Indian clothes were hanging off me. I looked terrible.

I bounced back to the ashram in a good mood. Recently, Rudra and I had taken to meeting in the morning, because doing so side-stepped the issue of alcohol. It seemed a perfect compromise. We both knew that Rudra was still drinking in the afternoons and evenings, and so, in an unspoken agreement, we shifted our meetings to the only time he was sober. In this way, we could pretend that everything was fine, and our arguments had lessened considerably. Again, it reminded me of the childhood relationship I had with my mother, who only drank secretly in the evenings.

I showed Rudra the photographs I had taken and we marveled at the bright-eyed cuteness of some of the children. Today, being with him was like in those very first precious days that seemed elusive like a distant dream now. Sitting huddled together on his bed behind those familiar woolly curtains, we laughed, joked, spoke, and soon began to kiss.

Unsurprisingly, passion started to take over. Swiftly, fluidly, we undressed each other. I looked up briefly, and for the first time, I saw raw desire in its full manifestation on his face. Whereas Rudra had tried to maintain a certain composure and self-control in our previous encounters, this time, he really allowed himself to let go. Like two wildcats, we rode on the wave of repressed desire that was emerging with full force now. Nothing apart from Rudra and I existed; there was only the moment.

Just as we were about to physically unite, there was a knock on the door.

'Swami-ji! Swami-ji!' one of the ashram boys cried. Rudra was needed in the office. Startled, we looked at each other. I saw Rudra's disheveled hair and giggled.

'It's a sign,' I half-joked. 'You better get dressed.'

'Right, it's a sign.' Rudra looked at me earnestly and jumped up. 'Guru-ji intervened. We must heed his call.'

He threw on his crumpled clothes and left the room to assist his staff. I dressed as well and waited, sitting demurely on his bed. I jumped as a big hairy spider crawled leisurely across the wall and disappeared behind the bed. Maybe Guru-ji was really trying to tell us something.

Yet, when Rudra came back into the room, we immediately started to kiss again and ripped each other's clothes off. This force was stronger than us and any imposed notions of restraint.

'Fuck self-control!' I murmured defiantly with a sideward glance at Guru-ji, and we started to make passionate love. This time, everything was different. The intensity of our lovemaking was urgent, untamed and primal. We both knew it would be for the last time.

But duty still prevailed in some way. As I was approaching orgasm, Rudra tensed slightly. 'Don't scream!' he whispered into my ear anxiously and tried to put his hand over my mouth, evidently remembering the night we first made love. I bit his fingers and scratched his back to pieces instead. This was an absurd situation, and thus, made our passion all the more intense. We never knew when the moments we spent with each other would be interrupted or end.

Of course, just as we were both about to climax, somebody knocked on the door again. This time we had no choice but to ignore it. 'You can't go now!' I insisted. 'Right, I can't,' he groaned, and we continued, as did the knocking on the door. Poor Rudra, I thought, torn between never-ending ashram duties and his illicit lover. Even I could see the comical side of the situation, and burst out laughing. I imagined the ashram workers coming through the door and seeing us lying entangled on the holy *sannyasi*'s bed. They would be horrified.

Eventually, Rudra tore himself away, kissed me and left me lying on the bed as he went to attend to the by now very disgruntled caller. I wondered if he could smell the sex on his body. I covered myself with one of his *dhotis* and smiled to myself.

1.33: Heartache

When he returned, we lay next to each other. Tenderly, he looked at me. 'It is my greatest joy that I have given you pleasure.'

Delight flooded my being. Was this really about to end?

'Are you satisfied?' he asked. Without waiting for my reply, he answered the question himself. 'Yes, you are. I can see it in your eyes.' We continued to gaze at each other, face to face, heart to heart. It was in these moments, when Rudra's tender, caring self shone through, that my heart melted. These were the moments when I really saw him, felt him – when his austere conditioning fell away and he did not try to control himself, or what he said.

'Let's forget about the consequences and make a child,' he suddenly said, nostalgia flooding his eyes.

I snorted derisively. 'A child. Are you mad?'

'Wouldn't that be wonderful?' The shimmer remained in his eyes.

'Sure. And then what? I'd never see you again.'

'No! I would marry you!' he protested. 'I would take care of you, the child, and we'd raise him together.'

'Hmm, yes,' I responded sarcastically. I made some joke about delivering the baby to his Swami-ji in a Moses basket after it was born.

Rudra always confused me with these comments. On the one hand, he was so attached to his status and position as a *sannyasi*, and yet, he was talking about marriage and babies and my coming to live in India an awful lot. At other times, he'd say exactly the opposite.

'In other circumstances, we would be married,' I mused once.

'No,' he shook his head, 'marriage is not for me. After four months, I would be gone.' Nostalgically, he added: 'This austerity is for me. I want to die here'. He suddenly smiled. 'When I am old, with a long white beard, still here, and you come to visit me then… can you imagine?'

I didn't want to imagine.

'So,' I said, as I was getting ready to leave his room. 'Shall we just part on a good note now and call it a day? Shall this be our last meeting and then I leave tomorrow?'

Rudra bit his lip. 'Tomorrow already?'

An uncomfortable silence filled the room. My flight was not until the middle of next week, and Rudra had asked me to stay as long as possible at the ashram. The *yatra* season would soon come to an end, which meant fewer pilgrims and less chaos, and we would therefore have more time to spend with each other. Perhaps the tension between us would ease when external stressors decreased.

I, however, wanted some kind of finality, a last pretence of certainty and control in a situation in which I had lost control of myself completely. I had not yet arranged my jeep back into civilization, but my departure was imminent. Sooner or later, I would have to leave.

My official reason for being in the ashram, teaching, had ended today. And with things as they were, I was scared of staying, of prolonging the inevitable separation that hung over us like a Damoclean Sword. Part of me couldn't wait to get away, to what I perceived to be normal life, away from the emotional ups and downs of the past days. I felt run down and craved a good night's sleep, some peace and space to reflect. I was longing to talk to somebody who understood the turmoil I was experiencing.

Yet, I also harbored dreams of returning to the village in the winter. Deep down, maybe I still hoped that somehow things could work out between us. This was not the only reason, however. In the few weeks I spent at the ashram, I had fallen in love not only with Rudra, but also with the children, the villagers, and the beautiful simplicity of mountain life. I felt at home here, and loved my teaching job.

I had ideas of how to teach more imaginatively through theater, creative writing, yoga and extra-curricular activities. I also had visions of working with the village women, maybe in rural development and microfinance. When I came back, I reasoned, I would not stay in the ashram. Things would be different. I would rent a little house near the ashram and only come in to teach, and possibly for *pranayama* and the *aarti*. I had already discussed these ideas with Kavindra, who said he could help me to find a nice place to stay.

I shared my ideas with Rudra. To my surprise, he looked uncomfortable.

'Look,' I said, 'I am not trying to make your life difficult. I know how you have chosen to live your life, and I respect this. I will not come to the ashram if you don't want me to. But I have made many friends in the village, and I would like to return and do some more work here.'

He shook his head sadly. 'You are always so caring about me.'

'Don't you want me to come back?' I asked.

'You fool,' he said, half-heartedly. I could see the uneasiness on his face. I think deep down he yearned to get back to normality, to regain control of his life, just like me. In his better moments, Rudra tried hard to be a good *sannyasi*.

The heartbreaking thing was that we loved and respected each other as friends who had a great deal to learn from each other, but that the spiritual paths each of us had chosen essentially did not match. We were in a Catch 22 situation, unable to co-exist as platonic friends; and equally unable to live out the natural flow of the passion we felt for each other.

A few days previously, I had suggested that, with the school term over and teachers leaving to go back to their respective homes, I could live in one of their apartments in the school building. It would be quiet there and maybe I could finally sleep for more than a few hours a night.

'That is a very good idea!' Rudra nodded. 'Yes, you could do this. But it would mean that we could not meet anymore at night.'

I hadn't thought about that. If I didn't live at the ashram anymore, I'd have even less reason to roam around its dark stair-cases at night than I had now. If the staff really knew nothing about our affair, this would change the situation for sure. Suddenly it didn't seem like such a good idea anymore.

'How can we go back to being just friends now?' I asked. 'I don't really want that.'

'Is our relationship only physical?' Rudra replied crossly. 'It is not. Ours is a spiritual relationship, beyond the confines of time and space. We can practice *pranayama* together, you will come to the *aarti*, and we can talk in the office.'

I was not convinced that I could go back to being just friends and colleagues after what we had experienced. It would be too difficult. My renunciation skills were not that advanced.

'Will we see each other tonight?' I finally asked.

'Sure,' he mumbled, but again, his body language told me something different. He did not seem particularly enthused at the prospect of seeing me again later. In fact, he looked apprehensive. Not knowing what to make of it, I kissed him and left.

Miserably, I had my lunch alone in the canteen. I wasn't hungry, and felt guilty that I had missed my farewell lunch with Rakesh and Uday by now. Picking at my food, I gloomily looked at the portrait of Guru-ji that towered over the serving pots, and grimaced.

When I returned to my room, it looked like a hurricane had torn through it. My altar had been knocked over; books, clothes and toiletries lay strewn all over the place. *What happened?* I wondered, as I perused the chaos. Had an intruder broken into my room? But how? The door had been locked from the outside. When I found some empty banana skins on one of the beds, it all made sense. A monkey had climbed in. I looked at the barred window and remembered my orange breakfast companion. How did it get in? It was far too big to squeeze itself through the bars.

'It was a baby monkey,' said Rudra, when I told him what had happened. 'The mothers send their babies into the room to steal food. Always keep the shutters closed when you leave the room.'

After the beautiful morning we had spent with each other, I was now feeling the pain of my imminent departure with full force. I was having a hard time letting go, and not being able to share my hurt with anyone was making it all the more difficult. I reflected on all those stolen, interrupted, delusional moments Rudra and I had shared, and the attachment this drip-supply had created. All this, the bliss and the drama, would be over tomorrow – I would be gone. I hoped that I could leave on a good, happy note but somehow, the heartache was killing me already. Why was it so hard to let go? And why, I asked myself despairingly, did I have to let go?

I lingered around restlessly. Not able to sit still, I went to the kitchen, the canteen, then to my room again. I tried to go for a walk but returned again after several minutes. A sharp pain had begun to manifest in my solar plexus. Eventually, at a loss as to where else to go, I ended up in the temple. I sat down in the back, averted my eyes from Guru-ji, and began to focus on my breath. I counted my *japa mala*, I meditated, I tried *pranayama*. Nothing helped. All I could feel was the excruciating ache in my solar plexus and heart, and it almost took my breath away. I knew this feeling only too well.

I found no peace in the temple either, as some of the ashram staff came in to do repair work. Agitated, I got up and left. I passed the office and saw Rudra on the inside. Parmod was with him. Trying to make light of the despair I was feeling, I entered the office and half-jokingly asked Rudra for a remedy that could ease the pain in my heart. He remained professional and poured a dose of tiny pills into my hand. Pokerfaced, Parmod remained rooted at Rudra's side. With nothing left to say, I returned to my room.

It suddenly hit me what leaving Rudra meant. It would be like cutting my arm off. But what were my options?

1.34: One More Night

To distract myself, I walked up to the market in the afternoon, hoping to see Rakesh and Uday in the village. Instead, I ran into Kavindra, who was having a cup of *chai* with Manoj in the little computer shop. Together with his friend Dharam, we visited my friends in the shops so that I could wish them farewell. We shared cups of *chai* and exchanged promises that we'd see each other again soon.

While we were walking through the marketplace, my mobile phone rang. Rudra. I excused myself and sat down on a flight of steps to talk to him. He sounded strange.

'Where are you?' I asked.

'I am in my bathroom.' I could hear him drag on a cigarette. 'I escaped the pilgrims for a few minutes.'

'Aha. So, what's up?'

'Darling,' he slurred, 'I want to take alcohol tonight. And I thought to better tell you this now because we said we would meet tonight.'

My feelings were mixed. I had half-expected this and hence it didn't come as a surprise; yet equally, I felt a small voice of disappointment which I tried to silence. Mainly, though, I had had enough of the dramas and was resolved to leave the village, if not in perfect equanimity, then at least in something resembling contentment.

Thus, I remained reasonably calm. 'Okay, in that case I think I will have an early night.'

'But why?' he said.

'It's simple,' I responded tiredly, 'and I've said this to you many times. You can drink as much as you like, but I don't want to be around you when you do. I don't like your energy when you are drunk.'

But Rudra wasn't happy with my response. It seemed as

though he was looking for a quarrel, and he tried to convince me to see him anyway. Today, though, I wasn't in the mood for our usual circular arguments. We had spent such a beautiful morning together and I did not want my memories to be marred by more futile arguments.

'Rudra, look,' I said impatiently. 'It's simple. If you want to see me tonight, then stay sober for a few hours. If you prefer to drink, that's fine, too, and I'll go to bed. It's your choice.'

'Yes, it is so simple for you,' he interrupted me. His voice was dripping with sarcasm. 'What you are saying is that if I will take alcohol, then this means that I do not love you.'

'I know you don't love me,' I responded sharply.

He laughed wryly. 'I would not be so sure about that.'

The conversation was clearly going nowhere. Exasperated, I ended our exchange with 'I think we both know where we stand' and hung up.

I rejoined Kavindra and Dharam, and together, we collected my new dark red *kurta* outfit that I'd asked a lady tailor to sew. '*Sundari!*' she enthused. 'Beautiful!'

It was getting dark, and Kavindra wanted to take me to his house to meet his family. I, against my better judgment, wanted to participate in the evening *aarti* one last time. The two men grimaced – they were not particularly enamored with the ashram or Guru-ji, and Dharam in particular was a declared atheist. 'He does not like these things,' laughed Kavindra. However, to please me, they acquiesced. Afterwards, I wished I hadn't bothered.

There were only a handful of people in the temple when we arrived. To my surprise, two of them were Rakesh and Uday, my teacher friends, who had made a special effort to come and see me one last time. I felt both touched and guilty. Due to all the emotional ups and downs with Rudra, I had neglected them.

'Ma'am,' moustachioed Rakesh proclaimed, genuine disappointment in his eyes, 'I was waiting for you loooong time at lunch today. You said you would come!'

I felt terrible.

'I'm so sorry,' I managed to say, 'Swami-ji wanted to speak to me about school matters. This delayed me. I was very sad to have missed you.'

I felt even worse that I was lying. But what could I say? That I was in bed with Rudra at the agreed time?

It was a strange evening. The *aarti* felt disjointed and unfocused. Rudra looked disheveled and ill and, for some reason, neglected to go to the altar to anoint Guru-ji's sandals, as was protocol. He simply remained seated at his harmonium and recited the Vedic mantras from there. With a confused frown creasing his forehead, Mr Chaudhari, the temple assistant, glanced at Rudra. I was confused, too. Rudra didn't appear to notice it. At some point, he got up to perform the knife dance.

I turned my head to look at Kavindra's friend, who sat with his mouth open. Then he whispered something in Kavindra's ear. Kavindra leant over towards me with a twinkle in his eye. 'He just asked me whether this *aarti* was supposed to be a joke.'

I stifled a laugh. How comical that an Indian person, who was surely used to such religious rites, would ask this question.

In the dark, Kavindra and I climbed up the precarious mountain path that led to his home, illuminated only by the weak light of his mobile phone. Wealthy for village standards, he lived in a spacious stone house with a large balcony and a garden that contained blossoming trees. When we arrived, his dark-eyed wife Anjali and her sister were crouched in saris on the ground outside the house, cooking vegetables over a little fire and rolling out *chapattis*. They both turned to greet me with wide-mouthed smiles.

Two children, a boy and a girl, ran towards me and gazed up at me curiously. Kavindra laughed. 'This is Pritesh, my son. He is seven. Deepika,' he pointed at the little girl, 'is my daughter. She is four years old.' He patted her head.

Together, we went up to the house. The walls of the large white living room were covered with devotional pictures and family photographs, and contained an altar, a TV and a few chairs. There were two bedrooms and an austere kitchen, which was situated beneath the living room.

Kavindra and I sat on the veranda in the cool mountain air and sipped sweet *chai* while the giggling children ran circles around me. To amuse them, I pretended to be a zombie that was out to catch them every time they passed, which caused them to hide beneath the table and fall exhausted to the floor in fits of laughter. In stark contrast to my outer enthusiasm, inside, my heart continued to sink.

'One more night,' it whispered in a continuous mantra, 'you're leaving in the morning!'

1.35: Kali's Dance

It was late when I returned from Kavindra's house, and the canteen was jam-packed with pilgrims. Feeling nauseous, I sat down next to a Bengali family with three young children. Even though I had arrived last and many families were already waiting for their food, I was, as usual, served first. This preferential treatment embarrassed me greatly, in particular as I wasn't even hungry anymore.

I offered my *rotis* to my Bengali neighbors. They politely declined. Despondently, I moved my food from side to side and took half the tray back to the kitchen. Halfway through the meal, Rudra appeared in the canteen and spoke to the serving staff. Upon seeing me, he smiled and asked cheerfully, 'How are you? Okay?'

'Yeah, okay,' I forcibly returned his smile.

'Please come to the office after you have eaten,' he said. 'I would like to say goodbye to you.'

When I arrived at the office, it was full of chattering pilgrims. 'Please sit,' Rudra instructed and gestured towards the seat to the right of his desk. I did as he asked, and he continued his negotiations with a group of plump Bengali women. Like a *murti*, a devotional statue, I sat with him for a while, but eventually grew bored and went upstairs to pack my bags.

When I returned, Rudra was furious.

'Can you not just sit quietly for a few minutes?' he snapped at me. 'What were these people to think, with you jumping up and running away?'

'I don't think they thought anything,' I replied defensively. 'What is it to them whether I sit next to your desk or not? I don't think they even noticed me.'

Scowling, he glared at me.

'You did this just because I was not paying any attention to you.' We eyed each other challengingly.

Parmod had entered the office and now sat diagonally behind me on a chair. I felt increasingly uncomfortable. Even though he didn't speak English, he surely realized that we weren't exchanging polite banter.

'Well,' Rudra said finally, faking a gracious smile. 'Thank you for all your service to the ashram. Have a great journey back home. Goodbye and many happy returns.'

I fell into the trap.

'Is this all you're going to say?' I hissed. 'I'm leaving in the morning and this is what you're saying to me? *Many happy returns?!*'

I jumped up and left, beyond caring what Parmod thought. I shot Rudra one last dagger-look and stormed up the stairs into my room.

Pain tore through my body like a wildfire as the demons of rejection and abandonment sprang forth to taunt me. Not knowing what to do with my intense emotions, I grabbed my mobile and punched in Rudra's number. His phone was switched off. Furious, I threw mine onto the bed. Within a minute, it rang.

'Yes, dear?' Rudra asked sweetly.

I exploded and started to shout at him.

'I can't believe you're acting like this. You can't treat people like that! People are not toys! I can't believe I wasted even a moment of my time with you. You're not worth it. I'm so glad I'm leaving tomorrow.'

'I am sorry, I am sorry,' was all Rudra could say.

It was too late. I ranted and raved and accused him of deceiving me, of using me for his own ends, of playing with my heart. I vented all the frustrations I had held in for so long, about the injustice of the situation, our power games, and the pain in my heart that I didn't know how to soothe. In my violently erupting anger, I said many things I later regretted deeply.

'Are you enjoying this?' he asked quietly when I had finished.

He sounded hurt. It didn't make any difference. I didn't know how to stop.

'I want to meet you. I am not keeping all this anger inside of me.'

'Okay,' Rudra agreed and suggested that we meet at ten thirty pm. I wanted to meet at ten. He said he would ring me when he was free. We argued again and, feeling more powerless than ever, I hung up.

I wished I had heeded my intuition and just gone to bed. Instead, the energy of Kali, Goddess of Destruction, took hold of me. In a wild dance, I completely lost any control I believed I might have still had.

Frustrated, I threw my phone against the wall and started to take my anger out on the ashram room. It was like I was watching myself in a movie. These days, I hardly ever got angry, but that night, I lost it completely. I kicked doors and beds and tables and slammed the window shutters.

I cursed Guru-ji, the ashram and the *sannyas* tradition. Looking out into the black sky, I cursed Rudra and wished that he would feel the pain I felt. 'You're going to get this back,' I prophesied. 'One day, you will feel what I feel.' It was like I was possessed. I felt righteous in my anger and expressing it in this way gave me some momentary relief.

After I had exhausted my energy, I sat down on the bathroom steps and started to cry. I felt small and foolish and very alone. To top it all, there had been another power cut. Hugging myself on the bathroom step in my cold, dark room with the rose-covered pillows, I cried for a long time, releasing tears of sadness, regret, guilt, shame and anger. I cried for myself, I cried for Rudra, and most of all, I cried about the absurd, hopeless situation I had managed to get myself into.

1.36: Shiva's Surrender

When I had calmed down, I gathered everything Rudra had ever given me: the small *tulsi mala*, the *Bhagavad Gita*, a book on Guru-ji and some pamphlets. I took the pile and stormed down the stairs with it, intent on thrusting it back at him, thus ending our relationship on a final, dramatic note.

I purposefully strode into his dark office, where, to my dismay, three of the ashram boys sat, drinking *chai*. I was not deterred. 'I need to see Swami-ji,' I firmly addressed one of them. He looked uncomfortable and indicated through sign language that Rudra was asleep.

'Wake him up then,' I retorted and pointed towards the hidden door. The boys looked at me skeptically, but moved towards Rudra's room hesitantly. I accompanied them. To my surprise, the door was locked from the outside. Damn.

'Tell him I'm looking for him if you see him,' was all I could manage before I left. Thinking that he was hiding from me, I was outraged. Back in my room, I tried to call Rudra again. Both his mobile phones were switched off. I sank to the floor. This night was getting worse by the minute.

Rudra called me a few minutes later. One of the ashram boys had told him that I was looking for him. He said he was downstairs in the canteen with the pilgrims. Even though I had been so convinced that I never wanted to see him again mere minutes ago, it was now as though my life depended on it. He, by now, had changed his mind.

'No,' he said finally. 'I am not going to meet you tonight. I am busy with the pilgrims.'

I resorted to desperate measures.

'If you don't meet me in the next ten minutes, then the whole ashram will know that you have had an affair with me.'

I heard Rudra inhale sharply.

'Okay,' he said curtly. 'I will meet you in fifteen minutes.'

'No,' I replied, 'we will meet in five minutes.'

'No, ten!'

It was ridiculous. Even in this dire situation, one of us tried to gain power over the other. We were impossible.

Within a few minutes, my telephone rang again.

'Come and meet me now,' said Rudra.

Highly charged, I stormed down the stairs, ready for a massive confrontation. He opened the door to his room and I stood facing him, suddenly feeling not so sure of what I wanted to say anymore.

'So,' Rudra said.

I half-heartedly tried to start a fight, but Rudra, who was by then sitting on his bed, interrupted me swiftly.

'I have just one thing to say to you,' he said, running his fingers through his cropped hair with an air of exasperation. 'Just *one* thing.'

There was a pause. Confused, I glared at him.

'I love you.'

Stunned, I stopped dead in my tracks. I looked at him in disbelief. *What* had he just said?

He continued, emotion tainting his voice. 'I'm trying to forget you! Do you think this is easy for me? Yes, I did not want to meet you again this evening, because you are leaving tomorrow. I thought, if I meet you once more, I'll become even more attached to you. Do you think I can forget you, my first girl?'

He began to cry.

His outburst took my breath away. Defeated, I sank down next to him on the bed. All my anger had vanished in an instant.

1.37: The Final Night

'Let's stay here and talk all night,' Rudra suggested. We spent the next few hours lying tightly embraced on Rudra's bed, talking, crying, kissing, but mainly talking. That night, we *really* spoke.

'What a horrible evening. You were so angry.' Rudra shivered. 'And despite all of that anger, there is always so much love. There is always love between us.'

He was right. Our souls loved each other, but it was on the human level – with our cultural differences, with our egos – that we couldn't cope.

'I'm so sorry.' I felt awful. Not only was I leaving the ashram in a few hours, but I also felt that I had managed to ruin our final night with my rampage. Why had I not gone to bed? I just wanted to wake up from this bad dream and make it all go away.

'Shhh,' Rudra said. 'Nothing happened. Everything is fine.'

He stroked my face gently. 'You're wonderful,' he murmured. 'Wonderful... a thing of wonder. Your beauty is different in the mornings, in the afternoons, and different again in the evenings. An angel from heaven visited us for a short while.'

'But why did you say this to me in the office earlier? Why did you say all this "many happy returns" crap? When you knew this was our last night?'

'I was really angry, too. I was angry that you didn't stay in the office when I had asked you to, and anyway, I knew I would see you in the morning before you left.'

Dejected, I shook my head. It still didn't make sense to me. Not much did at this stage.

He traced my body with his finger. 'Inside your body, there is a matrix. It runs up and down, from here to there, and in the center is an empty space.'

I nodded silently.

'I noticed it from the beginning. There is something... not

right. There is an inner emptiness in you that you are trying to fill,' he said. 'Repair this. It's important.'

Rudra was right. We both carried this inner emptiness, the black hole, inside of us. I suspected that somehow, this was the reason we had connected so deeply and understood each other's minds so accurately and intuitively. He filled his empty space with alcohol and work; I tried to fill mine with the drama of co-dependent love.

'Yeah,' I said tiredly, 'I suppose none of this is really about you. It's about my father.'

'Your father?' Rudra sounded surprised.

'Yes. My father was just as unavailable as you are, and my mother… Well, I told you that she was an alcoholic.' I didn't elaborate further but I was swiftly beginning to grasp something vital that had eluded me before. Could this be why I was so powerfully attracted to Rudra? Why he felt so familiar? Because he reminded me of… my *parents*?!

What really puzzled me about my discovery was how we could have been so drawn to each other without knowing the other's background. Our family histories and resulting behavioral patterns fitted like a hand into a glove. I sensed that, in an old script, Rudra was still escaping an overly controlling mother by joining the *sannyas* order, while I was still trying to stop my mother from drinking and win the love of a distant father, twenty years after I had left home. Hence, we pressed each other's buttons with an uncanny precision.

But how had we recognized this? When I met Rudra, I believed him to be a deeply spiritual man with integrity. I had no idea about his alcoholism, his struggles, and the lie he was living. Likewise, he did not know that my mother was addicted to alcohol and that I probably displayed many of his mother's character traits. How was this possible? Was this really karma, a soul mate relationship, or was it simply that we unconsciously sensed each other's shadows? Or could it be both?

Rudra turned to look at me. 'Promise me something. This is the last time you're getting involved with an unavailable man. After me, no more unavailable men.'

I promised this only too gladly. At this point, I could not imagine loving anybody ever again after him, let alone somebody unavailable.

'Why did you get involved with me? Why didn't you just leave it alone?' I wanted to know.

'Remember when you said "You're playing with fire", right at the beginning? It was not something I could control. It was stronger than me. And, I thought the same about you. I thought you were "the unavailable woman". I did not think that we would be together and that it would be so... strong.'

I told him that, despite everything, I was happy I had met him, though.

'Meeting you confirmed to me that men like you exist,' I said. 'It showed me that dreams do come true.'

He smiled. 'Had you wished for it?'

I nodded. 'Yes, for a long time. And I knew that I would meet you. And even if we can't be together, at least we have met in this life.'

'Correct,' he said, 'and I got a lot from you. You told me to always keep my heart open, and I will try to do this. And I promise you that I will stop all these habits, the liquor, the smoking. This will be your legacy. I will never forget you.'

'You'll forget me sooner than you think.'

He grew angry. 'What are you talking about? Maybe you can forget this in a week or two. I cannot. I am Indian. This, *you*, will stay with me forever. Every time from now when I think of you at a particular time of day and you are not there, it will be like a knife in my heart.' He could talk so well.

'Leaving you will be like cutting off my right arm. It doesn't feel right. It'll be awful,' I said and turned my head away from him.

'Don't you think I will feel that?' he asked. 'If you are in pain out there, don't you think I will feel that in my own body? My own pain I can bear. But yours? Is it not always the pain of the nearest and dearest that hurts the most? Please,' he implored me, 'try and be happy.'

'You know what's even worse than leaving you?' I replied, turning back to face him. 'Knowing that you do, that you did love me. That's worse than thinking that you were just an opportunist who deceived me to get laid.'

'See! The unavailable man *did* love you!' He paused, emotion coloring his voice. 'Do you believe me now? For a moment, this *sannyasi* loved you.' He hugged me tightly to his chest.

The pain in my heart intensified. This night was swiftly becoming as dramatic as a Shakespearean play. But whichever way my mind turned, I couldn't see a way out of the situation. All solutions sucked.

'Do you want me to leave?' I asked.

'Well, could you stay? Could you tell your mother that you are not coming home and will stay in India?'

'I *could*...' I said.

There was a pause.

'We could get married.'

'And then what?' I asked.

And indeed, what would happen if I decided to stay in India, Rudra left the ashram and we got married? It seemed ludicrous. Despite the intensity of emotion between us, our relationship had mainly consisted of drama and chaos so far. How would that be, if I married an alcoholic ex-monk from Varanasi? What were the chances of the relationship surviving? Would we have to live in his mother's house, as is custom in India? How would I cope with his feelings of guilt, failure and loss that would invariably follow such a decision? And besides, how could I ask him to do this for me; to break his vows, to leave the ashram he had helped build, to leave the children who loved and needed him? To leave everything he loved behind for the sake of a volatile relationship? It seemed too risky.

Moreover, I knew myself too well. In the evocative setting of the snow-capped Himalayas, our love story seemed ethereal, so strong that it could have overcome all obstacles. In truth, I did not want this responsibility. I loved him, but equally I was afraid that reality would set in all too soon, and that the odds were stacked impossibly high against us. And maybe, just maybe, I was scared of what might become the greatest surrender and transformation of my life.

Rudra could read my thoughts. 'Yes, and then what?' he asked. In the semi-dark of the room, I could see the pain and despondency on his face. 'The last good thing about me would disappear also.'

For him, the situation must have been even more extreme. Contrary to me, he had everything to lose. I remembered the day I told him something I had read about in Tibet. Apparently, it was fashionable among some female travelers to 'break monks' – to have sexual relationships with them – and then drop them once reality kicked in. This was irresponsible, the book had said, as the monks often had nowhere to go after breaking their vows and leaving the monastery. In retrospect, I do not know why I told Rudra this, who then lay on his bed and looked horrified. Maybe I wanted to warn him, maybe it was self-sabotage. 'I am not going to leave *anything* for you!' he'd said strongly, half-jokingly.

'I am not asking you to,' I'd replied defensively.

We were both too aware of what our options were. We knew that we could take that step and trust that eventually, love would conquer all, but the reality was that neither of us was prepared to do so. We were both too scared, and perhaps, too sensible to take this step.

'I think we both know it is impossible,' Rudra said finally.

My stomach cramped. Beyond all reason, this was not what I wanted to hear at all.

Trying to make light of the situation, we started to joke.

'Imagine if we were married,' one of us began.

'If you were my wife,' Rudra said, 'you would have to change. No more traveling around the world. You would just be with me all the time.'

'What?!' I asked, slightly disturbed. 'But you know that traveling is my thing.'

'Well, you could travel, but not alone. Just with me. And all your male friends, all of that would have to stop.'

I was beginning to feel uncomfortable. Was he still joking or was he serious?

'Forget it,' I replied defensively.

'You would always wear a sari, not Western clothes. Beautiful, with the *Sindoor* color of the married woman on your head. You would wear only what I want you to wear.'

I shook my head and smirked.

He continued. 'I told you, I am very conservative. Very jealous, very possessive.'

'But this is not love,' I protested. 'If you're trying to control and change somebody, that's possession, not love.'

'Maybe,' he said, 'but this is what it would be like if we were married.'

'Thanks for this information,' I responded wryly. 'I am now sure that I don't want to marry you.'

Now that my departure was nigh and the need for pretences gone, our cultural differences began to become more evident. Since our relationship had primarily been conducted within the confines of Rudra's room, there had been little opportunity for them to emerge. For Rudra, his visions of married life were probably perfectly normal and justified; to me, with my liberal Western background, they were anathema.

Naturally, as a visiting Western woman, I could do as I pleased. I knew Rudra was not too fond of my friendships with the ashram boys and other men of the village, but his ego did not permit him to openly admit it. And besides, what could he do? To Rudra, I must have seemed like a wild woman, roaming through India by myself, talking to and joking with strange men, carrying condoms, and having an extra-marital sexual relationship with him. It must have seemed unfathomable to him; alluring on the one hand, but perhaps frightening, too. He had said as much after we had made love for the first time. 'I was really scared of you that night,' he had joked afterwards. 'I thought, What is she doing? You were like a creature from a different planet.'

'What do you want with me, really?' he asked now. 'There are so many nice men out there, with good characters. Men who do not drink, who do not lie. *Good* men. Why do you want to be with me? I told you so many lies, really. Why don't you marry a *nice* man, rather than this poor *sannyasi?*'

He had a point. What *did* I want with him?

Rudra got up and stretched. It was about three am, and it seemed like we had lived through a lifetime of experiences in a day.

'If you are going to stay, then I will really need to smoke a cigarette.'

'Okay, I'm going then.' My inner control freak kicked in again.

In my distraught state, I took his request to smoke personally and believed it to be a sign of provocation, another confirmation that he did not really care about me and wanted me to leave. He knew I hated cigarette smoke, and to my clouded mind, his wish to smoke meant that he did not love me. The thought that his addiction had absolutely nothing to do with me, that the world did not revolve around me, did not occur to me.

'*This* is your problem,' he said suddenly. 'You are always thinking that I am sending you away!'

Startled, I looked at him. He was right. Deep inside of me, I harbored an old insecurity complex, an ingrained feeling of not being wanted, and I spotted evidence of this everywhere, even where there was none. I had never seen it so clearly. My God! No wonder our relationship was so capricious.

I got up, too. We stood embraced for a while and looked at our reflection in the bathroom mirror.

'Look at us,' he said. 'You are so white, I am so dark. We are *totally* mismatched.'

Wryly, I remembered the first time we had looked into the same mirror together, on an afternoon that seemed to be in a different lifetime now.

'So what is happening now?' I asked. 'Will we just part ways and never see each other again?'

Despite my better judgment, I wanted to maintain our connection. I still believed that we could transform the powerful energy between us into something stronger that transcended sexual desire. Maybe with some physical distance, we could be friends. Rudra, however, wanted to simply bring it to an end. He was an 'all-or-nothing' person. We would either get married, or 'cut it off' and discontinue all contact with each other. For him, there was no in-between. 'It is best to just cut it off,' he said. 'And I am well used to doing this.' That, I knew, he was.

Looking at me imploringly, he added, 'Please do not go back to your country with a broken heart. Forget me. Remember me, of course, but live your life. Be free.'

When dawn set in, I left his room. By now, we had said all we could, and still nothing had changed. I was still leaving. Rudra stood at the bottom of the staircase and watched me disappear upwards. This time, I wasn't looking back at him. I was crying too much.

1.38: Disentanglement

After an hour's sleep, I got up again. At this stage, I was beside myself and wanted to see Rudra one more time. I wanted to ask him whether he meant what he said. I wanted to ask him whether he really wanted me to stay in India.

The temple was locked. I rang Rudra, who was still sleeping, and asked him to open it. The atmosphere between us was tense. We hardly spoke and he pretended to practice *pranayama*. He was detached and business-like. I, in turn, somehow could not bring myself to talk to him. The moment passed and Rudra left. Now I felt even worse than before.

Knowing that the jeep driver was to arrive at ten am, I returned to my room and began to pack. Simultaneously, I started to throw up. Every item took an eternity to place inside of my bag, and I had to keep sitting down because I was exhausted and the pain was too intense. Surely I was overreacting. 'The pain was already there,' Rudra had said the previous night. 'I am only helping to trigger it.' It seemed that way.

There was a knock on my door. Hoping it would be Rudra, I opened it, but it was merely the jeep driver, who had arrived too early. Irritated, I sent him away again. With a deep sigh, I dragged myself to the bathroom to pack up my cosmetics, avoiding my reflection in the scratchy mirror.

I hoped that Rudra would come up to my room, hug me and tell me that it was all a nightmare. When I later told him that, he said, 'What, come and help you pack? No. I do not have the guts for that.'

When I had finally packed most of my things, I prepared an envelope that I planned to give to Rudra when I left. Inside was a photograph of my favorite shrine in Kathmandu, Nepal. The intricate stone carving showed the naked Shiva and Parvati sitting side by side. Shiva's left hand was wrapped around

Parvati's waist beneath her voluptuous breasts, while her right arm rested on his left thigh. The deities, with open legs displaying their genitals and faces covered with red and yellow *tilak* powder, looked united and relaxed as though they had just made love. I loved this carving for its natural eroticism and the warm glow it radiated. On the back of the photograph I wrote, '*Don't cry because it's over. Smile because it happened.*'

I also left him the red and white *mala* I had bought from the South Indian women at the market, and a card depicting Tara, the Buddhist Goddess of Compassion. I had carried this card with me throughout my journey and it seemed an appropriate gift for Rudra. Inside, I wrote words that came straight from my heart, words that I could not convey to him in any other way.

'*Thank you for everything you taught me,*' I wrote, '*and thank you for giving me the opportunity to look at myself and my own addiction – my addiction to unavailable men, and the resulting pain of trying to win that elusive love. Thank you for showing me that I am still playing out the old drama of getting my mother to stop drinking, and thank you for showing me, once again, that I need to let that go. Thank you for all the beauty we shared, the moments of intimacy, understanding, connection, tenderness, joy.*

'*Thank you also for everything else – the pain I caused myself by fighting an impossible quest, as pain brings awareness, and with awareness, misery disappears. Thank you for allowing me to teach and to discover the joy of working with children. Thank you for the beautiful ceremonies, the beautiful music, and for allowing me to be part of this ashram for a while. Most of all, thank you for being yourself, for your courage, your vision, your strength, empathy, attention to detail, and for all the work you do in this community. You are an inspiration – keep on shining.*

'*Despite everything I may have said in moments of anger and drama, I see you as you are, and that is as a person I respect and admire tremendously, a beautiful mixture of darkness and light.*

'*Let me close this by saying that it's been wonderful to meet you. In many ways, you are the man I've been hoping to meet for a long time, and I'm glad that I did. It's time to let go now, to let go of attachments and desires and agendas, but know that you'll always be in my heart. The love I feel for you, which, in its better moments, is above all desires, passions and needs, will be there always, even if we never see each other again.*

'Many blessings on your path, wherever it may carry you in the future. I pray and I know that you will always be safe and protected.'

1.39: Departure

And then it was done. I had packed.

Wearing my new dark red *kurta*, and with my messy hair scraped back, I took a deep breath and walked to Rudra's office to return the books he had lent me. He stood near his desk, alone. When he saw me, he smiled regretfully.

'You look beautiful,' he said, and I could read in his eyes that he meant it. 'Do you want to come into my room for a few minutes, to say goodbye properly?'

'Sure,' I replied, and followed him into the little room, the secret cave in which we had lived so intensely over the last few weeks.

Once in the room, he hugged me tightly with tears in his eyes.

'I am sorry,' he said. 'I am sorry for everything I have done to you.'

I started to cry as well. 'I've just gathered myself together, and now you say that.'

We had forty-five minutes until the driver was due to arrive. In those minutes, we held each other and reviewed the time we had spent together.

Final words, final kisses, final reminisces. Our eyes connected, and our hearts danced towards and away from each other.

Don't go, heart implored me. *Go!* instructed mind.

I had always advised Rudra to follow the path with heart – but, what if, as I had come to experience over the last few days, head and heart didn't agree? What if heart believed that it could conquer everything, and head said that it would be a crazy, self-destructive, egoistic choice? And what if the path with heart meant to want what was best for the Beloved, even if this meant that I had to let go?

'If I put this… thing inside you,' Rudra smiled as he held my hand from his cross-legged position opposite me, 'a small Tiziana will come out. Or maybe a small Rudra.' I saw a moment of flickering recklessness in his eyes, a sort of 'Come on, let's do it' – his wild side wanting to follow the heart's desire, to go with the flow, brushing aside all thoughts of consequences. Life is simple, really: it's us who make it complicated.

'Mind you,' he added, 'there is only one knife that fits into the sheath. There can only be one Tiziana.'

I wasn't sure how to take this remark. 'And only one Rudra?'

'No!' he replied. 'There should be *lots* of Rudras. An army of us could change the world for the better!'

I laughed. Even now, his ego prevailed.

He hugged me close to his chest. 'It was wonderful to meet you, and it was...' he whispered the last word into my ear, 'delicious.'

'It was,' I said, 'it was.'

'Let us go to the temple,' Rudra suggested when the departure time had crept uncomfortably close. 'I want to give you something.'

'Give me one last good kiss,' I said, and our mouths tasted each other for the last time.

We walked to the temple, side by side. A man was sitting near the altar, praying. Rudra picked up a fragrant dried red rose, placed it in a little envelope, and gave it to me.

'This is for you,' he said, 'with the blessings of Guru-ji. You will always be blessed by him.'

He recited some mantras, poured holy water into my hand and put a dot of white *tilak* paste on my forehead.

After that, we walked back towards the office together. 'I did something for you earlier in the temple,' Rudra confided with a low voice. 'A ritual, so that you can be in peace.'

'Thanks,' I responded. 'I might need it.'

Kavindra was leaning against the landing outside the office, waiting for me. When instructed by Rudra, Azar, one of the ashram boys, leapt up to my room and carried my heavy bags down to the waiting jeep. In departure fever, I ran down to the kitchen and said goodbye to Keshava the cook, the vociferous *chaiiii* man and the ashram boys who waved at me cheerfully.

Trying to put on a brave face, I also ran across the road to my beloved Moustachio Place to wish my friends there farewell. Rudra watched me from the front of the ashram next to the running jeep. I came back and took a seat in the back of the vehicle, next to Kavindra, who had decided to travel with me. For this, I was grateful beyond belief. Although Kavindra knew nothing of my relationship with Rudra, I felt supported by his presence.

The driver unlocked the handbrake and put the jeep into gear. This was it. We were leaving. Rudra stood outside the ashram gate next to a teacher who had come to say goodbye, and our eyes connected. I will never forget the look in his eyes that contrasted his smile. The car began to move. My eyes darted from Rudra to the teacher, and back to Rudra. Our gaze spoke volumes.

'See you,' he said.

'See you,' I echoed, as though I was only going to town for the afternoon, and would return later.

The jeep drove down the small mountain road and around the bend. I turned to take a last look back, and suddenly the ashram, the place where I had lived through heaven and hell in a matter of weeks, had disappeared from my sight.

Part 2

The Return

We are all masters of our own destiny. We can so easily make the same mistakes over and over. We can so easily flee from everything that we desire and which life so generously places before us.

Paulo Coelho

2.1: The Mountain Road

The main thing I remember from the long drive back into civilization is a sense of unreality. Quietly, I sat in the back of the jeep with Kavindra and looked out of the window as we descended from the mountain. I took in hills, rocks, woods, rivers and waterfalls as we drove through the different villages, some bustling, some deserted. We crossed bridges and passed landslides.

I felt like I was watching a movie. Physically, I was in the jeep, and yet at the same time, I wasn't. Faintly, like background music, a range of different emotions passed through me: relief, sadness, denial, despair and confusion. The main sentiment however was numbness. I could not believe that I had left the ashram, that I had left Rudra.

I was glad for the company, however. Kavindra's calm, reassuring presence was like balm for my bruised heart and shocked psyche. It gave me a sense of stability and the pretense that I was merely a tourist who was leaving a remote village in the Himalayas after an exhausting, but satisfying holiday. Had I been on my own, I feared I might have lost it completely.

As it was, I kept it together quite well. I vaguely remember stopping at a roadside canteen, where we had lunch and I was reprimanded by a group of Indian pilgrims for inadvertently stumbling over their imaginary picnic 'table' (an empty space on the ground) on my way to the grim lavatories.

After a day's driving, we were back in the sweltering heat of Rishikesh and the yoga ashram. Again, it seemed unreal. The lively ashram that had been my home for two months was now deserted, like an empty shell. With soaring temperatures of up to 42 degrees Celsius and the approaching Monsoon, most students had packed their bags and left for the colder climates of Dharamsala and Kashmir. I felt disconnected from the few remaining people – a couple of acquaintances, the ashram staff – I had said goodbye to only a matter of weeks ago. On the surface, everything was the same, yet somehow, it was completely different, too. This was mainly because I had changed, and could not communicate the enormity of what had happened to me in the Himalayas.

I was settling back into my old room with mixed feelings, when MJ strolled through the door. She smiled and gave me a big hug.

'How are you?' she asked, as she perused me with a raised eyebrow.

'Wounded, but still standing,' I grinned. 'Good to see you, MJ.'

That moment, my mobile rang. It was Rudra. My heart jumped.

'Where are you?' he asked, and I could hear the smile on his face, seven hours away on the mountain I had left behind.

I told him that I had just arrived at the yoga ashram.

He paused. 'I was not sure whether I should call you. But I had to.'

'I'm really happy you did,' I said. 'I miss you so much already. What are you doing?'

'I am sitting outside the office, moving my belly in and out. I am doing my *pranayama*.'

'How are you feeling?' I asked.

'I think you can tell by my voice how I am,' he said simply. 'I slept for a long time this afternoon, with the clothes you left behind in my bed. Your scent is still with me.'

I wanted to cry. He continued: 'Today, people asked me all day, *Are you ill? You look disheveled.*' He laughed briefly, without mirth.

Suddenly, I was cursing myself for my decision to leave, for the plane ticket I had booked, for the impossible situation that had made me depart in the first place.

Rudra sighed. 'In a few days, this will all just be a memory. Everything will become normal again. Life will continue as usual.'

He sounded melancholic. I forbade my heart to feel what it wanted to feel. Instead, we talked a bit more, me being more chatty than usual, and then ended the call.

'See you,' Rudra said.

'See you,' I echoed.

The line cut.

My final three days in India passed like a blurry dream. Initially, the yoga ashram cocooned me like a safe, quiet haven after the turmoil and austerity my life had consisted of in the Himalayas. For the first time in weeks, I got a full night's sleep and eased back into my yoga practice. I enjoyed singing *kirtan* and lighting sacred fires with a small group of Indian friends. And to my surprise, I was hungry, too. My heart was sore, but at the same time, I felt grounded, happy to have escaped the chaos.

With some distance, I could see that this was not the time for hasty decisions. To marry a man, monk or not, with an alcohol problem was simply not wise. The future would take care of itself. For now, I wanted to go home and address the underlying issues that had led me to engage in this crazy situation in the first place. If it was meant to be, I'd meet Rudra again one day, maybe when we were both in a better place emotionally. Pain was transient. This, too, would pass. Or so I kept telling myself.

My feeling of relief at having left the mountains was short-lived, however. After the initial respite, I began to feel wretched. With too much time to think, my mind went into overdrive. I was haunted by memories, images, smells, feelings and sensations. Most of all, I felt lonely. Kavindra had left to visit some relatives in a nearby town; MJ was ill and asleep most of the time; the internet was down; and I consequently had nobody to talk to about what I had *really* experienced. And talking, sharing my story was what I needed to do more than anything else. Ironically, it was the very thing that evaded me. I felt tempted to call Rudra, but what was the use? It would only be a temporary fix, and do nothing to change the situation. I tried to surrender to what was, but everything inside of me resisted it forcefully.

A numb despair clung to me like a shadow. Alone, I wandered aimlessly through the dusty heat, emotionally frozen, not caring where I was going or whom I met. I sat by the Ganga for hours on a remote rock and let the water wash over me. I hoped it would soothe and carry the pain away. 'Let go, let go, let go' was my mantra. Why was it that, despite everything that had happened and the feeling that it could probably never work between Rudra and me, my heart broke every time I thought of him, and I wanted nothing more than to be with him?

A casual meeting I had on my second afternoon back in Rishikesh gave me some perspective. Swami Vasyudevananda, a middle-aged American renunciate who lived in a *kutir*, a small hut at the banks of the Ganga, visited the ashram. Tall, lean and attractive, he sported a stylish goatee beard that looked slightly at odds with his orange monk's robes. I'd met him on previous occasions and found the Swami, and especially his inflammatory temper, endearing.

After lunch, we drank a leisurely cup of *chai* together on the ashram steps. Soon enough, perhaps through synchronicity or my desire to share some of what I had experienced in the Himalayas, our conversation turned to relationships, cultural differences and renunciation. Knowing that I'd traveled in Pakistan, the Swami told me an interesting story.

'Y'know,' he said in his American twang between swigs of

chai, 'a good female friend o' mine from the States married a Pakistani. He's a very conservative, traditional man from the Frontier-area, and they met while she was traveling over there. She's a lively, independent and modern woman who runs her own business in New York, and I could not believe it when she told me that she was marrying this guy.' He shook his head. 'What was she thinking?'

I knew what he meant. Pakistan's North-West Frontier Province was the Wild West of the country, where warlords ruled a rugged terrain that was exempt from Pakistan's national law.

'It was okay initially,' the Swami continued. 'While she was in Pakistan, they got on fine, also with his family, who were happy with the marriage. But after a year or so, they decided to move to New York for some time. And there, it all went terribly wrong. He just couldn't cope with the way she was behaving in the West. She had close male friends, was used to enjoying her freedom and wearing Western clothes. It was too much for him, in particular because in New York, he could not tell her what to do – unlike in Pakistan. So he turned violent. I can't say I was surprised.'

I was eerily reminded of the conversation I'd had with Rudra during our last night.

The Swami turned to look at me through clear, blue eyes. 'But my friend is a bit strange. She really believes that relationships are a spiritual path, a path to transformation.'

'Well, they *can* be,' I offered. 'Some yogic texts say that marriage is a *sadhana* in itself. By learning to live with another human being and seeing God in one another, great transformations can occur.'

The Swami pursed his lips. He was not convinced.

'I told her that this was a bad idea from the start. How can you expect to live harmoniously with somebody from such a different culture? In Pakistan, a woman is expected to obey her husband. She has to veil herself, not look at or talk to other men, live a life that is primarily housebound. *You* know that – you have been over there!'

I nodded. 'I know what you mean. It's hard. I don't think I could do it.'

We sat in silence for a while.

'Why have you renounced relationships?' I asked him suddenly. 'Why do you choose to live like this?'

The Swami smiled. 'It wasn't so much a choice. It was a calling. I met my Guru when I was in my twenties and knew that this was it. I'd been living on the streets, was involved in drugs and drink, and then a friend and I started to hitch around the United States to search for meaning. It was then that I became aware of spirituality, and it turned my life around. When I eventually met my Guru at a yoga center, I knew that I wanted to dedicate my life to his teachings. I asked, no, *begged* him to take me to India. He did and I never looked back.'

'So you've lived here for how long?'

'Oh, over twenty years. I was living at my Guru's ashram for a long time, but in recent years I have become a teacher myself and started living alone at the Ganga. I teach internationally now.'

'Do you think it is natural to live a renounced life devoid of personal and sexual relationships?' I asked.

'I tell you one thing.' He looked straight into my eyes. 'Sexual desire remains. It never leaves. But we are trying to overcome it with our yogic practices. It's not easy.'

'But why? Why are you forcing yourself to renounce something you secretly desire? Is this healthy?'

'Well,' he said crossly. 'If you see a cake in a shop, you don't just buy it and eat it all in one go, do you? It is not good for you!'

'Isn't that slightly different?' I continued my interrogation. 'Just because you have a healthy sexual desire and want to be in a relationship with a woman doesn't mean that you have to become a porn star or sex addict. Surely there is a middle path?

I mean, you could just eat one slice of cake and enjoy it, rather than eating it all and feeling sick.'

'But we don't need this!' The Swami seemed exasperated. I obviously wasn't getting the point.

'If you don't need it, why do you still have sexual desire then?' I really wasn't getting the point.

'We do not need this type of interaction. We yogis are man and woman in one body. *This* is what we are trying to achieve: the perfect union of Shiva and Shakti, the masculine and the feminine energies, inside one human body. This is what all of our practices lead towards. Why would we need a partner if our ultimate goal is transcendence of mundane human desires? We want to advance so that we can escape this cycle of death and rebirth and become liberated.'

'I don't know,' I said. 'From what I have seen so far, renunciation can also backfire. I have recently met a Swami who was an alcoholic, smoked cigarettes and enjoyed sexual affairs with women.'

The American Swami didn't seem surprised. 'Yes,' he sighed. 'Unfortunately, this happens from time to time.'

'Really?' I pricked up my ears. Was my experience with Rudra not unique? Did other *sannyasis* do this, too?

'Yes, of course. We had a very capable Swami in my tradition. He was pretty high up in the order, and well respected. But... unfortunately, he allowed himself to get involved with a woman.'

'Really? What happened?' I asked with as much nonchalance as I could muster. The incredible synchronicities that seemed to happen when one travels, particularly magnified in India and other power places such as Glastonbury, never failed to amaze me. I'd noticed that if I remained open, I always heard the information I needed to hear and met the people I needed to meet at the exact right time.

'You have to understand that this Swami was a *pujari*, a priest, also. Normally, we *sannyasis* are supposed to live a life that is somewhat secluded from other people. We are meant to stay detached, and y'know, not get so involved with other people and the materialistic world. This Swami was in contact with many people from the public all the time, because he was leading rituals for them. And so one day, a woman fell in love with him, and they began an affair that lasted for a long time. They even got married.'

'They got married?! So he left his post?'

'No,' he smirked. 'They got married in secret, and he carried on a double life. Until one day, the lady had enough of the secrecy and told his superior what was going on. And then all hell broke loose. He was instantly dismissed from the ashram and our Swami-ji absolutely demolished him in public when he did so. Here, it's a great shame to leave *sannyas*, and even more so if deceit is involved, of course.'

'Wow. Did the marriage last?'

'For a while. But not very long. The last thing I heard was that he had gone back to some type of religious post.'

'Hmm,' I mused. 'But it seems like the *sannyasi* wasn't so convinced about his chosen path, or otherwise he would not even be interested in women, right?'

'It's not so simple. We're only human beings at the end of the day. Temptation is always there. Imagine that you are trying to grow a big strong hedge around your house. This hedge is there to shield you from intruders. But when you first start to grow it, the plants are still young and tender, and so, intruders can get in easily. It is only after many years of growing and nurturing that it is strong enough to withstand whatever temptation comes its way.'

I could appreciate the analogy. Maybe it wasn't so black and white after all. Rudra was actually still very young.

'So you're always asking yourself: where is your center?' the Swami explained. 'If you keep returning to your *sadhana*, your spiritual practice, then you will eventually succeed in leaving human desires behind. But it takes time, lifetimes in some cases.'

I reflected about the Swami's words for a while in the still afternoon heat.

'I'm still not so sure about this, Swami-ji,' I said eventually. 'In particular with young men. Why do you have to renounce *anything* to love God? I mean… look at what happens in the Catholic Church. We often hear about celibate Catholic priests who abuse children. Can't we love God *and* love a woman or man as well? Why do we have to choose?'

'Because we Swamis dedicate our life to God, to our spiritual practice, and to the good of humanity. There is no room for anything else. Please understand that this path is only for the very few who really desire it, and not for the lay person.'

'But it's bad karma though, to take a vow and then break it in secret,' I pressed on. 'You're deceiving others and you're deceiving yourself!'

'Yes, and what about the karma of the woman who lets herself get involved with a monk?' the Swami challenged me with blazing eyes. 'Why would she do that? Does she have low self-esteem? Does she let people walk all over her? You have to ask yourself this as well.'

Ouch. Yes, what about my karma? And why would I do such a thing indeed? I averted my eyes, afraid that the Swami could see right through me and knew that I was speaking about myself.

I still couldn't let it go. 'But… This Swami I met, he was also addicted to alcohol. Isn't this a sure sign that he is unhappy and would be better off doing something else?'

'Well…' The Swami directed his gaze wistfully over the ashram gardens. 'That's between him and God. Otherwise brilliant people can sometimes have big problems. I once knew a Tibetan monk who drank a lot of alcohol. But he was an excellent scholar and a gifted teacher. And yet, alcohol was his weakness.' He paused. 'I don't know what the answer is. I only know that we are trying to do our best, and that none of us is perfect.'

2.2: Leaving India

After three days that seemed like they would never end, it was time for me to leave India. MJ, somewhat recovered from her illness, helped me to pack my bags by candlelight, as there'd been another power cut. In semi-darkness, we reminisced about our days in the Himalayas and my encounter with Rudra. 'Forget him,' she said. 'Move on with your life.' I wished it was that easy.

Thankfully, my friend and fire ceremony teacher Sanjay offered to accompany me on the five-hour taxi ride to Delhi airport. He'd hopped onto the first bus from his hometown when he heard that I was back at the yoga ashram. Although I did not feel able to share my story with him, his mere presence soothed me. We climbed into the taxi at eleven pm and waved farewell to MJ, who performed a wild knife dance in my honor on the ashram steps.

As I sat in the dark taxi, thoughtfully looking out of the window onto the still busy streets, my phone rang. Rakesh, my ex-yoga teacher, as well as Al Pacino and a couple of other friends called to wish me farewell, although I had not told them when I was leaving. In the midst of all the confusion inside me, I felt taken care of, as though the Universe was telling me: 'Your relationship with Rudra may be over, but other people love you and think of you.' A warm glow filled my body. Maybe everything was how it was meant to be after all.

We started our trip, a jerky, irritating ride that was accentuated by a cacophony of honking and the driver's constantly ringing mobile phone. I lay in the back of the taxi in my pajamas, trying to sleep, while Sanjay attempted to do the same in the front seat. After what seemed like a very long time, I heard Sanjay's voice from the front seat.

'Tiziana,' he said gently. I reluctantly opened one eye to look at him. 'We are nearly there. Wake up.' I stretched and gathered my belongings together. After a quick wash in the airport restrooms while Sanjay guarded my bags, I hugged him goodbye and walked past the armed guards to check in.

I still carried a slight feeling of unreality inside of me. Somehow, I still couldn't believe that I was leaving India and that my long trek through Asia was over. And, I was somewhat ashamed to admit, I still irrationally hoped that Rudra, who knew that I was flying home today, would turn up at the airport, tell me that everything had been a misunderstanding, and implore me to stay. But, as I knew only too well, such things only happened in romantic movies.

I wandered around the airport for a while and then sat down to wait for my plane to Frankfurt. Even though I knew it was a bad idea, I tried to call Rudra to say goodbye. There was a network failure on both of his mobile phones, and however much I tried, I could not get through to him. Frustrated, I gave up. *Okay okay*, I mumbled, *I know I should let go. But can't I just have one final conversation?!*

As I sat waiting and observing the other passengers in the departure hall, I caught a glimpse of saffron in the corner of my eye. Surprised, I turned my head. A young man dressed in saffron-colored robes made a beeline for me and took a seat opposite me. My heart missed a beat. Who was this monk? Was he a messenger from Rudra? A quiet, pale young woman wearing a cotton sari followed the monk and sat down beside him. With downcast eyes, she counted prayer beads with her right hand.

The monk smiled cheerfully at me. 'Are you going to Frankfurt?' he asked.

'Erm… yes,' I replied. 'Are you?'

He nodded and handed me a little card. A dancing Krishna smiled at me from glossy paper. '*Pure Bhakti*', the red words on the card read. '*Chant Hare Krishna and be happy!*'

Oh fuck, I thought, *it's a Hare Krishna! That's all I need right now.*

'Come and visit us at our temple in Stuttgart,' he invited me.

'We have a feast there every Sunday.'

'Yes, thanks, I'll think about it,' I mumbled.

I was delighted. *Not.* Feeling like I was starring in a bizarre *sannyasi* soap opera, I shook my head. The Gods had a strange sense of humor sometimes.

Rudra had prophesied that I would be crying on the plane home. To my delight, I wasn't. Mysteriously, as the plane started to move smoothly over the runway, a feeling of joy and great peace saturated my Being. When the pilot took off and gently lifted us into the sky, I cast my glance over a hazy, smoggy India, the country that had so challenged me over the past five months, one last time.

I smiled when the many adventures and lessons I had experienced here passed before my mind's eye. I remembered moustachioed masseurs who offered me breast massages, suicidal rickshaw rides, deformed beggars with the most beatific smiles, slowly swaying women in colorful saris, preaching Gurus with their disciples gathered around them at the banks of the Ganga, children that cried 'One rupeee please!', meditative cows, thieving monkeys, the infectious smiles and dreamy eyes of Indian boys, and the many people I had come to know and love here. What a crazy, vibrant world India was! With all its madness, contradictions and irritations, I had utterly, irrevocably fallen in love with the country.

And ultimately, did it not all make sense? I came to India looking for a tantric teacher and my soul mate. In a convoluted way, it had all come true, albeit not at all how I had envisaged. As we lifted higher and higher into the clouds, I suddenly slapped my forehead with my palm. The moustachioed German with the Shiva wristwatch beside me cast me a bewildered glance. I ignored him. Why hadn't I thought of this before? In

Tantra, it is always Shakti, the female, who initiates Shiva, the male, into the mysteries of the tradition. Had I not met and initiated an austere *sannyasi* into the mysteries of love and feminine energy? And wasn't Tantra ultimately about non-attachment and transcendence of duality?

Perhaps, I thought, I carried all the knowledge I needed already inside of me and it just needed unlocking. Maybe that was my tantric lesson. I realized that, in some weird way, I had completed my Himalayan tantric quest and found my Shiva – but how differently from how I imagined it would be! I chuckled to myself, suddenly elated by the divine comedy I had lived out during the past weeks. From up here, seen through the detached eyes of a soaring metal bird, it seemed almost hysterically funny.

I now felt light-hearted and ready to go home, excited to meet all the people who loved and supported me. I was not leaving broken-hearted as I had feared, but stronger, wiser, enriched and happy. Back home, I resolved, I was going to enjoy myself, and cherish the memory of the *sannyasi* who had given me a fragrant rose as a parting gift. Yes, everything was indeed perfect.

2.3: Broken Heart, Blossoming Heart

It was wonderful to be at home with my parents at first. After the chaos of India, I relished the tranquility of the small village in which I'd grown up. Strange as it may seem, in the sixteen years that passed since I left my native Germany, I had not once missed my country of birth. Sure, I had returned from time to time, but only for short, fleeting visits and with a great deal of resistance, too.

The fire ceremony *sadhana* I participated in at the yoga ashram just before I met Rudra changed all that. I remembered sitting up in surprise on Day Four in the middle of relentless chanting when I realized that, for the first time ever, I actually really missed the wild woods and fields of my childhood days.

In the years that followed my leaving home, my parents had calmed down considerably. My mother stopped drinking, my father gave up smoking, and their arguments lessened. Now, they still bickered, but the violence of my childhood days had subsided. Subsequently, I'd managed to develop a good, adult and loving relationship with both my parents, and liked to visit them from time to time.

In my first days back in Europe, I mainly slept, practiced yoga and went for long walks in the forests that surrounded my parental home. After my big journey, I needed to ground, connect with my roots, and find the space to process everything that had happened to me. It was now early summer, and the gardens and fields were in full bloom. Colorful flowers, especially red roses, sprouted at every corner and in every orderly garden. I drank it all in, the lush smells and sounds of nature, grateful for the beauty as though I was seeing it for the very first time.

At the same time, I felt disoriented and alienated. The shops with their many products bewildered me, as did the people wearing what seemed like bland uniform clothing to me. I resented spending more money in a day here than I did in almost a month in India. Like probably every other traveler who returns from a Third World country, I was painfully aware of our material affluence and the many seemingly unnecessary products that lined the fluorescent, packed supermarket aisles. And, of course, I was annoyingly self-righteous, too, as I soon realized after I compassionately comforted my mother's neighbor, who complained about her boyfriend's uncomfortable sofa, with a stern reminder that at least she didn't have to live in Afghanistan.

As much as I might have cursed India in various moments of frustration, I was sorely missing it, too. I'd vowed that I'd never eat lentils again after the thrice-daily *dhal* of India, and yet, here I suddenly was craving Indian food. Everything made me nostalgic. I wandered into Indian clothes shops and struck up melancholic conversations with the owners. I continued to wear Indian clothes, including a headscarf, much to the dismay of my father, who was convinced that I'd converted to Islam. I loudly recited Sanskrit prayers before eating food while my parents exchanged concerned glances. Every day, I wistfully pored over my photographs of India and sent equally wistful e-mails to my Indian friends.

I couldn't quite fathom my longing. It wasn't exactly like I had spent the most wonderful time of my life in India – often I'd been frustrated at the noise, the harassment, the traffic, the fatigue, the heat and the scams. But somehow, India got under my skin, and I couldn't shake it off. It was ever-present, calling me, loud and strong, like a persistent lover. In a way, this wasn't news to me – other travelers had told me many times about the love–hate relationship they harbored with India. They loved it, hated it, vowed never to go back to this crazy country, only to book the next plane ticket as soon as they returned to Europe. I just never thought it would happen to me.

Even my spirituality changed significantly after India. For

almost twenty years, I had followed the Pagan Goddess path of ancient Europe. I'd worshipped and prayed to Celtic and Mediterranean Goddesses for most of my adult life. Since immersing myself in yogic practices in the Himalayas, all this had shifted. Suddenly, I had transmuted into a strange hybrid you could call a Hindu-Pagan. The Hindu Gods, primarily Shiva, Parvati, Kali and Ganesh, now dominated my altar; and the strangest thing was that I had in fact whole-heartedly accepted a male God into the Center of my altar. Whereas before, I had almost exclusively invoked Goddesses in my prayers and rituals, suddenly I was addressing both masculine and feminine deities in perfect union. It was as though something very deep inside of me had changed forever.

My main occupation in those days, however, was moping. More than India, I was missing Rudra. Desperately. With hindsight and a few thousand miles between us, I was convinced that I had made the wrong decision. I agonized *ad nauseam* over what would have happened if I had stayed in the Himalayas. Would it have been more of the same, or could we have transformed our troublesome relationship? After all, had Rudra not asked me to stay in India on several occasions, and even suggested marriage? Why had I not explored this further?

I felt that I had finally found the man I was looking for, and then gave up too soon when things became difficult. It was driving me crazy. I tortured myself mercilessly with doubts, regrets and guilt. I deeply regretted my lack of compassion towards Rudra when I found out about his alcoholism, my harsh and often insulting words and my self-righteousness. To top it all, I felt self-indulgent, which only added to my guilt. Why couldn't I just let it go and instead enjoy what was? And why did I miss this man so much as though my life was depending on it?

Mornings were worst. Every day, I woke at the crack of dawn with a sharp pain in my heart, akin to a raw gaping hole that had a large knife planted in it. Unable to get up, all I could do then was to place my hands on my chest and breathe for an hour or so to soothe the pain. This pain was like a wild animal, disappearing one day, just to pounce back with double ferocity the next day. I also dreamt about Rudra every night without fail. Actually, it wasn't Rudra I dreamt of. It was his absence that crept into my dreams. Every night, I was looking for him in classrooms, ashrams, the mountains. He was never there.

'You have two options,' said Mum, sorry to see her daughter in such obvious distress, even though I tried to hide it as best as I could. 'Either you forget him, or you go back to India.' I knew she was right, of course, but still couldn't make up my mind. Could I really go back there, now? And what would happen if I did? As usual, heart and mind were locked in a fierce battle. Heart was urging me to go back to India, mind told me to stay in Germany. Could these two not ever agree?

In moments of clarity, or at least that's what I perceived them to be at the time, mostly after meditation, I knew that all I wanted was to go back to the Himalayas and Rudra. I told myself that I was willing to work on our relationship and do whatever it took to *make* it work. I felt that there were valuable lessons Rudra and I could learn from each other. We could grow together, master our fears and demons together, and heal our wounds together. Yes, it was going to be hard, but it would be worth it in the end. As long as we were honest with each other and communicated, we could do it. In my desperation, I convinced myself that I was willing to sacrifice everything for this relationship, even if it meant living out my love in a platonic friendship.

In my more ostentatious daydreams, I saw myself heroically living a hermit-like existence in the Himalayas, performing austerities for Rudra like Parvati had done for Lord Shiva. Like Parvati, I'd be sitting, unmoving, in the freezing winter with barely any clothes on, reciting '*Om Namah Rudraya*' while pouring cold water over myself. In the heat of the Indian summer, I'd build fires around myself and chant mantras, my sole focus being on Rudra and the love I had for him.

In India, I would gain fame as the undeterred Western woman *yogini*, whose sole aim it was to win the heart of an Indian *sannyasi*, just like Parvati had become highly respected for her *tapasya* in the realm of the Gods thousands of years ago. Even other *sannyasis* and Swamis would be touched by my unwavering devotion for Rudra, and implore him to marry me. Rudra, upon hearing the stories about my severe penances, would eventually become so impressed with my single-mindedness that his heart would melt and he'd have no choice but to love me and live with me happily ever after. (In an alternative version of my vision, he called the police and instructed them to remove the mad stalker woman from his vicinity.)

You might wonder as to why I wanted to go back there. Read, black on white like this, it seems ridiculous that I even entertained the thought of being with an alcoholic monk who'd lied to me and held attitudes that were almost diametrically opposite to mine. Looked at logically, our relationship had very little chance of surviving or even coming off the ground.

But the attraction I felt for Rudra was stronger than anything else I had ever experienced before. Rationally, it didn't make sense; emotionally, to me, it made every sense in the world. In a way, I knew that our differences could be the key to our healing. I felt that if Rudra and I side-stepped our egos and pooled our energies and strengths, we could do great work together. We were opposites and complemented each other perfectly. Rudra had chosen the masculine path of the Sun. I had chosen to walk the feminine path of the Moon, but that was precisely why I felt that we could learn so much from each other.

I wanted to share my life with him, not just as spouses, but as creative partners as well. I dreamt of uplifting poor communities together through education, healing and inspiration, just as he was already doing in his *sannyasi*-post. The difference was that I wanted to do this work with love in my life, working with the natural forces and desires, rather than against them. Could our paths converge? Maybe he could ground me, and I could help him to live more freely.

Yet, time and again, doubt held me back and kept me stuck in the hell that is called indecision. Did Rudra want me to return? Could I handle the pain of going back into the chaos that had been? What about his addictions? And then there was the reality check, of course. Had he called me since my departure from India? Had he asked for my address? Had he asked me to come back? Wasn't the writing clearly on the wall?

I was swinging from letting go to holding on, certainty to doubt, joy to sadness. In my better moments, the distance between us didn't matter and I could feel myself connected to him. In my worst moments, it was as though he had died. I realized that I found it so hard to let go because I was not sure whether Rudra still loved me or not. If I knew for sure that he did, I'd go back to India. But, afraid of what the answer might be, I was scared to ask him that question. Yet, I also knew that I had to take the bull by the horns to get some sort of resolution. I needed certainty, and I needed closure.

So, one morning, after a long week of fretting and obsessing back in Europe, I gingerly dialed Rudra's number on my parents' telephone. I felt sick. The phone rang a few times, then suddenly –

'Hallo?' His familiar voice resounded through the crackling phone line. My heart missed a beat.

'It's me,' I said.

'What? Who?'

'It's me. Tiziana.'

'Ah, okay. It's you. Hello.' He sounded distant. Not exactly the euphoric '*Wonderful to hear from you!*' outcry I was secretly hoping for.

'You don't sound too happy to hear from me,' I said.

'No, no, it is not that. I am happy to hear from you. But I was a bit irritated, because the phone has been ringing all day and I was just about to take some rest.'

'You sounded like you didn't recognize me at first.'

'Well, I did not expect you to call,' he answered. 'And...' – there was a pause – 'I was not thinking about you.'

'You weren't thinking about me,' I repeated slowly. *Great.* I was barely gone for a week and he'd already forgotten me. Just what I wanted to hear.

'Yes... no, no... I have to be honest with you. I was not.'

I suppressed an impulse to mock him with the '*I'm* Indian. *Do you think I can forget you? My first girl? My life partner?*' speech he'd presented me with only days ago. I also silenced my heart that sank deeper and deeper into my stomach.

Instead, I pretended that everything was normal and that I was talking to an old friend, not the intimate lover I'd just left behind in India. We exchanged pleasantries, asked each other how we were and what we were doing. After a while, I had the feeling that I was talking to my uncle and changed tone.

'Come on, Rudra,' I asked. 'How are you *really* doing?'

'Okay. I am okay now.' He sounded confident. 'It took me a few days after you left, but now I am fine.'

'A few days,' I replied, trying not to tear the telephone cable into pieces. 'How did you do that?'

'Well... every time thoughts of you came, I distracted myself with work. I got busy. I chanted *japa*. Always distractions. It worked.'

'That was quick,' I offered, badly concealed sarcasm tainting my voice.

'You will see, time is a great healer. It is early. After one month, two months, you will be fine also. Practice your yoga, your meditation. This will help you a lot.'

The way this conversation was going, all my best intentions to ask him a direct question as to whether we should give things another go went straight out of the window. I felt completely out of my depth, overwhelmed to speak to him after what seemed like an eternity, and finding that perhaps everything had been an illusion after all. I hinted at it, though.

'I'm sorry I left India,' I started.

'Well, I could not ask you to stay, really, either.'

'Maybe I should have stayed... Maybe it could've worked after all.'

He guessed what I was trying to say. His reply was swift.

'No, I can't. Really,' he said decisively. 'My Guru-ji, my Swami-ji. It is not possible.'

He continued: 'I think maybe you are lonely somehow. This is why you want to be with me. Why don't you get married? Find somebody nice, settle down. Or do you want to stay single your whole life?'

'Certainly not!' I retorted quickly, trying not to react. 'Meeting you has made me more determined to be in a relationship, even if we can't be together.'

He remained silent.

Even though his words were crystal-clear, I still didn't get it. Or didn't want to get it.

'You know,' I said, 'things would be easier if you just told me to go away. What makes it so hard is the knowledge that there was something tangible and strong between us. A real connection.'

'Yes, I know.' He sounded thoughtful. 'The separation created a loss. Also for me.'

'It did,' I agreed, and, almost as if to soothe both of us, quoted him a passage I had just read in Paulo Coelho's *Brida*: '*People give flowers as presents because flowers contain the true meaning of Love. Anyone who tries to possess a flower will have to watch its beauty fading. But if you simply look at a flower in a field, you will keep it forever.*'

Brida was a book that had literally fallen into my hands just hours before I left India. I'd wandered into a bookshop with the firm intention of buying *Shantaram* by Gregory David Roberts. As I held the book in my hands, a sales assistant approached me. 'Don't buy this book,' he instructed me. Confused, I looked at him. He reached to his left and lifted another book from the shop window.

'Here,' he said, 'this is much better. It's Paulo Coelho's new book. Buy this instead.' In the sorry state I was in, it was too much hard work to argue with him. And besides, I loved Paulo Coelho. Hence, I acquiesced and bought *Brida* as advised.

When I began to read it in the plane on the way home, I understood why. It was another one of those utterly synchronistic moments. The book was all about love, the freedom of unconditional love, and conveyed the message that soul mates, despite the strong connection they shared, weren't always meant to stay together. I read it within a couple of days and underlined many passages that spoke straight to my heart and seemed to sum up so perfectly my relationship and parting with Rudra. *Brida* was the start of a long line of awakenings about the meaning of love that were just about to make their way into my life.

'Hmm, yes, that is a good analogy,' Rudra said.

'Yeah. Maybe the lesson is to keep loving you, even though our paths are separate again now. Maybe I should just look at you like I'd look at a flower in a field, and appreciate you from afar.'

'That is beautiful.'

We talked a little more, reminiscing about the time we spent with each other. I apologized to him for my Kali-esque behavior on the night before my departure.

He laughed. 'You are welcome. But there is nothing to apologize for,' he said. 'I mean, it was not exactly like I behaved like an angel with you.'

'Yes, but still.'

As the conversation carried on, Rudra began to sound blurry

and his language became increasingly amorous and sexual. I had the feeling that he was drinking. After all, it was afternoon, his rest – and drink – time.

'Are you still drinking alcohol?' I asked.

'No,' he said. 'I have stopped all of those habits two, three days after you left.'

I didn't believe him but kept quiet. It didn't matter anymore.

'Is there anything I can do for you, Tiziana?' he asked finally, charmingly. 'What can I do to make this easier? You know your wish is my command.'

'Can I call you from time to time?' I asked feebly. Enchanted as usual by his velvety words, I wanted to believe that maybe some of our connection could remain, however slight.

'Yes!' he replied. 'Of course! Please do. Please call.' And, after a pause: 'Thank you for calling me today. You have given me energy once again, and I need to thank you for that.'

'Thanks,' I said, and meant it, holding on to his voice like a drowning woman to a lifeline. 'Anyway, I've got to go now.'

'My dear, dear, dear Tiziana,' he sighed. 'Be free. Forget me. I do not mean *forget* me, but do not be attached. Live your life.'

'I'll try,' I said, unconvincingly. 'Take good care of yourself.'

'Yes, you, too,' he said. 'See you.'

'See you,' I echoed, and slowly put down the receiver.

After my initial excitement of having spoken to Rudra faded, the meaning of his words sank in, and I exploded with anger and disappointment. Although I preferred to close my eyes to it, it was clear that it was over between us. He'd moved on with his life and didn't seem to want me back. I felt deceived. In my rage, I considered writing to his Swami-ji and telling him about what had happened, but scrapped the idea as soon as I had calmed down. It wouldn't bring Rudra and me back together, even if I was believed.

Instead, I tried to adopt a compassionate approach and under-stand that Rudra did what he did in the moment, in the haze of desire, and that any deception that happened did not stem from ill will. And ultimately, if I was taking the moral approach, then yes, he should not have allowed himself to get involved with me; but likewise, I should not have welcomed his advances either. We'd both been playing with fire.

I was beginning to ask myself why I had fallen for him, a monk that had the words 'unavailability' stamped all over him, in the first place. Had our affair not been doomed from the start?

This time, my escape had backfired. Maybe for the first time, because Rudra didn't pursue me like all of the other men had and thus gave me the space to reflect, I saw the massive healing potential of relationship. Suddenly, I was seeking the alchemy, the magical meeting and merging of opposites I had always been so afraid of. It wasn't so much that I had lost my fear, but that I was determined to keep on walking despite the fear. Where I had always cut off and stoically said 'Next one!' after a failed relationship, this time I could see beyond myself.

It dawned on me that, inadvertently, Rudra was teaching us all a lesson. Everybody wanted something from him. His mother wanted him to take care of her. His patient and her mother wanted him to be the father of a spiritual child. I wanted to set up an ashram with him and elevate my own spirituality through the combined strength of alchemical love. We all thought we knew what was best for him and projected our desires onto him. Yet, none of us seemed to respect his chosen path. On the contrary, we all tried to pull him away from it to fulfill our own needs, and he only too happily played along with it for a while. It was ironic that he, who was walking the path of renunciation and detachment, should be the one that was teaching us – women in 'love' – the greatest lesson about the true nature of love. Wasn't true love unconditional?

In the weeks that followed my conversation with Rudra, an intense growth process began to unravel in myself. Through my meditations, ponderings, books I discovered and through the open doors of my broken heart, I learned a lot about love. I came to understand that what I had believed to be love for most of my life had actually not very much to do with love at all. I began to see and feel that love was liberty, not possession or need or attachment or any of the other feelings and restrictions we humans liked to place on it. Love, I was beginning to comprehend, was freedom. It included supporting the Beloved on his chosen path, even if those choices conflicted with one's own needs and desires.

It seemed that I needed to reprogram all I had ever learnt about love.

2.4: Finding Myself Again

After hibernating for three weeks with my parents, I packed my bags once more and jumped on the train for a short trip to Sweden. I was invited to the Baby Naming Ceremony of my Goddess-son Alvar, the one-year-old baby of my friend Kerri. Although tired of traveling, I was glad for the change of scenery. In Germany, I'd been feeling unable to express the rawness of my emotions, the grief and anger that were consuming me from the inside, out of fear of worrying my parents. Consequently, I felt like a pressure cooker for the whole time. This holding back consumed my energy and overshadowed the days I spent with my family. I was hoping that some distraction and the company of my friends would do me good.

On the long train and boat journey, I was in a reflective mood. Insights and inspirations poured into my awareness incessantly, as though I was breaking free from a shell. I was detangling my connection with Rudra, and saw that what hurt me was not love, but something within me that was screaming for attention. Most importantly, it seemed that the sole purpose of my encounter with Rudra was to shake me awake and open my heart.

I recognized that it wasn't just Rudra I was missing. I equally missed and felt envious of his lifestyle, so filled with rituals, prayer and spiritual practice. Having shared it, however briefly, with him showed me that I wanted to live in that way, too. If nothing else, Rudra had helped me to gain clarity on what I wanted in my life and where I wanted to go.

My heart was still telling me, persistently, that it loved Rudra and that we could overcome our challenges, but at the same time, it was a mature partnership I was after. Rather than from a place of need, I knew that, for any relationship to work, it needed to come from a centered place of authenticity and awareness. And for this lofty aspiration, I still had a long way to go. But, I comforted myself, even if it hadn't worked out between Rudra and me, at least I could take all of this knowledge into my next relationship.

In Stockholm, I stayed with Elsa, a friend I had first met at Kerri and Johan's wedding in the south of Sweden two years previously. Back then, her husband had just passed away after a short, intense battle with stomach cancer at age forty. A young widow, Elsa had been grieving intensely. I remembered being impressed, as well as intimidated, by her ability to honestly express her feelings, no matter how raw. She didn't put on a brave face and pretend that she was alright, but instead allowed herself to be with what was, for however long it took. Although Elsa felt much better these days, she was still mourning Rob's loss and going through the last stages of letting go by contemplating the idea of moving out of the apartment they had shared, and passing on his paintings to his family.

Somehow, our reconnection could not have been timelier. I didn't have to pretend with Elsa, a woman who knew the loss of the Beloved like no other, and instinctively understood my grief. To be with her was like a warm, soft hug for my bruised heart. It was in Stockholm, in Elsa's big, airy period apartment, that I found the space to stand still and feel my emotions fully. The pain, though it had lessened temporarily, was still my companion. But a new freedom, compassion and softness now accompanied it. Most of all, I felt stronger and more trusting in the ways of the Universe. Though uncomfortable, all was as it should be.

I also found my way back to my priestess roots. Through the long conversations Elsa and I shared, I realized that I was on the right track. My path, my heart, was certainly not that of a renunciate: it was that of a woman deeply entwined with the path of the Divine Feminine, of Mother Earth, and of balancing the earthly existence with spirit. I didn't want to renounce the Earth and all its wonderful gifts.

Neither did I want to deny my body, the temple in which my spirit resided, sensual and sexual pleasures. I saw the human body as a bridge between Heaven and Earth, where both energies met and mingled in the heart center. Neither was better or worse than the other; both were necessary and to be cherished. I saw the Divine as dwelling within each and every one of us, all of creation, and not apart from us 'out there' somewhere.

And something else became clear to me. The deeper I dug into the subject, the more I came to the conclusion that renunciation, in particular of the body and of sexuality, had something to do with the loss of the Divine Feminine in the world – the very path I'd been trying to reclaim for so long. It seemed as though at some point, somebody somewhere decided that sexuality was a threat to spiritual progress. Above all, female sexuality was seen as frightening and too 'out of control'. It could lead men astray and therefore needed to be controlled.

And maybe this was how the story of the Snake and the Apple was invented, along with that of the Immaculate Conception. Gradually, Goddesses became whores, Gods became devils, priestesses became priests, temples became churches, and snakes and dragons became seductresses and monsters. Wise women were condemned and their knowledge extinguished, and before long even the very act of giving life, birth, was ruled over and made sterile by male physicians. Some say that this was a time when life changed from holistic to monotheistic.

The implications of the loss of the Divine Feminine – of respect for life and the Earth – were far more wide-reaching than I had initially thought. Everything, anything, seemed to be affected by it. The way we farmed and the damage this caused to the soil. The way we ate and how we acquired our food. The distribution of the Earth's resources. The poisoned rivers and polluted landscapes. Wars over oil and religion. The low restricted status of many women in the so-called Third World. In the patriarchal system, the emphasis was on profit, speed and greed, on production and cost-efficiency, regardless of the effect it had on the land and its people. I eventually came to the conclusion that almost everything that was out of balance in today's world could be traced back to the negation of the life-giving Feminine Principle.

It slowly dawned on me just how much the loss of the Goddess, and all she represented, had wounded us all, women and men alike. Everywhere around me I could sense the repercussions of a deep cut: a split between head and heart, heart and womb, sky and earth, earthly life and spirituality. We had completely lost touch with Nature and failed to see the interconnectedness of all life. I felt it was *this* that was at the root of all our problems. Organized religion seemed to be just a small by-product of a huge cultural and global imbalance, one that favored a 'masculine', left-brained way of being over a more intuitive, creative, life-affirming existence. It was a path that was built on subduing and dominating the Earth instead of living in tune with her.

I was amazed. I'd never thought about it in that way before. Sure, I had been on the Goddess path for a long time, but I'd never before understood just how deeply it was intertwined with the way the modern world worked. Surprisingly, all I was learning from my affair with Rudra was pushing me firmly back onto my path. Maybe I had to see who I wasn't in order to remind myself of who I was.

2.5: Wales: Three Months in the *Sadhu's* Cave

I left Sweden more healed and optimistic. Still, I limped back to England feeling not unlike a war veteran. I had to laugh at myself. On my trip, I'd survived bombs, extreme weather conditions, high altitude challenges and food poisoning, and in the end, it was love that ambushed me.

Back in Leamington Spa, I reconnected with my friends, who were eager to hear all about my adventures. Although it was wonderful to see them again, it was challenging, too. Everybody expected me to be happy, excited and glowing. Instead, I was somewhat more fragile and melancholic than they remembered me, and all I could talk about was my ill-fated love affair with Rudra.

In early July, after a few busy days in Leamington Spa, I took the train to Wales to meet Tony Crisp. Tony was a healer I'd met a few years ago at a retreat center in Devon while recovering from my breakdown. During my fire ceremony *sadhana* at the yoga ashram, I'd received a strong impulse to work with him. Following a martial arts injury in my early thirties, I'd been suffering from chronic lower back pain, something I managed but hadn't been able to cure with yoga. Tony was a body worker who specialized in chronic pain, and had written books about yoga already in the 1970s. If anybody could help me, it was probably him. Just before leaving Rishikesh, I had decided to go to Wales for three months to study with him.

Tony collected me from the train station in Neath, a small town in South Wales, in his car. It felt bizarre. In many ways, Tony was a complete stranger: I had only met him twice before, and suddenly I crossed continents to spend three months in his company, based on nothing more than a hunch I had received in my *sadhana*.

As we were driving through the overcast countryside in the drizzling rain, my heart sank. What exactly did I think I was doing here, in Wales, where I knew nobody? Where would I stay? Reality hit me in the face like a wet flannel. I had envisaged living in a small cottage in the midst of enchanting mountains, wild woodlands, and lush meadows. Instead, I saw bleak, rocky hills, dilapidated shops and petrol stations. What had I let myself in for?

Tony was a tall, lean and active man in his early seventies with sparkling, alert eyes and an engaging personality. Like me, he was half-Italian and had a fairly hot temper. He loved to communicate, in particular about spiritual matters and what he called the 'inner life'. Fond of the pre-war expressions of his youth, he used peculiar words like 'knapsack' (meaning backpack) and 'wireless' (as in radio, not internet) with great gusto. Tony had spent much of his life working as a therapist, teacher and writer, and, most significantly, as a personal explorer of the strange worlds that lie beneath everyday waking awareness. These days, he lived a quiet, secluded life in a small cottage with his son Quentin.

After a night on Tony's living room floor, I rented a furnished house in a nearby village. I wept after signing the letting agreement. So that was it? My trip was now definitely over? Suddenly, I had mundane responsibilities again: cooking, shopping, cleaning, and most crucially, bills. A *gas* bill. And in Wales out of all places? Damn. Not really what I had envisaged.

There were four houses on Heartbreak Close, as I called the *cul-de-sac* that was my new abode. Edwina, the older woman next door, instantly befriended me. She was a musician whose husband had passed away several years ago, and she was still grieving him. The wife of George, the man living adjacent to Edwina's house, had just absconded with another suitor after twenty years of marriage. Consequently, the abandoned husband sat in Edwina's kitchen every night, recounting his misfortunes.

Keith, the gentleman in the house opposite me, was single, drove immaculate Jaguars, and lived a seemingly dreary existence with his housebound mother he sometimes referred to as 'Godzilla'. And then there was me. We made a cheery gang.

It was bleak in Wales. Heartbreak Close towered above a depressed ex-mining village that consisted of deserted stores, Fish & Chip shops, Chinese Takeaways, charity shops and pubs. Young people with blank eyes loitered around aimlessly on street corners, while adults cradling cans of Strongbow cider sat on their porches and greeted me with a cheery 'Alright?' whenever I passed. After the colorful exuberance of India, I felt completely alienated.

The thing I remember most about my three months in Wales is the rain. That summer, it rained every single day, sometimes so hard that it was impossible to leave the house. It was as though the Monsoon had decided to escort me all the way from India. It provided me with plenty of time to think, in particular as I had chosen to live without telephone or internet access, true *sadhu*-style. I just wanted to be with myself, without distractions of any kind, and concentrate on the healing work with Tony. Maybe it was what I needed after my big trip; maybe it was just a tad too austere emotionally.

In the long days that were to follow, I spent hours sitting in my conservatory, which I had converted into a yogic temple. Under slate-grey skies, I stared at the giant bare hill that loomed over the house like an ominous shadow. And I wrote. I wrote reams and reams of journals and notes, pouring out from my fingers synchronous with the rain and the tears from my eyes.

2.6: LifeStream

In retrospect, it was extraordinary that I ended up working with Tony when I did. Somehow, because of his background in yoga, I had imagined that he'd be teaching me advanced yogic practices that would finally shift the pain in my back. However, when I arrived in Wales, heartbroken and disoriented, my back pain was the least of my worries. And in fact, our work would focus on something completely different, and it was exactly what I needed.

We agreed to meet three afternoons a week to see where our work would take us. 'I don't like to have much of a plan when I work with people these days,' Tony explained, leaning back comfortably in his armchair by the window that overlooked The Sleeping Giant, a large mountain in the Brecon Beacons. 'I trust that I will be shown what we need to work on.' This statement threw my analytical mind slightly. There'd be no plan? No objective? No, said Tony. We would 'explore', as he called it.

In our first session, one of many that were to take place in my living room on Heartbreak Close, Tony introduced me to something he called LifeStream. It was a dynamic process that, he said, could release energy blocks in the human body. It consisted of simply allowing the body to move in the way it wanted to, and learning to listen to what the body was saying. The practice was to be completely unstructured and self-directed.

'What, just move?' I wanted to know, perplexed. 'And then what?'

'Just try it,' Tony smiled.

To help me, he took me through a strange series of arm circling and rib-cage swinging movements. I wasn't too impressed. I wanted instruction, knowledge, and to do something my intellect could grasp. Instead, Tony bypassed my intellect completely.

'Just sit there and close your eyes,' he said. 'Direct your awareness inside of your body. How does your body want to move right now? Does it *want* to move? Just sit, lie down, stand up, move around – do whatever your body asks you to do. If you want to make a sound, do so. You may feel like curling up into a ball, or maybe you'll want to yawn, or scream, or cry... Just explore and trust the process.'

'Okay,' I mumbled and did as he said, feeling more than just a bit self-conscious. Sitting on the fluffy floral carpet, I tried to 'surrender', as Tony called it, but my mind was having none of it. *What is this supposed to do? This is crazy. I don't want to do this. Can't we do some yoga?* – in particular when I heard Tony singing a strange Arabic-sounding chant and speaking, as it seemed to me, in tongues.

Not much happened for me in this first session – I was far too uncomfortable and critical to allow myself to participate fully in this alien process. I feared that if I really let myself go, all hell would break loose and once I started to release my grief, I wouldn't be able to stop it. Would it consume me? Annihilate me? I was scared of Tony's reaction. Would he be able to cope with my outburst? What would he think if he saw how much sadness and anger were really inside me? Would he be freaked out? Judge me? Reject me? Find me pathetic?

My shyness surprised me. I'd always seen myself as relatively open and expressive. This process taught me that I had done a great job of pushing down my uncomfortable feelings, in particularly grief and anger. Anger was especially hard to express for me – it was an emotion that wasn't 'spiritual', and so, more often than not, I internalized it and pretended that I wasn't feeling it.

Tony smiled and shook his head gently when I eventually confessed my fears. 'This is the ideal place for you to access your deepest emotions,' he encouraged me. 'And let me tell you, I've seen it all. In some of the LifeStream sessions we did back in the 1970s, you would have thought that you were entering a mental asylum. Some people were thrashing about on the floor, screaming their heads off, making the most bizarre noises... So, a little bit of anger is certainly not going to freak me out.'

I still found it hard to fully let go. Yet, over time, something strange happened. It was as though an internal controller took over my body and moved me in ways it wanted me to. And this controller seemed to know exactly what the movements I needed were. Suddenly, my arms moved, my back arched, I twisted and stretched on the floor, and strange hissing sounds came out of my mouth. Sometimes, memories and visions flooded my consciousness.

Soon, my body instinctively knew how to express itself, and after some practice in letting go, I'd enter into an altered state of awareness. As my body contorted and stretched, I'd often cry and release pent-up emotions, mainly sadness and anger. LifeStream was like opening a Pandora's Box, filled with memories, emotions, visions and sounds, all of which my body seemed to store. Though painful, I found it liberating and after every session, I felt a little lighter.

After a few weeks of practice, I managed to experience the full power of LifeStream for the first time. Tony and I had started to 'surrender', and I was moving around on the floor, stretching and hissing. I felt like a snake that was oozing poison from her mouth. Eyes closed, I suddenly found myself in darkness, in what I soon recognized to be my mother's womb, overwhelmed with fear and sadness. From afar, I heard screaming, and felt as though my mother had been kicked in the stomach. I experienced a crushing feeling of wanting to get out and escape, but this was not possible. Instead, I had to stay where I was, and felt trapped. There was no escape. *I can't even die!* I thought, outraged. In the end, I curled up, and went to sleep in resignation.

When I emerged from my visions, shivering intensely while Tony held me, I was amazed. What had just happened there? As I shared my experiences with Tony, I suddenly made an important connection. Four months into her pregnancy, my mother had nearly miscarried me. Back then, the gynecologist asked her to make a choice: either she'd lose me, or I had to be kept in place by an oval, black hard plastic ring that was to be inserted in her womb. She chose the latter option.

Through my early childhood, I had one near-death experience after another. Only several weeks old, I developed a life-threatening illness which saw me hospitalized for three weeks. As a toddler, I swallowed a piece of cardboard and was already blue in the face when my sister noticed and saved me. I nearly drowned twice, got lost on a regular basis and was almost run over by a car had it not been for my uncle who lunged at me to pull me back.

These incidents diminished with adolescence, but I developed a fascination with death instead. As a teenage Goth, I romanticized death in all its forms, primarily through music, literature, art, and later by buying a house next to a graveyard. As a young adult, I had often been confused by my restlessness. I always wanted to leave, wherever I was. Places, jobs, relationships. I always wanted to be somewhere else. Was this where it had all started? Before birth, in my mother's womb? Bewildered, I looked up at Tony.

'What is this, Tony? How is it possible to have such vivid memories coming out of nowhere?'

He smiled and leaned back against the sofa.

'It's a powerful process,' he said. 'We used to call it Self Regulation at first, because it appears that these movements regulate the Self in the same way that the body's natural functions do, such as crying, or vomiting. It's a type of cleansing process. The way I understand it is that we store traumatic memories in the tissues of our bodies. If we don't express our feelings right away, and often we don't because we're too scared or shocked, they get locked in the body. Often this results in tensions and even disease. This simple practice can help us to release these tensions and help the blocked energy in our bodies to flow freely.'

'Heavy stuff, isn't it?' I was still reeling from what I had just experienced.

'Of course, at first it's likely to release some very uncomfortable feelings. Not in everyone, but in many people,' Tony explained. 'It sets something in motion, and what is remarkable is that you don't tend to have much control over what comes up. The emotions and memories that surface live deep in the unconscious, and when they are ready to surface, they will. And to face them, to really look at them... well, it takes courage.'

I could see why.

'But they're better out than in. The rewards are worth it in the end.' Tony stretched and got up from the floor to make us some tea. While he was boiling water in the kitchen, I stared out into the garden. What an incredible process. LifeStream was like a deeper form of psychotherapy. At first, it was excruciating when the emotional body started to open up, perhaps for the first time, but ultimately, it could be a greatly liberating experience.

Tony returned with two cups of herbal tea in his hands. We sat down on the big sofa and sipped the hot liquid, facing each other. We sat in silence for a while.

'How did you come across LifeStream?' I asked after a few minutes. 'Did you invent it?'

'No, not at all. I discovered it through trial and error, back in the 1970s. But when I started to do some research later on for the books I wrote about the topic, I realized that many comparable practices exist all over the world. For example, the Indian practice of *Shaktipat* seems to be a very similar process: spontaneous movements arise in the practitioner in this state, and sometimes they perform previously unknown yogic postures to perfection. *Shaktipat* is usually 'given' by a Guru to a disciple, but the descriptions I have read of the practice are extremely alike. And the end result is the same: you let go of your conscious ego enough to let an internal energy flow freely through your body.

This leads to the awakening of *kundalini* energy, the life force that is dormant in all of us, in your body.'

'So is this what happens? The release of *kundalini*? Wow!' I exclaimed excitedly.

Kundalini is the Sanskrit world for 'coiled'. In yoga, the word is used to describe an unconscious, instinctive force, often envisaged as a sleeping serpent coiled at the base of the spine. Yoga and Tantra propose that this energy can be awakened through spiritual practice, such as *pranayama* and mantra chanting. Upon awakening, the energy rises from a point at the base of the spine up a subtle channel called *sushumna* to the top of the head, where it merges with *sahasrara*, or the crown chakra. The awakening of *kundalini* energy brings about an expansion of consciousness. Ultimately, it leads to the attainment of divine wisdom and infinite bliss – the state commonly described as enlightenment.

'Have you discovered this method anywhere else?' I wanted to know.

'Yes, also in Japan in the system of *Seitai*. But in *Seitai*, there is not much use of sound and it is often done with a partner. *Subud* in Indonesia, and Reichian therapy, named after Wilhelm Reich, are very similar. That's obvious though – it's such a simple process actually, so simple that we can't see it most of the time! We think that we have to go to doctors, therapists and healers, to be fixed by somebody else, and sometimes that is helpful. But the truth is that we have everything we need already inside of us. And that in itself, because it is so empowering, can be scary.'

'But how did you find out about this?' I was curious. 'Did somebody teach you?'

'The way I discovered LifeStream,' Tony recalled, 'was by simply surrendering. For years, I had been practicing and teaching yoga, meditation and relaxation, and still I was a very unhappy man. It just didn't help me. I was depressed, and completely blocked emotionally. So one day I said to God, *Look*

God, I am just going to sit here now. I don't know what to do to release my pain, so I will simply sit and wait until you tell me. And then, gradually, it started to happen. The movements began to flow through me, and they took me onto the most incredible journey.'

Tony took a last sip from his cup, and gently placed it on the table next to the sofa.

'I was running an ashram in Devon at the time,' he recalled with a smile. 'Together with some friends, I started to surrender in a group. We just sat in the meditation room and experimented. We'd journey inside our Beings and explore our emotions, with movement and voice, to see what our bodies wanted to express. Quite a liberating thing to do, really.'

He paused. 'And then, one day, something big happened. You know, I was suffering from this most horrific neck pain for almost thirty years. Again and again I had tried to relax it away, with not much of a result. And that day, in our surrendering session, I suddenly began to tremble. I thought it must be tension, and carried on calmly.

'After a little while I started to tremble again. But I didn't feel cold, and I didn't feel nervous enough to cause this type of tension. So I moved back from the group and lay down to let the trembles happen. First of all it was just vague, but gradually, my head pulled back hard. The movements became very sponta-neous. And suddenly, my mouth clamped open, and my arms were in a position of being strapped to my side. Slowly the pattern of shaking changed, and I cried out in pain. My whole body contorted into contractions as this happened.'

Tony paused in thought. 'My poor friends just sat there, not knowing what the hell was going on, until I was done.' He laughed. 'I soon realized that I was reliving the effects of a tonsil operation I had when I was six years old.'

'Really? Wow!'

'Yes... maybe I wasn't fully anesthetized back then. But the fact was that I carried a lot of tension, stress and shock inside my body from that time until I was thirty-five, resulting in my chronic neck pain. And the most incredible thing was that from that day on, after I relived and released the original experience, I never again suffered from neck pain.'

I was amazed. 'What, you think you carried this tension inside your body for all that time, and that is why your neck was always hurting?'

'Yes. Our bodies are incredible. Whenever we repress an emotion, it tends to show up as body pain or disease. That incident, that huge release of tension I experienced on that day almost forty years ago in Devon, inspired me to experiment more with the practice. And over the years, I released a lot of blocks in my body and from my unconscious mind with LifeStream.'

He looked at me. 'As I said earlier, we really do have everything inside of us. We carry all the wisdom we need in our bodies and in our dreams. It is all there for us to explore – but we have to make the effort to connect, to listen to ourselves.'

'Isn't it strange how you discovered this all by yourself, without any guidance?' I asked.

'Hmm, maybe,' Tony nodded. 'Perhaps it was because I didn't like authority or Gurus. Plus, it was a necessity. I couldn't afford expensive therapy. I had a wife and five children to support. I *needed* to find my own way out of the misery in which I was living.'

I was amazed, to say the least. Coming to Wales at this time made more and more sense. Whereas I had mostly beaten myself up for starting the work with Tony in such a state of misery – *great*, enchanting company I was at the moment – I now sensed that my fragile state could actually be conducive to what we were trying to do. Maybe I was here to heal not only my body, but also the underlying issues that seemed to make sure that I ran from one romantic drama to the next? Could this method help me to get to the root cause of my chaotic relationship history? Time would tell the tale.

2.7: The Original Wound

Tony and I had much more in common than I initially thought. Although he was so much older and more experienced than I, his life story resembled mine in many ways. Therefore, it wasn't surprising that he understood only too well the pain and lovesickness I was going through. I felt blessed to have this grounded man by my side who was ready to help me find the root cause of my problems and support me on what he called 'The Hero's Journey'.

In many ways, we had a wonderful relationship. We talked deeply and intensely about our lives, our spiritual experiences, relationships and beliefs, for hours at a time. With Tony, I felt safe enough to share my innermost feelings, and knew that I could tell him absolutely everything without fear of judgment or ridicule. I trusted him completely. This was a big step for me, considering the mistrust I'd held towards men for most of my life. But there was a natural, strong bond between Tony and me that didn't even allow doubt to enter. I simply knew with every fiber of my being that he had my best interests at heart. Here, head and heart agreed completely from the very first day we worked with each other.

Tony shared his wisdom generously with me. He often talked to me about his two long-term marriages, the second of which was very significant for his healing. Tony had left Brenda, his first wife, with whom he fathered five children, upon meeting Hyone, an Australian woman. With Hyone, he shared a strong, irresistible connection, out of which a strong partnership ensued.

'Meeting Hyone was where my healing journey really started,' Tony said one afternoon, as we sat in my conservatory. 'I married Brenda when I was very young, and I was emotionally crippled then. I didn't know what love was until I met Hyone.'

'In what way was she so significant for your healing?' I

wanted to know.

'Oh, it was mainly what we mirrored to each other. We had a shared interest in exploring and healing, and in that ours was a very fruitful partnership. But at the same time, I was eaten up by guilt about leaving Brenda, and my children. I still visited the children every day, but that did nothing to ease my conscience. It was a miserable time.' He laughed. 'As could be seen when, early on in our relationship, Hyone went back to Australia for a couple of months.'

'What happened?'

'I was missing her so much, I was beside myself after she left. I had no idea why, or what was happening to me, but I was crying for seven weeks! That time, I felt like I was having a nervous breakdown. I was crying most days, couldn't sleep, and was besieged by a never-ending ache. That, together with compulsive thoughts, anger, despair and terror. I was just crying and crying, uncontrollably, like a baby; day and night, can you imagine? I had to go to the grocery store like that, sobbingly telling the woman what vegetables I wanted!'

'Really? Gosh.' I laughed.

'Really. In those days, there were no telephones as there are now. We only had a payphone outside our flat, and Hyone had left me a number in Australia to reach her on. But I just couldn't get hold of her. Every day, I went to that payphone and dialed her number.'

'You must have really missed her.' I stretched out on my sheepskin and looked up at him.

'That's an understatement.' He smiled. 'But here is where it gets interesting. Do you know why I was going through this? It wasn't because I was missing *Hyone* so desperately. Rather, our physical separation triggered a deep, unconscious wound I held in my core from when I was a young boy and very ill. My mother left me in a convalescent hospital for three days, and I felt completely abandoned. And now, with Hyone being away, I was reliving all of the anger and despair that I harbored at my mother for leaving me when I was small. I didn't know it at the time, but it soon became apparent when I explored it and the memories started to flood in.'

I remained silent, thinking about what Tony had just told me. Something about this story resonated very deeply with me.

'Of course, as a child, I repressed these powerful emotions to survive, as I could not make sense of them at the time. I buried them deep inside me, and this love relationship brought them out.'

He continued. 'I went through so much stuff in those weeks. Out came terror that I had done something awful to cause Hyone, who represented my mother of course, not to love me. And anger, anger that anyone should apparently treat me as if I didn't matter, and could be casually left. As a child, I experienced a strong desire to divorce my mother out of my soul, rather than have her treat me that way. This whole sequence of terror and pain had come about because of Hyone's absence, and because of my ability to stay present with it. And I gradually saw how this buried convalescent incident had negatively influenced my whole way of relating with women in my adult life.'

'That's pretty incredible,' I said, looking at the bare mountain outside the window. 'I mean, how many times do we experience emotional pain in a relationship and think the other person has caused it? It's happened to me lots of times. Who'd think to relate it back to childhood, and with such precision? And yet, it makes so much sense when you look at it.'

'Exactly,' Tony enthused, 'and this is what the whole projection business is all about. We project so many of our unresolved childhood injuries onto our partners, when really, most of the time, they have absolutely nothing to do with it and are bewildered at our reactions! But there is a way out of this emotional treadmill.'

'So what happened in the end with Hyone and you? Did she

phone you?' I wanted to know.

'Eventually, I did get hold of her on the telephone, and told her that I felt something strange going on and needed to know when she might be coming back. She said she would let me know. So I waited for a telephone call, a letter, something. Nothing came. That's when the crack widened and all hell broke loose from within me. Thank God! Because I needed to go through it to let go of the latent feelings I had inside of me from that convalescent hospital incident. After that, the pressure was gone. I gradually learnt how to forgive and trust.'

He laughed. 'And guess what – Hyone sent me one postcard from Australia telling me she'd be back in a couple of weeks!'

'Wow,' I said. 'And what happened when she came back?'

'Nothing. It was out of my system by then. I had dealt with it, and in retrospect it was good that I couldn't reach her. It forced me to experience the full extent of the pain, realize what it was really about, and release it. I believe that this is the only way. Acceptance and release.'

After Tony left that day, I sat quietly in my yogic temple for a long time. His vivid account of abandonment had triggered something inside of me. Had this not happened to me, too? I knew that I had been gravely ill as a baby, and put into intensive care for three weeks when I was barely a month old. In those days in the 1970s, hospitals kept babies in strict isolation.

'We were only allowed to visit you once a week, for one hour on a Sunday,' my mother told me when I spoke to her some days after my conversation with Tony. 'And we could only see you through a window. I asked the nurse, *Can I hold her?* and she said, *No, no, don't do that – she'll only start crying when you leave and then we won't be able to calm her down.* You poor thing lay there all alone in your little bed and we couldn't get to you.'

Was *this* why I now experienced such excruciating pain at the separation from Rudra? Was this what the constant ache in my heart, the despair, my feeling of inability to reach out to him were really about? Was I not just missing him, but reliving the feelings of being left by my mother when I was a baby?

It certainly made sense – nobody could understand the intense emotional turmoil I was experiencing for a man I had only been with for a matter of weeks and with whom interactions had been so volatile. Sure, there was the theory that Rudra was my soul mate and we were twin souls connected through different lifetimes that had karma to resolve with each other. And perhaps that was also true.

However, I could not ignore the fact that energetically, he reminded me too much of my mother and the early imprint of love – extreme closeness followed by abandonment – I had experienced. As a baby, I knew, *felt* that my mother loved me, and hence experienced such incomprehension and confusion when suddenly, after six weeks of intimacy, she was not there anymore. Instead, I found myself all alone in a clinical hospital ward, surrounded by strangers in white uniforms who smiled down at me.

I continued to follow the thought. Was this why I had this ingrained belief that I was not wanted and that I had to do every-thing by myself? I closed my eyes and tried to imagine what it must have been like for a small baby. What would her reaction be? Initially, I thought, a baby would cry and scream, but what happened when this did not help and the mother wouldn't come back? It would probably give up eventually and retreat into its own little world. And what emotional message would it receive following such a traumatic separation? 'I am not wanted'; 'I must be unlovable to be left like this'; 'I don't need any of you' were likely contenders.

Although I'd known the story of my illness as a baby for many years, I had never paid much attention to it, or at least not made any emotional connection. Yet, through my degree in psychology, I knew that human development was most strongly influenced during the first seven years of life, and that the way we were nurtured by our caretakers was particularly significant. If we didn't feel secure attachment and consistency in the bond with our parents, problems in interpersonal relationships were likely to develop in adult life. It gave me much food for thought.

Further explorations in LifeStream showed me that I was on to something. In a spontaneous regression that happened in one of our sessions, I had visions of being in a hospital bed and repeatedly smashing against a window pane. It was as though my spirit wanted to fly out of the bed, out of the window, but was repeatedly being thrown back down. I continued to be overwhelmed by feelings of abandonment and incomprehension. Only now, I was starting to dive below the surface.

Although it was difficult, the awareness of what had happened to me was a huge relief. I could suddenly see the abandonment pattern I had experienced with men clearly: the feelings of despair and terror when they did not call, my tendency to just crumble, and my inability to eat when I was going through emotional difficulties. Previously, I had thought that there was something wrong with me because I reacted so strongly in intimate relationships, that I was just clingy or needy for the sake of it, oversensitive, emotionally disturbed. I'd never really understood *why* this was the case or whether I could do anything about it.

My coping strategy thus far had been to overcompensate for my vulnerability by putting up a tough front, and cutting off relationships at crucial points in an attempt to stay in control. More than once, I had ended the relationship with a man I really cared about when I couldn't cope with the closeness and the anxiety it evoked in me, even though it'd cut me up inside for the next two years to come.

It was as though a veil had lifted. I'd lived through several weeks of intense closeness with Rudra before the incision followed. And Rudra, though he said he loved me, had decided not to be with me because of the *sannyas* rules that forbade him to do so – just like my mother who had accepted the hospital rules that said she could only see me through a window once a week. I was dumbfounded. So I was inadvertently re-creating that pain over and over again? Because it wanted resolution?

The more I thought about it, the more logical it seemed. From an early age, I'd been attracted to men I couldn't reach. It was always the unattainable that brought me the bittersweet, familiar feeling of longing I understood as 'love'. When I was older, I only felt safe in long-distance relationships, even though they caused me immense pain also. Again, they echoed those short, intense bursts of intimacy and bliss, followed by long periods of sadness and longing.

I knew that my boyfriends loved me, and yet something – something I had unconsciously chosen and co-created – prevented us from being fully and consistently together. And when the distance was removed, and we decided to live together, I became scared and found a reason to run. Consistency and true intimacy didn't fit into my experiential picture of love. I was looking for evidence everywhere that I was not wanted, because my identity depended on it.

2.8: Simply Love

The insights continued. When Tony had to travel to France for work, I decided to take the opportunity to be completely silent for a week. I wanted to go deep to the root, without distraction, and see what I would find inside of myself. Feeling utterly depleted, I had no wish to talk to anybody anyway. I didn't want to be confused by other people's opinions any longer. In stillness, I urged my soul to speak.

The continuous, flood-like rain was helping the process. It gave me an incentive to stay in my cave and explore my inner worlds. Besides, it seemed that I had no choice. I did not want to, could not live anymore like I did before, running from one painful drama to the next. I didn't want to be driven by the past any longer.

Instead, I wanted to learn what love was so that I could love fully, unconditionally and without fear. I wanted to grow conscious, aware and blissful. For that, I sensed that I needed to acknowledge and feel my sadness, anger and despair to their full extent, to be able to let them go. In the midst of the wretched state that was so familiar to me, I was driven by a passionate desire to heal myself, not only for my sake, but also for the benefit of everyone around me. This desire gave me the courage to face the demons that lurked in the dark recesses of my mind. It was a knife's edge, but I knew that I would come out stronger when it was over.

And, rapidly, as the silence removed all external distractions, it started to sink in what my fateful encounter with Rudra had really been about. Soon, I was no longer asking, 'Why did he do this to me?' Instead, I moved the focus from Rudra and his faults to myself. Now, the question was: 'Why did this happen to me?' Why did I allow myself to become involved, over and over again, with men who could not, would not commit to me, had addiction issues, and did not treat me with respect? What was it inside of me that was scared of commitment?

It was clear to everyone around me, including myself, that I wasn't making wise choices when it came to potential partners. But whereas I had always blamed the men in the past for their perceived faults (read: behaviors that did not conform to my wishes and made me feel unsafe) and the breakdown of the relationship, this time, I was looking inwards. Deeply, and perhaps for the first time. What I found was a common denominator – me – and a clearly emerging pattern.

Much of my rapidly growing awareness was due to books that had almost magically fallen into my hands, most notably the work of the German psychotherapists Katja Sundermeier and Eva-Maria Zurhorst. Books I probably would have never looked at before, had I not been in the crisis I was currently experiencing. These authors said something quite radical, something that was relatively new to me, and equally something I grasped instantly because it spoke straight to my heart.

Among other things, they proposed that intimate relationships were catalysts for all our buried childhood wounds, fears and negative patterns. The relationships we lead on the outside, I learned, were exactly the relationships we needed because they showed us the relationship we have to ourselves. That it was never the other person, the irresponsible, commitment-phobic spouse that caused our pain, but that the pain was already there, waiting to emerge and be healed through our intimate encounters.

One book was to become especially poignant on my Welsh inner journey. *Simply Love*, written by Katja Sundermeier, examined and demonstrated how partner selection really works through a number of unique and often uncomfortable exercises. These exercises focused on what Katja called the 'cellar child', a metaphor for our buried childhood injuries and needs, and how to bring them into conscious awareness. She explained how these old, redundant life scripts often dictated our responses in current life situations and also determined which partners we chose. Though I was at first skeptical, this book turned out to be one of the greatest gifts on my healing journey.

I worked through *Simply Love* in a week, lying on a sheepskin rug in the glass conservatory with the rain sliding down the windows. Like a detective, I was fascinated by every little clue I discovered. Prompted by the playful, but deeply profound questions and exercises in the book, I was encouraged to take a really good, honest look at my belief systems and my early conditioning that led to my choosing the men I did. I was often astonished, deeply saddened, and relieved at the same time that everything suddenly made sense to me.

I discovered that many of my adult responses and patterns were indeed influenced by my hospital stay as a newborn baby. Time and again, I had re-created the unhappy life circumstances that reinforced the loneliness I felt deep in my core: leaving home aged sixteen, moving into empty houses in new areas where I knew nobody, living alone, traveling alone, working alone. Even though I still felt awful, my newfound knowledge was exhilarating. It was as though somebody had given me a key and the door to freedom was now wide open.

Other exercises in the book were quietly amusing, such as the 'advertising slogan' in which Katja asked us to become aware of the unconscious messages we send out to potential partners. I laughed out loud when I read mine. '*Attention!*' it blinked at me in red letters. '*I find it difficult to tolerate intimacy and generally make a swift exit when things become too painful for me. I'm therefore looking for a man who is just as fearful as I am, and even better if he can also confirm to me that men lie, betray and are scared of commitment.*' My God! Was this really my billboard? No wonder I always ended up in such messy relationships!

I loved working with my newfound 'cellar child'. Katja illustrated this metaphor with endearing drawings of a little person that lived in the belly of the adult. 'Hello,' it said. 'I am your cellar child, I live inside of you. I have experienced many things that hurt me. I urgently need somebody who listens to me, sees me, and who, above everything, can give me now what I did not receive back then. Because you up there don't see or hear me and don't take any notice of me, I'm now going to find somebody who fits into the script that I am holding in my hands. I am looking for a suitable actor in the episode: *Nobody wants me.* And when I have found him, then I'm giving you the opportunity to look at and especially feel again all that is contained inside of my script.'

Gosh. Was this really how and why we chose our romantic partners, to bring our old childhood wounds to the surface and heal them? Was this why we were sometimes irresistibly attracted to people who were completely unsuitable? And if this was really so, why did nobody tell us? Why were we brought up on diets of romantic novels, books and songs that reinforced an illusion? Why were so many people stuck in bad relationships or divorced?

And, most importantly, was there a way of doing things differently? Was there a way of engaging *consciously* on this path of relating? Could we purposefully become aware of and heal our wounds and then choose somebody different, a partner that was more healed, too? It made sense – once our needs were attended to, once we knew how to take care of ourselves, then perhaps we did not need to be with partners who triggered all our wounds. Maybe we could then make a conscious choice of who we actually wanted to be with, rather than being driven by the unresolved issues that lurked in our unconscious minds.

The more I grasped the concept, the more excited I grew. Of course! We, our unconscious, chose the very people who triggered what we most needed to heal in ourselves, which made intimate relationships often so difficult. And because love and intimacy triggered so many painful, inconsistent memories in me, I had constantly chosen men who reflected that same wounding, the wounding I was not aware of, to me through their actions. How clever!

And what did this mean for love? Did romantic love exist at all? If it didn't, then what were the intense, uncontrollable emotions we experienced when we fell in love? Was the irresistible attraction we felt towards another really just nature's way of healing itself? And if so, where did the people in happy marriages fit in? Did it mean that they had managed to heal their issues, or came from happy families and did not have so much to process? No matter what the general answer was, in my case, the theory certainly made sense.

Like Tony, I'd repressed my painful childhood emotions for most of my life. My way of coping when my father was beating my mother, and when my parents were screaming at each other, was to shut down. The one time I'd tried to interfere and jumped in front of my mother to protect her when I was seven, my father had violently attacked me, too. From that point onwards, I felt it was safer to keep out of it. Consequently, I had avoided family meal times and eaten my meal in front of the TV ahead of my parents so that I could leave the house as soon as they started their evening meal. I would seek refuge at my best girlfriend's house and pretend that everything was okay. From what I can remember, I told nobody how I was feeling, and neither did anybody ask, even though the whole village must have heard what was going on in our home.

I shut off emotionally, sought solace in books and music, and pretended, best as I could, that everything was normal and as it should be. Inside of me, a deep despair simmered. Love, for my cellar child, meant pain, disappointment and loneliness. The most difficult task for me now was to transform my resulting, unconscious feelings of guilt and worthlessness into real compassion and love for myself.

Now, in my current healing crisis, all of this was begging for resolution. I looked at my 'scripts' with my mother, father and sister, and all the patterns that had formed in my family of origin. Love, in the Stupia household, equaled violence, control and power struggles. With such a blueprint, what chance was there for me to sustain a happy, fulfilling partnership?

There was only one way forward: I had to become fully conscious of my life script and rewrite it. Katja called it the 're-parenting process', and it consisted of learning to give myself what I had not received as a child. Now I was an adult and not dependent on my parents anymore, so instead of looking at a partner to fill the empty spaces inside of me and cure my loneliness, I needed to take responsibility and heal myself. This healing could of course also take place within a relationship, but without due awareness, it often meant that old scripts were simply played out again and again, resulting in emotional mayhem.

Awareness, it seemed, was everything, as was taking respon-sibility, and acting without guilt or blame. I had to learn to accept that I, like many other people, had been wounded, and that it was not my fault. Neither was it my parents' fault who had been wounded themselves and not had the good fortune to become aware of their issues before they decided to have children. There was no fault. I had to learn to love and forgive myself, for, deeply ingrained in me was the belief that I was not good enough and not wanted, otherwise my parents would not have abandoned me nor acted in the way they did. It was time to let that old, outworn script go and journey into authenticity.

It was as though a big hammer had cracked my head open for a new consciousness to emerge. I was sad about the many oppor-tunities for transformation I had not realized but equally felt lucky that I had found this knowledge now, aged thirty-six. It'd been a long journey but at least I knew now that I was not condemned for things to stay that way forever. More than once, I was overcome with deep feelings of gratitude for Rudra for inadvertently bringing me this awareness, coupled with sadness that it was its lack that had torn us apart.

More insights started to pour in. When I back-tracked my past boyfriends, I concluded with amazement that all, without fail, had issues with their mothers. Mainly, they were the sons of mothers who were absent either through death, mental illness or divorce, or conversely, mothers that were still around but overly controlling. I recalled that even one of my very first boyfriends, when I was thirteen, only had a father to look after him. The mother of my first long-term boyfriend, a skinhead called Bernd, had left the family after an affair and I remembered the bitter terms with which he used to describe her.

It was those men, the men with the absent mothers and the deep-seated, simmering hatred against women, that I loved the most – seemingly because our wounds matched perfectly. I'd harbored a deep resentment towards men, triggered by my violent, emotionally absent father, which mirrored the hurt and anger those men felt towards women. And hence I had sought solace in the feminist Goddess movement, and Rudra had embraced an entirely masculine spiritual path.

Tony was thrilled when he returned from his trip and I shared my discoveries with him. Understanding interpersonal relationships was one of his major passions, too. He introduced me to the 'Imago' work of Harville Hendrix which echoed many of the same concepts. According to Hendrix, human beings have a composite image of all the positive and negative traits of their primary caretakers deep in their unconscious minds. He calls this image the 'Imago' – a blueprint of the person one is likely to marry someday.

People tend to marry Imago matches, that is, somebody who matches up with this composite image of their primary caretakers. This, says Hendrix, is important because people marry for the purpose of healing and 'finishing the unfinished business of childhood'. The rationale is that since parents were the people who wounded us, they were also the only ones who could heal us – not literally, but in proxy through a love partner who matched their traits. Through conscious communication and exercises in awareness, the unconscious becomes conscious and profound healing can take place in intimate relationships.

This resonated strongly with me. Fascinated, I was learning all I could about the alchemy of love and the reconciliation of apparently irreconcilable forces. I was spurred on by an intuitive knowing that this was all part of a greater plan, that all this, even the pain – especially the pain – was perfect and would lead to happiness eventually. I took this knowledge from my previous journeys to the Underworld, and I knew I had the strength to return. This was not a descent; it was integration.

I loved the growth process my broken heart had set in motion. For maybe the first time in my life, I wanted to stand still and feel it all, explore the pain and know it. It was a wonderful opportunity for healing what was at the heart of the matter. Paradoxically, through the loss of love, I was discovering what love really was.

2.9: Full Moon Eclipse: The Last Call

You would have thought, or at least hoped, that after all the awareness I gained in my work with Tony, my lovesickness for Rudra was waning. It wasn't. Despite the frequent and often exciting insights, my pain and longing didn't subside. Even though I now knew why Rudra and I had been so powerfully attracted to each other, it didn't change the fact that I was still hopelessly, desperately in love with him and wanted nothing more than to find reconciliation with him. I still dreamt of him most nights, and often woke up in tears. At least now I knew that I wasn't just crying for him. This insight didn't stop me from feeling utterly pathetic, though.

I spoke to Rudra one last time on the Full Moon eclipse in August 2008. In astrological terms, eclipses are believed to be powerful times of big shifts and letting go. This one was particularly special, as there were two eclipses in one calendar month, one during the Full Moon and one during the New Moon. Synchronistically, this Full Moon was in Aquarius (Rudra's sun sign) in the period of Leo (my sun sign). That weekend, I felt compelled to speak to him and ask him once and for all whether there was a chance of us getting back together.

Of course, I knew that calling Rudra was a bad idea. I had not heard a single word from him since leaving India, and even though I had texted him my new mobile number, his only response was silence. Yet, although the facts spoke for themselves, part of me was still in denial. What if he had not received my message? What if he was ill? In difficulty? Dead? There was always the remote possibility that he did love me and was as tortured as I was about the situation. I needed to know. I had to speak to him for one last time.

I decided to call him on a dreary Sunday morning. Lying on my bed in the *sadhu*'s cave, I had my carefully prepared notes next to me. I knew exactly what I was going to say to convince him to come back to me. I was going to be so reasonable and make him an offer he could not resist. We'd set up an ashram together and live happily ever after. His life would transform from alcoholic *sannyasi* to blissful husband in an instant. Emotions are powerful, stubborn entities. Even though we know that something is not good for us, it doesn't stop us from wanting it. Badly.

In Wales, I had bought a mobile telephone which malfunctioned half of the time due to bad reception. I hoped I'd get through. With shaking fingers and a nauseous feeling in my stomach I dialed his number. After seconds that seemed like hours, I heard his voice. Rudra's voice.

'Hallo?'

My mind went blank.

'*Sannyasi!*' I said, stupidly, as though I was an old friend who called just to say hello. 'How are you?'

Rudra instantly knew it was me and sounded irritated.

'Yeah,' he said simply. Not 'Hello', not 'How are you?' 'Yeah' was all he could muster. Then the line cut. Humiliated, I stared at my phone for a few minutes. I was at a loss. Should I ignore his reaction and call him again? I tried, but could not get through. Now I was indignant. Was this how we should now be with each other, after everything we had shared?

I decided to text him. I told him that I wanted to talk to him one more time for 'closure' and 'clarity' and that I would appreciate it if he could call me. No response followed. I sank back onto the bed and stared out of the window. Half an hour later, my phone finally rang. It was Rudra.

'Sorry,' he said, 'I was doing my *pranayama*. So what is it you want to talk about?' He sounded cold and business-like.

My mind became blank. All my carefully prepared words, suggestions and manipulations flew out of the window like butterflies. I felt hurt that he did not ask me how I was, where I was, how I was coping. He was distant, as though he did not know me.

'I just wanted to talk to you for one last time. For me, things have not been as easy as they seem to be for you.'

'Why?' he asked. 'Did anything bad happen?'

What followed was a futile dialogue. Futile because for him, things were clearly over and he had moved on a long time ago. Yet, I still wanted to hear it from him.

'Tell me one thing: Is this story over for you now?' I asked, finally, exasperated.

'Well,' he laughed drily, 'it's not *over*... but...'

'Then what?' I asked, feeling like I was drowning slowly.

'Rudra,' I said in a final attempt. 'You said back then, in India, that it was impossible for us to be together. But it's not impossible. Nothing is impossible. We can make this work, if we really want to.'

He was unmoved. 'It is either all or nothing. You agree with that, right?'

'Yes,' I mumbled, not agreeing in the slightest.

'If we cannot do it one hundred percent, then we will not do it at all.'

'But why can't we do it one hundred percent?' I asked, feeling like a stubborn child. 'Why can't we have a relationship?'

'I do not want a relationship. Not in this birth. I am like an elephant with no tail. There is nothing to hold on to. Nothing will hold me back. And relationships, friends, they hold you back. Besides, I am really happy here. I love being a teacher, a *pujari*, ashram manager, a healer. I love my life here.'

He took a deep breath. 'I think there should be hardly any contact between us.' Bang. Words hitting me like a ton of bricks.

'I did not have the courage to tell you this last time, but this time, I have the courage. I have to tell you.'

'Right,' I said, slowly. 'Okay.'

'This is becoming a pain for you,' he said, now sounding

exasperated. 'And it is becoming a pain for me, also.'

'It's already a pain,' I sneered cynically. 'You can't add much to it anymore.'

'What if I come back to India? Could I stay at the ashram and teach?' I was now grasping at straws.

'You will always be welcome here,' he said, using carefully measured words. '*Always*. But about teaching, I am not so sure. We actually have enough teachers right now.'

It gradually started to sink in that he really did not want me to come back into his life, in whatever shape or form.

'But I really like you!' I whimpered feebly, by now feeling like the most pathetic person on earth. He said all this and I still liked him! What was the matter with me? 'Can't we be friends?'

That dry laugh again. 'We will *always* be friends.'

'How can we be friends if you tell me not to contact you again?'

He snorted derisively. 'Tiziana,' he said slowly, 'that is for *normal* people. *They* need to talk and stay in contact. We are always connected. Don't you know that?'

I wasn't convinced.

He continued. 'What happened between us was in the book. What is going to happen next is already written as well. What are you worried about? Just trust in the Almighty.'

I had to admit that he had a point. And yet, despite paying lip service to it, I envied and resented his faith in the unseen script of life.

'Well, I had to call you to hear this. I would never have forgiven myself if I had not called you and tried one more time.'

'I understand that,' he said.

'I always had the faint hope that maybe you do love me.'

The mirthless laugh again.

Defeated, I gave up. I could say what I wanted. He had made his decision. Crushing as it was, I had to accept that I was not included in his life anymore.

'It is raining so much here,' he said suddenly.

'Yes, here too,' I replied.

'Oh, and I need to tell you something else. All these habits, I left them a couple of weeks after you went away. No more alcohol, no more cigarettes. Just meditation.'

'Great,' I enthused. 'Well done!'

'Yes, but,' I heard him grin, 'but, there was also another reason for that. The guy who was supplying me left the ashram.'

'Right,' I said.

'I have to go now. Pilgrims are coming.'

'Okay,' I said.

'See you,' Rudra said, 'see you.' I heard the tiniest flicker of emotion in his voice.

'Bye,' I said.

The line went dead.

It was still raining outside. I was still in my bed. I was staring at the telephone in my hand. So that was it. I had asked and received my answer.

Dumbfounded, I texted Rudra a final goodbye.

'Thanks, Rudra. I can be in peace now and move on. I was in too much pain thinking of what could be and what we could have created together. Thank you for being my mirror and soul mate and teacher and for strengthening me on my path of unconditional love. I will love you always, in liberty. Take care, T.'

After this, I deleted his numbers.

The next day, I experienced a strange mixture of relief and sadness. And I felt stronger – because I had voiced my feelings, however feebly, and because I finally had clarity. There was only one way out now, and it pointed forward.

That afternoon, something strange happened in LifeStream. As we moved and I felt myself dropping into the energy, my awareness was transported into a different sphere. The room around me faded and it was as though I had astrally projected myself to Rudra's ashram in the Himalayas. I saw, heard and sensed it with astonishing clarity. I was back there, in the ashram's austere temple, and watched the *aarti* performed for Guru-ji by Rudra and several other people.

When I looked up at Guru-ji's portrait, I saw fat, white maggots crawling out of his face and eating their way out of his picture. I took the ritual knife from the altar and slashed the painting. I then sat down opposite Rudra and told him everything I had left unsaid. He listened to me in what seemed to be surprise and sadness. At the end of the conversation, I looked sharply into his eyes and uttered the following words loud and clear, three times:

'Husband: I divorce you. I divorce you. I divorce you.'

And:

'The karmic contract is over.'

When I came back to the 'real world', I felt dazed. What had just happened there? It had felt so vivid, as though I had really been in the Himalayas.

'There's still such a strong bond between you. Your soul is still hovering somewhere up there, in the Himalayas,' Tony said when I told him what I experienced. 'In a way, you really did get married out there.'

It made sense. In the shamanistic worldview, soul loss is one of the greatest causes of disease. Shamans assume that whenever a person suffers an emotional or physical trauma, a part of the soul flees the body in order to survive the experience.

'Soul', in this context, is interchangeable with life force, the energy that keeps us vital and flourishing. Maybe, in my vision, I had done just that: retrieved part of my soul that was still entwined with Rudra, and terminated whatever bond there still was between us? Whatever it was, it was incredibly powerful. Afterwards, I felt liberated. That day, I knew that my connection with Rudra was truly over and that I had to let go. My life was waiting for me.

2.10: Streaming Further towards the Source

From then on, the magic slowly wove its way into my life again. As layer after layer of old conditioning dissolved, I was discovering who I truly was underneath it all. Although I was still in a pretty bad space emotionally, I was getting a clearer picture of where I wanted to go. I resolved a lot of issues with my parents, mainly in my healing work, but also in frank, sensitive conversations with my mother. I understood that the way I had lived for much of my adult life was not how I consciously wanted to live at all. I had re-created my habitual isolation over and over again, and despite my self-image that had told me otherwise, it didn't suit me at all.

Since my ashram experiences in India, I knew that I wanted to live in a spiritual community. I wanted to share spiritual practices, creativity and food, and co-create a lifestyle that was based on a common vision, consciousness, love and joy. I started to dream about setting up my own community, and wrote down ideas. I yearned to live sustainably, somewhere in nature, grow organic food and have plenty of space for ceremonies. Like the Kalash tribe in Pakistan, my community would have a menstruation and birth house, a school, and a temple. Holistic living, personal development, healing and education were high up on my agenda.

Even though I knew I wasn't quite ready to set up this community yet, the thought inspired me, and I began to research existing communities in the UK and Europe I planned to visit. Now that I had no fixed abode and had liberated myself from most mundane commitments for my big trip, what could stop me? Now was the perfect time to try out new ways of living and stay free for as long as possible.

With the shedding of layers, our healing work also expanded into different territories. Soon, the microcosm of my limited emotional experience became a macrocosm and I could see, and most importantly, feel the connection between the personal and the archetypal. Wasn't the inner experience always a reflection of the outer world, and vice versa? Sometimes I glimpsed that it wasn't just my own personal wounding I experienced, but that it was related to the wider collective unconscious out there.

In particular, I connected to the collective pain of women. So many of us carried the memory of abuse, violence and suppression in our DNA. Sometimes, it was like plugging into a big, central computer and downloading all of the suffering that was stored there. It seemed that most of us were born with the imprints of ancestral wounds that we needed to clear in order to live a liberated life. Most significantly, I understood that when we heal ourselves, it has a positive effect on all of our relationships and therefore, ultimately, the whole world.

And, when I enquired deeper, it wasn't just the wounding of the feminine I connected with. In the end, gender didn't really matter. We were all human, on a quest to love and be loved, whether we admitted it to ourselves or not. The marriage of opposites, of the feminine and masculine energies in the Universe, had to take place within every one of us before successful, true outer union with another could be possible. If we wanted a peaceful world, we had to forget the past and come together to create a new equilibrium.

Towards the end of my time with Tony, something wonderfully strange started to happen. After some intense regression work, my body underwent extraordinary changes. I'd wake in the middle of the night with huge waves of energy passing through me. I can only liken it to a full-body orgasm that was centered not in the genitals, but in my heart. Enormous waves of bliss would spread from my heart towards my crown and my feet, and my body convulsed, coiled and pulsated. I had no control over these ecstatic sensations, other than to lie in bed, and watch the energy rise and fall in amazement.

When I gingerly told Tony about my strange experiences for the first time, he was thrilled. 'I am so pleased that this is happening to you,' he beamed and gave me a big hug.

'So it is normal?' I asked. 'But what is it?'

'Your Being is awakening. It's opening and blossoming. You are healing,' he responded. 'It is the life force, *kundalini*, which is starting to pulsate through you.' And, metaphorically: 'That was Krishna, making love to you.'

In those ecstatic nights, I had the impression that he was doing so indeed.

Before I knew it, it was time for me to depart from Wales. It was October 2008, and I left with mixed feelings. I was happy to escape this dreary, rainy place where I had felt so miserable and lonely most of the time, and start my search for an inspirational community to live in. Nevertheless, I was sad to leave Tony and stop the work that had become such a source of healing and inspiration to me.

Tony insisted that I was doing the right thing. 'You don't need me,' he said, reiterating what he had told me at the beginning of our journey together. 'You know how to access LifeStream now. Now go and tell others and carry it on in your own way.'

This, I promised myself, I would certainly do.

From then on, things happened faster than I expected. Within days of leaving Wales, I found my community – strangely enough in Glastonbury, the small Somerset town in which I'd trained as a priestess many years earlier. I had traveled to Glastonbury for the pagan festival of Samhain, intending to stay at a retreat center called Shekinashram for the weekend. I ended up staying for almost two years.

Shekinashram was a perfect fusion between East and West, combining Hindu practices with organic vegan food, a quiet location, and beautiful, cozy rooms. Elahn, the ashram's English owner, was a devotee of Radha-Krishna and Amma, the 'hugging Mother' from Kerala, and had visited India many times before opening the ashram.

Here, I learnt to play the harmonium and soon led the *kirtan* chanting in the mornings. I also performed the ashram's weekly fire ceremonies, ironically, on a Sunday, just like Rudra must still be doing thousands of miles away in the Himalayas. However, there was a big difference between our community and Rudra's austere ashram in India. There was much more freedom, and consequently, far fewer polarities. I chose to live in a community of people that honored truth, love, consciousness and communication above everything else. Loving partnerships, beauty and sexuality were as much part of life as were prayer, service and ritual. Life at Shekinashram integrated all aspects of life and thus felt complete and authentic.

Supported by Elahn, I delved deeper into the mysteries of Bhakti Yoga, Tantra and the archetypal myths, in particular the story of Shiva and Parvati. I began to understand it not just intellectually, but also intuitively and directly in my daily practices. Most poignantly, I comprehended why I felt such a strong connection to Shiva.

The austere ascetic reminded me of the emotional inaccessibility of my father. Shiva, sitting in deep meditation on remote Mount Kailash, resembled the father I couldn't reach; Parvati, the mountain daughter, reminded me of a younger version of myself as she performed extreme austerities to win Shiva's love in unwavering faith for millennia. Parvati's relentless 'Om Namah Shivaya' merged into my 'If only I work hard enough, become successful enough, rich enough, clever enough, he will love me'.

And for many years, I had played out this archetypal drama in my relationships with men, too. Rudra, the inaccessible *sannyasi*, was only the latest in a long line of emotionally unavailable men. At the same time, I realized that only Parvati could melt the ascetic's heart with her single-mindedness. Not only was Shiva the only one strong enough to surrender to Kali's ferocity; no – it worked the other way, too. Shakti, the feminine force, was the only one who could get through to Shiva, the *Mahadeva*. The one lesson *he* had not learnt in his ascetic, intensely spiritual life was how to open his heart and love. It was only through his union with Shakti that Shiva attained the power to become manifest, and that compassion for the human condition entered his heart.

I began to see liberation and enlightenment in a completely different light. Liberation, to me, didn't so much mean ascension to some type of heavenly realm. Rather, it meant liberating the Self from years, and sometimes lifetimes, of accumulated patterns and conditionings. Liberation meant to be free from all that so that we could be aligned with our true nature, which was bliss. *That* was heaven – in the same way that hell was to live in ignorance of our unconscious drives. Just like Tony said over and over again, everything was inside of us. There was nothing to attain or reach. Enlightenment was already here. We just needed to realize it.

One of the final missing pieces for solving my healing puzzle arrived during a LifeStream workshop I presented with Tony about a year after I left India. Through a series of events in the workshop, I was thrown into an excruciating process that triggered all of my rejection and abandonment issues.

Thankfully, with the awareness I already had, I was able to stay with my emotions and suddenly realized that, far beyond the separation from Rudra and even beyond the separation from my mother in infancy, it was something much older I was feeling. Something ancient that had its origins beyond time as I knew it. It was the 'original wound', the primordial pain of separation I'd been feeling all along.

I tracked the energy of the grief and abandonment I felt so deeply in my core back to its origin and found that it was the original separation from Source that triggered it. I recognized that on a cellular level, I deeply resented being born. I resented having to come back to Earth and live, and I carried this archetypal pain of being torn away from the original state of Being, of Bliss, in my DNA. With that came anger at myself for letting it happen. It went a long way to explain my many near-death experiences as an infant. Once I fully allowed myself to feel that deep, aching pain and accept it compassionately, I could let it go.

Rudra had not broken my heart. None of my lovers had. What I'd been looking for all along was my original broken heart. This discovery brought me great liberation, and a new, intense joy began to fill my Being. With every one of these healing crises, my wings started to spread a little more. I became more equanimous and, most importantly, more blissful. Love began to flow through me. I started to become an observer rather than a casualty of my emotions.

Now that I had found this awareness, it was up to me to make the 'original wound' sacred by healing it, transforming it, and sharing it through my writing, teaching and relating. I needed to learn to find that safe place within, a place that lay beyond my old, outworn patterns and in which I knew without a doubt that I was always wanted and loved.

2.11: Awakening to Love

Letting go was a gradual process. It took me about two years to get my journey to the East and especially Rudra out of my system. I continued to shine light into every dark crevice of my Being to understand what had really happened in the Himalayas, and most importantly, what I could learn from it. Gradually, supported by spiritual practices, rituals and inner exploration, I dismantled and let go, bit by bit, and discovered many treasures along the way. I forgave myself for the regrets I had and accepted that not everything was in my control.

Most importantly, I really understood that 'The Other' was an accurate mirror of myself. I became skilled at seeing and accepting all the things I did not like about Rudra and other people as denied aspects of myself. Along the same lines, I learnt to internalize and nurture the qualities I admired in others. Thus, I began to take responsibility for myself and the circumstances I created in my life.

One of the best gifts that emerged from my encounter with Rudra is my new appreciation about the true purpose of intimate relationships. I see now that a conscious partnership with another can be extremely healing if both partners are willing to look at and take responsibility for their personal issues. Ultimately, our healing work lies with each of us, but sometimes, our walls, through lifetimes of patterns and conditionings, are solid, and that is when a bulldozer might be needed to break them down. I know that this was certainly true in my case.

Like any growth process, healing is a journey, and one that I feel is accelerated enormously through the rollercoaster of intimate relationships. No knife cuts as swiftly, deeply and precisely as the blade of the Beloved. Like many others, I was accustomed to giving up and running when the going got tough, but I understand now that this is precisely the point at which staying 'in the fire' can bring about our greatest alchemical transformation.

I profoundly wish that somebody would teach us about the purpose and conduct of relationships when we are children, as well as about conscious, non-violent communication. We could spare ourselves a lot of pain if we understood the true nature of love from an early age, and weren't so trapped in the 'emotional treadmill' of reaction and illusion.

But maybe our journey into wholeness is meant to be arduous. Perhaps it is exactly the pain that cracks our hearts wide open and puts us firmly onto the path of self-awareness and growth. After reaping the harvest of my passionate liaison in the Himalayas, I am inclined to agree with Oscar Wilde that the heart was indeed made to be broken.

Epilogue

Every loss in life I consider as the throwing off of an old garment in order to put on a new one; and the new garment has always been better than the old one.

Harzrat Inayat Khan

At the time of writing, it is early 2012, and I am in Queensland, Australia. When I look back over the past four years, it is wonderful to see how much my life has healed since my big journey to the East and my difficult time in Wales. When I returned from the Himalayas, I mourned the loss of a lifestyle that was filled with magic, devotion and ritual, and thought I might never be able to have it again without Rudra. Instead, reality turned out much better for me.

Just as I visualized in my lonesome *sadhu*'s cave in the Brecon Beacons, I found a loving, conscious community that supported me on my quest for growth. My time at Shekinashram turned out to be one of the most beautiful, enriching periods of my life.

My passion for yoga and Indian spirituality eventually led me to the ancient healing system of Ayurveda, and I left England for New Mexico, USA to study with the Indian physician Dr Vasant Lad. I graduated from his Ayurvedic Institute in 2011 and am now an Ayurvedic Lifestyle Consultant and yoga teacher. And to share what I have learned about intimate relationships and healing of core wounds, I trained as an *Imago* Relationships Educator and am starting to lead seminars on the subject.

My own healing continues every day, one step at a time, sometimes intensely, but mostly gently. Perhaps there will always be issues to shift in my unconscious, but this is secondary, as long as I am aware and willing to look at myself and others stripped of the veils of projection. I continue to be deeply fascinated by the growth process we all seem to go through, and know that I will emerge stronger and wiser every time. Most of all, I am always feeling more love inside of me – a constantly deepening, objectless love that does not seem to depend on outer circumstances, and one that I am happy to share generously.

And most magically, I am in a loving relationship again. In the autumn of 2008, a little after I'd returned from India, a man called Sameer contacted me via the travel blog I keep online. He had read some of my articles on India and wrote to ask me some travel-related questions. Sameer was from Pune, India, and we exchanged some e-mails.

I don't know what made him different from all the other people who contacted me. But there was a connection, a certain spark, and from that point onwards, we wrote to each other frequently. We talked about our shared love for India, spirituality, our lives, our travel experiences, and a friendship ensued. It soon grew so strong that we were conversing by e-mail every day and told each other everything that happened to us. We skyped often, became acquainted with each other's friends and families, and shared books, passions, victories and defeats. This unusual friendship continued for three years and slowly, almost unexpectedly grew into love.

After I completed my studies in New Mexico, I decided to take a cargo ship from the USA to Australia, where Sameer now lived and worked, to meet him for the first time. In August 2011, we met and have been together ever since. He is a beautiful man, and though I still experience challenges with intimacy and my wounds surface from time to time, the work I have done since Rudra has enabled me to stay present. I don't need to run away anymore. I now have the courage to show myself fully as I am, with all my vulnerabilities and shortcomings, and my view of relationships is more realistic and compassionate. Intimacy, something I had always been so afraid of, has become one of the greatest adventures of my life.

As for Rudra, I feel gratitude for the brief, but incredibly intense and almost otherworldly connection we shared, and the beautiful transformation that unfolded within me afterwards. This gratitude is coupled with sadness that our journey with each other had to be so painful. Maybe it had to be, so that I could awaken and blossom. I hope that Rudra experienced similar awakenings as a result of our passionate encounter.

Inadvertently, or maybe by sacred contract, Rudra catalyzed the great gift of awareness for me. And that in itself, whether metaphysically or mundanely, makes him a Soul Mate in my eyes – a friend who helped my soul to grow.

Thanks

This book was over three years in the making and written in three different countries: England, France and Australia. I would like to thank the following people – my creative midwives – who prevented a number of untimely terminations and helped me to birth this book into reality with their unwavering support, especially when things were tough:

Sameer, for keeping me sane during the long hours of writing with your encouraging and enthusiastic messages throughout, your support and delicious food in the final stages of editing in Australia and England, and for being with me on every step of the way. May this journey lead us to our highest potential.

Tony Crisp, my teacher and extra-ordinary soul friend, for more than I can express here. My life would not be the same without you.

Tim Ward, *John Hunt* and all at *Changemakers Books* for their belief in my work. Special thanks to *Tim Ward* for your honest advice and encouragement. Your input made a huge difference.

Beth Forster for your sharp-sightedness and insistence that I had to finish the book.

Ben Huggan for your friendship, patience and interest, and for allowing me to write the first draft of this book in your peaceful oasis of non-duality.

Sheilagh Holmes for your loyalty, friendship, grounding support and patience, and for wonderful feedback on early drafts of this book.

Elahn Keshava and *Gisela Lirusso* at Shekinashram in Glastonbury for inviting me to stay in your beautiful space as a 'live-in fire priestess' and writer for a big part of birthing this book, and for furthering my tantric *bhakti*. I couldn't have written this book in a more perfect place. Further thanks and love go to my Shekinashram family: *Helen Shenstone, Paul Buck, Katie*

McPherson and all the karma yogis and friends who passed through. Haribol! Sri Caitanya Mahaprabhu ki jai!

The wonderful *Kassandra Knebel* for long years of friendship, wisdom and love.

My mother *Margarete Stupia* for being my No 1 supporter. Thank you for all the prayers, support and care during my many years of spiritual adventures. Keep praying without pause. I love you.

My father, the honorable *Don Santo Stupia* for your tolerance, support and coming to Glastonbury with me to sing 'Shiva Shambo'. Baciamo le mani! Ti voglio bene.

My dear sister *Claudia* for being my mirror.

My writing coach *Leda Sammarco* for being the first one to brave this material and comment on it wisely and sensitively.

My editor *Hayley Sherman*. Your insight, diligence and clear-sightedness have helped this book become what it was meant to be. Thank You. Your insistence that I 'stay in the moment' has made all the difference.

John and *Kerry* at the beautiful *La Muse* Writer's Retreat in Southern France, where my juicy creativity really started to flow.

Wendy Briggs, for availing your lush, evocative garden retreat to me for the final months of editing.

Jo Sutton for being instrumental in inspiring my tantric journey to the East.

Tanya Sheikh for sharing so much of your inspirational soul journey with me.

Kathy Jones, my first spiritual teacher who imparted so much wisdom to me and transformed my life forever.

Yogrishi Vishvketu and *Chetana Panwar* for being shining lights of inspiration.

Adrian Mitchell for steadily holding the fort while I was away on my travels.

Heeso Kim, my Korean soul sister, for sharing so much of India with me.

Ruth Guy for helping me to kickstart this project.

All the people who were test readers for this book: *Sheilagh Holmes, Paul Buck, Mike Jones, Donna Higton, Pete Duckworth, Amodini Gaganavir, Emilie Nicole, Ben Huggan* and *Hansje te Velde.*

All the men I have loved and who have taught me so generously through their mirroring.

My trusty red *Sony VAIO,* on which this book was written.

Lord *Ganesh* for helping me to write. Om Gam Ganapataye Namaha!

And most importantly, my Guru *Swami Satsangi Saraswati* and her Guru *Swami Satyananda Saraswati* for welcoming me back home.

Love and gratitude to the rest of my soul family, too numerous to mention here, for being who you are.

And finally to all the brilliant writers who have taught and inspired me over the years and encouraged me to write this book:

Jonny Bealby, who motivated me to go to Pakistan, a country I had thus far not harbored the slightest interest in. Your adventurous writing changed my life for good. Thank You.

Daniel Odier, whose book *Tantric Quest* made me dream and feel the true essence of Tantra resonate in every cell of my body.

Tim Ward, whose insightful, brutally honest writing inspired me beyond words.

Jay Ramsay. Crucible of Love is a masterpiece I still relish like a rare, exquisite delicacy.

Katja Sundermeier, whose *Simply Love* book literally opened my eyes.

Harville Hendrix for his groundbreaking 'Imago' work that came to me after I returned from India.

Eva-Maria Zurhorst for her unwavering belief in love.

Sarah McDonald, whose *Holy Cow* gave me a first glimpse into the bizarre world that is India and kindled my interest before I set foot into it for the first time.

Sarah Lloyd. It was your beautiful book *An Indian Attachment* that was the final confirmation I needed to start writing this book.

Elizabeth Gilbert, for showing me what writers can do for themselves and others, and for encouraging me to see writing as a 'holy office'.

Asra Q. Nomani for her soul-searching, brave and heartfelt writings on Tantra.

Muriel Maufroy for making me weep with recognition, wonder and relief when I read *Rumi's Daughter.*

Ramesh Menon for his emotive *Siva Purana* that furthered my understanding of the relationship between Shiva and Shakti so much.

Lyndsay Clarke for introducing me to the concept of the *Chymical Wedding* long before it made any conscious sense to me.

The amazing *Paulo Coelho* for all his work, for inspiring me to go traveling after I read *The Alchemist,* and for popping up on my path periodically and often prophetically just when I needed him. Likewise for insisting, through *By the River* and *The Zahir,* that I *had* to write this book. Your books showed me what writers are capable of, and that it's never too late.

Glossary of Terms

Aarti – a Hindu ritual in which light from wicks soaked in ghee or camphor is offered to one or more deities.

Agni – Sanskrit for 'fire'. Also Hindu God of Fire.

Ajna – one of the chakras, located between the eyebrows. Often referred to as 'third eye'.

Angrezi – Hindi for 'English'.

Ashram – a religious hermitage.

Atman – often used to describe a person's soul.

Bhagavad Gita – one of the holiest scriptures in Hinduism.

Bhai – Hindi for 'brother'.

Bhakti – devotion.

Black Metal – a type of extreme Metal music, often associated with Satanism and death.

Brahmachari – a young, celibate man.

Chai – Indian tea.

Chakra – Sanskrit for 'wheel', used to refer to vortices which, according to traditional Indian medicine, are believed to exist on the etheric human body.

Chalo – Hindi for 'Let's go'.

Chapattis – unleavened flatbread used in India.

Dhal – lentil stew used commonly in Indian cuisine.

Dharma – Hindu concept, meaning 'one's righteous duty'.

Dhoti – a traditional Indian men's garment. It is a rectangular piece of unstitched cloth, wrapped around the waist and legs and knotted at the waist.

Dupatta – a long scarf that is essential to many South Asian women's suits.

Ghat – a series of steps leading down to a water body, usually a holy river.

Ghee – clarified butter, often used in Hindu fire ceremonies as well as Indian cooking.

Gita – short for *Bhagavad Gita*, one of the holiest scriptures in Hinduism.

Gopi – Sanskrit for 'cowherd girl'. Often used to refer to the cow girls that were devoted to the Hindu God Krishna.

Guru – a spiritual teacher and guide.

Gyan mudra – A *mudra* is a gesture, usually done with the hands, which focuses and directs energy in a yoga pose or meditation. *Gyan mudra* consists of a joined index finger and thumb, while the rest of the hand's fingers are outstretched.

Hare Krishna – term commonly used to describe a member of the Hare Krishna movement, followers of the Hindu God Krishna.

Harmonium – a free-standing keyboard instrument, often used in Indian devotional music.

Havan – a Hindu fire ceremony.

Japa mala – Hindu prayer beads.

Karma – the concept of 'action' or 'deed', understood as that which causes the cycle of cause and effect; originating in ancient India.

Karma yoga – the 'discipline of action'. A concept outlined in the *Bhagavad Gita* and used to refer to selfless actions without attachment to outcome.

Kirtan – Hindu devotional chanting.

Kundalini – Sanskrit for 'coiled'. In yoga, it is used to describe an unconscious force that lies coiled at the base of the spine and can be awakened through spiritual practice or the grace of a Guru.

Kurta – a loose shirt falling either just above or below the knees, worn by both men and women in India.

Kutir – a small hut or cottage.

Laddoo – a round Indian sweet

Lakh – a unit in the Indian numbering system, meaning one hundred thousand.

Langar – a Sikh community kitchen.

Lingam – a stone pillar representing Hindu God Shiva's divine phallus, symbolic of creation.

Mandala – Sanskrit for 'circle'. Used in Hindu and Buddhist religious art, it is often a square with four gates containing a circle with a center point.

Mangala Arati – a devotional practice performed by devotees of the Hindu God Krishna, which consists of dancing around the *tulsi* plant representative of the woods of Vrindavan where Krishna lived.

Masala – a mixture of spices used in Indian cooking.

Mauna – silence.

Moksha – Hindu concept of liberation from the cycle of life, death and rebirth.

Murti – a devotional statue, used for worship in Hinduism.

Nahi – Hindi for 'no'.

Namaste – traditional Indian greeting, meaning 'I bow to the divine within you'.

Panchagni – a Hindu spiritual practice in which the practitioner sits in the center of five sacred fires.

Paranthas – Indian flat bread.

Pooja – a Hindu form of worship.

Prana – Hindu concept of the 'life force' or 'vital energy' that sustains life.

Pranayama – a form of breath control used in Yoga to improve the circulation of prana in the body.

Prasad – blessed food, given away freely after Hindu religious ceremonies.

Puja – see 'Pooja'.

Pujari – a Hindu priest.

Puri – unleavened Indian bread.

Putain – French swearword, meaning 'whore'.

Rishis – India's ancient seers who are said to have channeled the Vedas, the most sacred scriptures of India.

Roti – unleavened Indian bread.

Rudraksha – seed of the blue marble tree, traditionally used for prayer beads in Hinduism.

Sabji – Hindi for 'vegetables'.

Sadhana – spiritual practice.

Sadhu – a Hindu term for a mystic, ascetic, yogi or wandering monk.

Sahasrara – chakra located at the top of the head.

Samagree – fragrant herbs used as offerings in Hindu fire ceremonies.

Samosa – a stuffed pastry and popular snack in India.

Sannyasi – a Hindu monk who has renounced material life to follow spiritual pursuits.

Sati – an ancient Indian tradition of the immolation of a widow on her husband's funeral pyre, now illegal.

Sattvic – pure, uncontaminated.

Shaant – Hindi for 'quiet'.

Shaktipat – conferring of spiritual energy upon one person by another, usually a Guru. It can be transmitted with a sacred word or mantra, by a look, thought or touch.

Shalwar kameez – traditional dress worn by both men and women in South Asia, consisting of pajama-like trousers and a long tunic-like shirt.

Sindoor – red powder, applied at the beginning or completely along the parting-line of a married woman's hair.

Smashan – Hindu cremation ground.

Sundar mooch – Hindi for 'beautiful moustache'.

Sushumna – one of the body's main energy channels that connects the base chakra to the crown chakra.

Svāhā – an interjection, approximately 'hail!', used to indicate the end of a mantra. Used with oblations in Hindu fire ceremonies.

Swami – an ascetic or yogi who has been initiated into a religious monastic order.

Tabernac! – French-Canadian swearword, meaning 'tabernacle'.

Tantra – an inter-religious spiritual movement from ancient India expressed in scriptures called the Tantras.

Tapasya – austerities, performed to attain physical purification and spiritual enlightenment.

Thik hai – Hindi for 'alright'.

Tilak – sandalwood powder used in Hindu religious ceremonies, worn as a mark on the forehead and other parts of the body.

Tulsi – holy basil, cultivated for religious and medicinal purposes.

Vedas, the – a large body of sacred scriptures originating in ancient India.

Vipassana – a term from the Buddhist tradition, meaning insight into the true nature of reality.

Wallah – Hindi for 'man'. It is often used in connection with a profession, for example, a *chai wallah* is a man who serves tea.

Yajna – Hindu fire ceremony.

Yak – a long-haired bovine found throughout the Himalayas.

Yantra – see 'Mandala'.

Yogi – a male practitioner of yoga.

Yogini – a female yogi.

Yoni – Sanskrit for 'vagina', in Hinduism used for the source of all that exists.

References

Part 1 title page
Sri Aurobindo, 'Savitri', Canto 1. Available from http://savitrithepoem.com/

The Three Stooges
Osho (1994), from *Osho Zen Tarot*, Newleaf, UK

Part 2 title page
Coelho, Paulo (2008), *Brida*, HarperCollins, India

Broken Heart, Blossoming Heart
Coelho, Paulo (2008), *Brida*, HarperCollins, India

Simply Love
Sundermeier, Katja (2004), *Die Simply Love Strategie: Ihr Weg zur grossen Liebe*, Piper Verlag GmbH, Germany

Epilogue
Khan, Hazrat Inayat. Available from http://www.hazrat-inayat-khan.org

Resources

If this book has inspired you to find out more about relationship dynamics and the healing of core wounds, please visit the following websites:

Imago Relationships: http://gettingtheloveyouwant.com/
Katja Sundermeier: http://www.simply-love.de/
Eva-Maria Zurhorst: http://www.liebedichselbst.de/
Tony Crisp (Dreams, Yoga, Healing): http://dreamhawk.com/
Donald van Howten (Ayurveda and Bodywork): http://www.lifeimpressionsinst.com/
Vipassana Meditation: http://www.dhamma.org/

About the Author

Tiziana Stupia is a writer, yoga teacher, Ayurvedic consultant and Vedic fire ceremonies practitioner. She has traveled the world extensively since 2007 and recently completed a circumnavigation of the globe by cargo ship. She keeps a blog called 'Travelling Priestess' about her travels, and has published widely in magazines such as *Mosaic*, *Yoga Magazine* and *Pagan Dawn* on the topics of spirituality, travel, health and personal growth.

Trained as a priestess of an ancient Goddess tradition, Tiziana spent many years leading transformational rituals in the community and in the UK's prison service, where she worked as a pagan minister. She now facilitates seminars about Ayurveda, Yoga and Imago Relationship Education and is planning to set up a spiritual community in nature.

To find out more and to contact the author, please visit www.tizianastupia.com

**CHANGE
MAKERS
BOOKS**

Changemakers publishes books for individuals committed to transforming their lives and transforming the world. Our readers seek to become positive, powerful agents of change. Changemakers books inform, inspire, and provide practical wisdom and skills to empower us to create the next chapter of humanity's future.

Please visit our website at www.changemakers-books.com